Maldives

Tom Masters

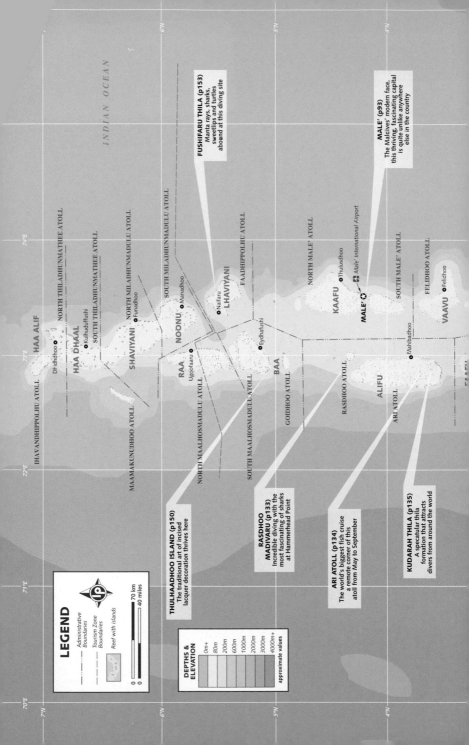

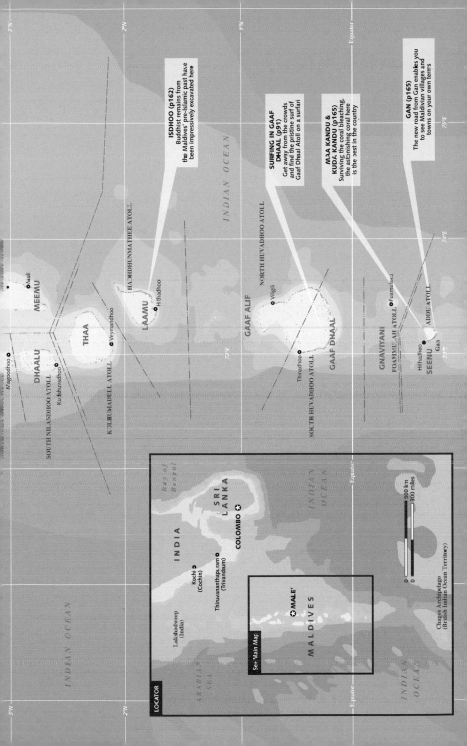

ISDHOO (p162)
Buddhist remains from the Maldives' pre-Islamic past have been impressively excavated here

SURFING IN GAAF DHAAL (p91)
Get away from the crowds and find the pristine surf of Gaaf Dhaal Atoll on a surfari

MAA KANDU & KUDA KANDU (p165)
Surviving the coral bleaching, the astonishing coral here is the best in the country

GAN (p165)
The new road from Gan enables you to see Maldivian villages and towns on your own terms

On the Road

TOM MASTERS Coordinating Author

This photograph was taken on a sandbank where a friend and I had just enjoyed breakfast at dawn. I hadn't been convinced until I did it, but coffee, croissants and fresh fruit on the sand with the warm Indian Ocean lapping the shore as the sun broke across the horizon was one of the most magical experiences of the trip...

MY FAVOURITE TRIP

I have been diving in the Maldives many times, but the last dive I did on this trip was easily the best of them all. Our diving boat arrived at Bodu Hithi Thila at around 8am, and we descended the dazzlingly clear water down to around 25m. Immediately we saw white tipped reef sharks (I counted five), a green turtle, three huge manta rays, two eagle rays, several tuna, stonefish, lionfish and moray eels – never have I seen so many large creatures in one short dive. I'll definitely be returning to Bodu Hithi Thila next time, and hope it wasn't just good luck!

ABOUT THE AUTHOR

A keen diver and lover of all things tropical, Tom was blown away by the Maldives on his first visit in 2006, where the friendly sharks, the great beaches and the relaxed vibe made for a good break from his usual haunts in Russia and Eastern Europe. Returning for this edition, he was delighted to find the country changed for the better, with a democratically elected government in place of the former dictatorship. Tom currently lives and works as a freelance writer in Berlin. More of his work can be found at www.mastersmafia.com.

Bodu Hithi Thila

Traveller Highlights

Your first glimpse of the Maldives is unforgettable – your plane breaks through the clouds and dazzling white sand islands and turquoise lagoons are revealed. Before you've even landed you're pretty sure this is paradise, but there's so much more to the country than just its beaches and clear waters. Whether it's underwater, on an inhabited island or in the buzzing capital Male', the Maldives repay anyone making an effort to see more than just the pool and the bar, though – perhaps the best thing of all – there's absolutely no pressure to do anything more than that if you don't want to!

TRACEY KISLINGBURY

MEERUFENFUSHI

Going on a night-time fishing trip from the island of Meerufenfushi (p115) was truly fantastic – we sat on a boat under a full moon on the calm, deep waters, each equipped with only simple hook, line and sinker. Patience and then strong arms were required to bag ourselves an impressive pile of fresh fish; very satisfying and definitely a night to remember.

Tracey Kislingbury, LP staff member

BREAKFAST WITH THE HAMMERS

Dawn; a boat bobbing in the middle of the southern atolls (p133). A group of divers descend the amazing, clear waters like skydiving, with no reference points, freefalling into the deep blue. We stop at 40m and wait. Before I know it, we are staring into a huge sea of hammerhead sharks lurking in the depths of the ocean, waiting to be fed. Breakfast with the Maldivian hammerheads. Absolutely mind-blowing.

Jo Stiebel, LP staff member

JAMES PIERCE/DREAMS

THULHAGIRI

It only takes 10 minutes to circumnavigate the island of Thulhagiri (p114). From our balcony we could see pure aquamarine water, while budgerigars entertained us at dusk. Snorkelling, straight off the beach through colourful schools of tropical fish and a turtle or two, was sublime, as was the French food with a twist of Indian spice.

Christine Morton, LP staff member

YANN ARTHUS-BERTRAND/COF

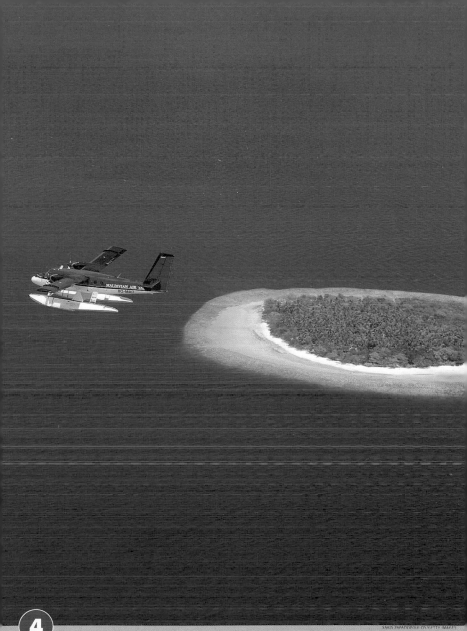

SAKIS PAPADOPOLI OS/GETTY IMAGES

4 FLYING OVER THE ATOLLS

My risk-averse, Westernised eyes scrutinised the seaplanes (p181) and told me they were things of great danger. I discreetly quizzed seasoned travellers: yes, I know they're like taxis round here but how often do they land upside down? Faced with little choice, I boarded my bobbing plane and it quickly became a secret joy. Like scootering through country lanes with no helmet, it felt naughty but wonderfully liberating.

Mike Christie, traveller

THOMAS HALTNER/PHOTOLIBR.

5 VISITING AN INHABITED ISLAND

A short boat hop from our resort at Kuda Huraa (p121) took us to a different world. Away from the spa and the bar, we found ourselves in a quiet Maldivian village, strolling the sandy streets, visiting local craft workshops and seeing the day's catch being unloaded on the dock. It was magical to see something of the 'real' Maldives, however fleetingly.

Zeeba Carrol, UK, traveller

MARCEL JOLIBOIS/PHOTOLIBR.

6 MALE'

Male' (p93) is definitely the best place to get to know Maldivians and see what makes them tick. The brightly painted houses, the crowded markets and the convivial teashops where you can chat to locals and share plates of delicious 'short eats' are my favourite thing about this bizarre capital city, the perfect antidote to the Robinson Crusoe experience in a resort.

Tom Masters, UK, Lonely Planet author

Contents

Regional Map Contents

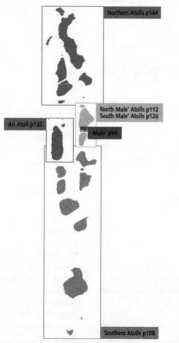

Destination Maldives

Positive change has recently come to the Maldives, making this a fantastic time to visit a nation in the ferment of transition. Having gone from authoritarian state to vibrant democracy in just a few short years, voting in its first freely elected government in 2008 and turning itself into both a beacon for environmentalism and a glowing, rare example of Islamic democracy, it wouldn't be an exaggeration to call the Maldives today one of Asia's most progressive countries.

Part traditional island nation with a staunchly Islamic culture and identity, part modern tourism emirate attracting over half a million well-heeled luxury sunseekers annually – and looking to increase this even further by building ever more resorts – it can nevertheless be more than a little difficult to put your finger on the 'real Maldives'.

The reality is, quite simply, that there are two versions of this country. When tourism got going in the 1970s, it did so without affecting the abstemious conservative village culture of the atolls one bit. A policy of separating tourists from locals meant that on one island scantily clad holiday makers cavorted on the beach sipping margaritas, while just across the lagoon the island elders drank tea in the shade of the palm trees and discussed the Quran. This remains the case today, though foreign influence is more and more keenly felt with the spread of mobile phones and the internet to even the remotest atoll islands.

Until the democratic election of Mohammed Nasheed in late 2008, the former president, Maumoon Gayoom, had ruled almost unopposed for three decades. His rule is credited with ensuring stability in the country while stimulating development, albeit in which few ordinary folk saw the benefits of the money pouring into the country. What was not so widely known abroad was that – according to international human rights groups such as Amnesty International, as well as the current president – torture, intimidation and imprisonment were commonly used against anyone challenging Gayoom or his policies.

By 2004 a pro-democracy movement was regularly staging anti-government protests and pressure groups abroad were advocating a boycott of government-owned resorts, culminating in Gayoom's own eventual decision to allow free elections in October 2008. Testament to his enduring support, particularly in the conservative atolls, neither Gayoom nor the Maldivian Democratic Party leader Mohammed Nasheed (known to one and all as 'Anni') won an outright majority in the first round of voting, but in the run off Nasheed triumphed, taking 54% of the vote to Gayoom's 45%.

The transfer of power after three decades was remarkable for its smoothness and, on the part of the new government at least, its lack of bitterness. President Nasheed, himself a victim of long imprisonment and alleged torture by the previous government, set a tone of national reconciliation when he told the nation that 'I have forgiven my jailers, the torturers. They were following orders... I ask people to follow my example and leave Gayoom to grow old here.'

Since assuming the presidency Nasheed has wasted no time in implementing sweeping reforms. Having inherited a country with, in his own words, 'empty coffers' – extraordinary for a tiny nation with a multi-billion dollar tourist industry – the key strategy has been to shore up the republic's finances. This is being done by privatising the lumbering state concerns that have run everything from construction to the electricity grid, a not

FAST FACTS

Area: 90,000 sq km (above water 300 sq km)

Percentage of the country that is water: 99.9%

Number of atolls: 26

Population: 299,000 (2006 census)

Percentage of population living in Male': 35%

GDP per capita: US$5000

Percentage of GDP spent on defence: 5.5%

Minimum number of Maldivians legally required to be employed at a resort: 50%

Inflation: 12.8%

Number of shark attacks since 1976: none

uncontroversial move that the president hopes will result in short-term liquidity and more efficient market conditions in the long run.

Perhaps most significantly for a nation that will be one of the first to feel the effects of rising sea levels caused by global warming, Nasheed has pledged that the Maldives will be the world's first carbon neutral country within a decade – an ambitious plan that will see oil imports replaced by the use of solar panels, wind turbines and other alternative energy sources.

Yet while Nasheed is feted on the world stage as the Indian Ocean's very own Nelson Mandela, he still faces enormous challenges domestically. Civil society in the country remains in its very early days, with the local media until recently totally unused to open debate or the concept of scrutiny, and there are still many powerful factions and corporations in the country who would be very happy to see Nasheed removed from power.

Even more pressing are the social problems the country faces. On paper the Maldives may be South Asia's richest country, but the lack of trickledown generated by the tourist industry means that an astonishing 40% of the population live on less than US$1 a day and some 30% of Maldivian children under the age of five are malnourished. Just as worryingly, there's a massive drug problem throughout the country – with anywhere between 10% and 30% of the adult population believed to be using 'brown sugar', a cheap unrefined heroin.

TEAM (Tourism Employees Association of the Maldives), effectively the first union of Maldivian resort employees, has stated that most Maldivians working in resorts earn between US$80 and US$120 per month, while most resorts make several million dollars profit a year at the very least. Indeed, the road ahead still looks bumpy for workers' rights in the Maldives, despite a recent amendment that included resort workers in legislation capping working hours and mandating overtime.

The legacy of the 2004 tsunami may no longer be visible in the tourist resorts or Male', but evidence of the devastation is still easy to find in the atolls, with many islands having been abandoned due to damage and several thousand internally displaced people remaining effective refugees on other islands.

You're therefore visiting the Maldives at a challenging but exciting time. While the problems the nation faces are by no mean insignificant, your presence is much needed to help generate tourist dollars that will hopefully now begin to filter down into the wider Maldivian economy. In addition, you'll discover a rich and peaceful people with a rich and fascinating culture of survival in the middle of the ocean, as well as incredible natural beauty and some of the most mind-blowing beaches and resorts in the world.

Getting Started

A country jealously guarding its cultural heritage and fragile ecology from the onslaughts of Western consumerism, the Maldives is almost exclusively a place for the package tourist. Despite most independent travellers' worst fears, coming on a package offers the best value for money, the easiest organisation and generally promotes preferential treatment – this is the way the Maldives is set up and everyone from the government to the resorts prefers you to travel this way. Fully independent travellers (FITs) are a rare species but, with good planning and some decent financial lubrication, this is an equally possible way to travel. However you arrive, you'll find the same astonishing white beaches, surreally blue water and good service.

WHEN TO GO

The Maldives specialises in winter sun for Europeans, making high season December to April, when the islands enjoy the dry monsoon with little rain and lower humidity while Europe shivers. February to April is the hottest period. Mid December to early January comes at even more of a premium due to Christmas and New Year and prices are even higher. Easter and the August holidays also attract peak prices at most resorts.

From May to November is the period when storms and rain are more likely. It's still warm, but skies can be cloudy and the humidity is higher. This is the low season, with fewer people and lower prices, with the exception of August.

Diving is good year-round, although a basic rule is that life on the reef is more varied and visibility better on the western side of any atoll from May to November and from the eastern side of any atoll December to April. This means you'd be wise to choose your resort accordingly.

The surfing season runs from March to October, which is great as this is when resorts are cheapest.

There is no bad time to visit the Maldives, although if you're interested in spending time in Male' or any other inhabited islands, Ramadan, called Ramazan locally (see p172), is a time to avoid as restaurants are closed and people aren't always in the best of moods. This won't affect you in a resort, however.

For climate charts, see p171.

COSTS & MONEY

The Maldives is no cheap destination – you'll hardly see a backpack the entire time you're here (and if you do it will most likely be being carried for someone by a member of resort staff). This is partly by design: the Gayoom government preferred it this way, maximising revenue while keeping out the stoned hippies who so outraged local conservative values when they began to trickle through in the 1970s. However, since the change of government in 2008 there has been talk of opening the country up to budget travellers and even building hotels on inhabited islands. For now, though, this is all very academic as even the folk here on budget packages are fairly well-heeled, and don't fool yourself – even if you do get a cheap flight and accommodation deal, unless it's full board you'll spend almost as much again on food and drink during your stay.

While it's possible to say that costs are high, it's hard to be much more specific, mainly because two travellers can pay vastly different sums for

HOW MUCH?

Male'-airport ferry US$1 or Rf10

Cappuccino US$3

Male' whale submarine ticket US$75

Bed tax per person per night US$8

Flat taxi fare in Male' US$1.50 or Rf20

the same deal at the same resort depending on how they book – one travel agent may have an excellent deal on the room rate, another a far worse one, while an FIT will just have to pay whatever rate they are quoted directly by the resort's reservations service.

Extremely roughly then, expect to pay at the very least $100 per person per day at the lower end for a room with full board. Midrange starts around $200 per day and extends up to $500, while for about $500 a day, you enter the heady heights of the Maldives luxury market, which currently seems to have no cap. As Male' offers very differently priced accommodation options, we've grouped them differently to those in the rest of the country. In Male' budget choices come in at under US$50, midrange runs from US$50 to $90 and top end is anything from US$90 per night.

For those with a modest budget, the best deal is a full-board or all-inclusive package (including certain drinks, both alcoholic and non) that includes flights and transfers. While it's still a lot of money, you'll spend almost nothing during your stay.

TRAVEL LITERATURE

While the Maldives has been covered in some detail by photography and nature guides, there's still precious little of any literary merit written about the place. This is perhaps unsurprising given the sun, sand and sea nature of most travel here, but the following titles are definitely worth a look.

Rudie H Kuiter's *Photo Guide to Fishes of the Maldives* is an indispensable book for divers and snorkellers, detailing some 700 species that live on the reefs of the country, all beautifully illustrated with photographs and descriptions of their habits.

The Maldive Mystery, by Norwegian explorer and ethnologist Thor Heyerdahl, is great for anyone wanting an overview of pre-Islamic Maldivian history and the numerous unanswered questions, although many of Heyerdahl's theories are now discredited.

Andrew Forbes' *Maldives – Kingdom of a Thousand Isles* is an odd mix of cultural overview, travel journal and resort guide. It's best employed as the first – the sections on history and traditional crafts are some of the most detailed available.

DON'T LEAVE HOME WITHOUT...

- Valid travel insurance
- Lots of sunscreen, sunblock and after-sun
- A good pair of UV-blocking sunglasses
- A sun hat
- Flippers, mask and snorkel – if you'd like to do much snorkelling; most resorts charge for the hire of a kit
- Plasters – small cuts on coral or sharp shells are not unknown
- Three-pin adaptors – the Maldives generally uses the UK-style electricity sockets (see p175)
- Lots of beach reading – don't rely on paperbacks left by other guests unless you're truly undiscerning
- All the medication and birth control you're likely to need
- Plastic bags for wet clothing and a waterproof jacket for the wetter months

Divers' Guide to the Sharks of the Maldives, by Dr RC Anderson, is another fascinating title that describes the various shark species divers can encounter in the Maldives.

Dive Guide The Maldives, by Sam Harwood and Rob Bryning, is one of the best dive guides in print, with reviews of all the main diving and snorkelling sites in the country.

INDEPENDENT TRAVEL

Independent travel in the Maldives is a challenge, but one risen to every year by many people, who decide that paradise on a package is not their idea of fun. As a fully independent traveller (FIT), you'll be a rarity, confusing hoteliers and transfer agents wherever you go when you tell them you don't have a tour operator. This is a great, if sometimes expensive, way to travel; however, while you're more independent than most package tourists, you're still not free to travel through the Maldives properly due to the restrictions on foreigners outside of resorts.

Male' is a great place to start for FITs – allow a couple of days in town to shop around several travel agencies and arrange onward travel, accommodation and even excursions and diving. FITs who want to get on a safari boat will certainly have to make arrangements in Male' (see p64), though they'd do much better to organise this before arriving. Due to the system of discounts offered to travel companies, even the most resolutely independent traveller determined to see untouristed areas will benefit from the help of a good travel agent or operator.

Male' has over a quarter of the country's population, relatively few tourists and is quite an interesting place in its own right. If you eat in local teashops, visit the market and walk around in the evenings, you'll meet lots of locals. English is widely spoken and people will be more than willing to chat. There are a few inhabited nonresort islands (Viligili, Hulhumale', Thila Fushi and Himmafushi), which you could reach and return from in a day.

It's perfectly feasible to use Male' airport as a transport hub from which you can take speedboat, dhoni, air and seaplane transfers to visit different resorts – all at your own pace. However, this will be an expensive way to travel and planning will be essential, particularly in high season (December to April) when many resorts are fully booked and last-minute changes hard to arrange. Inner Maldives (p96) continues to come highly recommended as the travel agency best set up to meet the needs of FITs.

It's still government policy to have tourists stay on island resorts or on boats within the 'tourism zone', though change is in the air, with the new government planning to open guesthouses on some inhabited islands, lift restrictions on travellers and even create a national transport network, the lack of which at present is another big impediment to independent exploration.

At the time of writing you still needed a travel permit to stay overnight on any nonresort island. To get a travel permit (see p176) you need a sponsor to invite you to the island concerned. If you want to visit islands that are occupied by Maldivians rather than tourists, you still have a few options.

Firstly, you can stay in a resort and make day trips. Most resorts offer 'island-hopping' trips that visit local fishing villages, though these villages often have conspicuous souvenir shops and persistent sellers. Some resorts are quite close to village islands; you can charter a dhoni to visit the village without a big group. Resorts won't allow you to use catamarans, windsurfers or canoes to visit nearby islands, but if you explain what you want and you find a sympathetic ear, you may get help.

The best resort to choose, if you want to visit local villages, is the Equator Village Resort (p167) on Gan, in the far south of the country. Gan is linked by causeways to four other islands with quite large villages and towns, including Hithadhoo, the second largest settlement in the country after Male', and you can cycle, taxi or walk through all of them.

The second option is to arrange a safari-boat trip to the areas you're interested in and make it clear to the operator that you want to visit fishing villages. The operator will arrange permits for all the people on the boat, and because you stay overnight on the boat, the accommodation problem is solved. You will have to charter the whole boat, so you'll need some other like-minded passengers to share the expense.

TOP FIVE WAYS TO SEE MORE THAN JUST YOUR RESORT

Many travellers are put off by the idea of spending a week or two on a small island and having little or no contact with the rest of the country. Here are five ways to see more.

- Take an excursion to Male' – the national capital is the best place to get to know the Maldives (p93).

- Visit an inhabited local island – nearly all resorts offer a half-day trip to a nearby inhabited island where you can see a small Maldivian town, buy local handicrafts and meet some residents.

- Take a photography flight – most resorts also offer the chance to hire a seaplane for a 30-minute swoop around the atoll – a great way to see more of the area and to get some great pictures.

- Take a dhoni cruise around the atoll – most resorts offer this and it's another great way to see other islands – ranging from local villages and other resorts to totally uninhabited islands.

- Chat to hotel staff – Maldivian staff are always happy to tell you about their country and share their impressions with you. In some resorts the staff quarters are nicely integrated into the resort, so you don't feel too cut off from the locals.

Adrian Neville's *Male' – Capital of the Maldives* is a beautifully presented coffee-table book with great photos of Male' and its people.

Mysticism in the Maldives, compiled by Ali Hussain, documents superstitions, encounters with jinnis, supernatural phenomena and weird stuff. Published by Novelty, it's out of print but still available in a few shops.

Classical Maldivian Cuisine, by Aishath Shakeela, is a fascinating and informative book with delicious recipes for fish soup, fish, coconut and curried fish – order from www.maldiviancuisine.com.

One holiday read that gives a fun behind-the-scenes account of what goes on at a luxury resort is Imogen Edwards-Jones's *Beach Babylon*. While it's not even explicitly set in the Maldives, it's allegedly based on Reethi Rah, one of the country's most exclusive resorts.

INTERNET RESOURCES

There's a huge amount about the Maldives online, though try a simple search and you'll find it's nearly exclusively travel agencies that come up. To find more useful resources, check out some of the following sites.

Inner Maldives (www.innermaldives.com) One of the country's best travel agencies has a great website packed full of information, particularly good for FITs.

Maldives Info (www.maldivesinfo.gov.mv) A government website providing the latest news on political developments in the country.

Maldives Story (www.maldivesstory.com.mv) A history site that tells the story of the country's development from ancient history to the present day.

Minivan News (www.minivannews.com) Excellent independent website reporting news and opinion from the Maldives.

Visit Maldives (www.visitmaldives.com) The official Maldives Tourism Promotion Board site has background information and data about virtually every resort, safari boat and tour operator in the country.

TRAVELLING RESPONSIBLY

Since our inception in 1973, Lonely Planet has encouraged our readers to tread lightly, travel responsibly and enjoy the magic that independent travel affords. International travel is growing rapidly, and we still firmly

---

TOP FIVE ECOTOURISM RESORTS

All Maldives resorts these days seem to be branding themselves as eco-friendly places for the green traveller. In most cases this is little more than savvy marketing, but the resorts below are some of the very best with good environmental records and a serious approach.

Banyan Tree Vabbinfaru (p122)

Coco Palm Boduhithi (p122)

Soneva Gili (p123)

Soneva Fushi (p151)

Nika Island (p138)

believe in the benefits it can bring. However, as always, we encourage you to consider the impact your visit will have on both the global environment and the local economies, cultures and ecosystems.

Of course, as you have to fly long distances from pretty much everywhere to get to the Maldives, you're already contributing to carbon dioxide emissions, which isn't a great start. Many offset schemes are deeply flawed, but still worth paying for to help offset your journey's carbon dioxide. On a more personal level, there are a few simple rules that all thoughtful visitors should adhere to.

There are plenty of steps you can take to help reduce the environmental impact of your visit: see boxed text, p43. In addition, most resorts are happy to answer questions about their green record, and many even have sections on their websites to explain their policy.

History

The history of the Maldives is that of a small, isolated and peaceful nation constantly trying to contain the desires of its powerful neighbours and would-be colonisers. It's also an incredibly hazy history for the most part – of which little before the conversion to Islam in 1153 is known. Indeed, the pre-Muslim period is full of heroic myths, mixed with conjecture based on inconclusive archaeological discoveries.

The Maldivian character has clearly been shaped by this tumultuous past: hospitable and friendly but fiercely proud and independent at the same time. It's safe to say that no conquering armies have got very far trying to persuade the Maldivian people of their benevolence.

Travels in Asia & Africa 1325-54, by Ibn Battuta, has been reprinted in paperback by Routledge Kegan Paul. Ibn Battuta, a great Moorish globe-trotter, was an early visitor to the Maldive islands and wrote this history of the early Muslim period.

EARLY DAYS

Some archaeologists, including the now much-discredited Thor Heyerdahl, believe that the Maldives was well-known from around 2000 BC, and was a trading junction for several ancient maritime civilisations including Egyptians, Romans, Mesopotamians and Indus Valley traders. The legendary sun-worshipping people called the Redin may have descended from one of these groups.

Around 500 BC the Redin either left or were absorbed by Buddhists, probably from Sri Lanka (known as Ceylon until 1972), and by Hindus from northwest India. HCP Bell, a British commissioner of the Ceylon Civil Service, led archaeological expeditions to the Maldives in 1920 and 1922. Among other things, he investigated the ruined, dome-shaped structures *(hawittas)*, mostly in the southern atolls, that he believed were Buddhist stupas similar to the dagobas found in Sri Lanka.

The Maldive Mystery, by Thor Heyerdahl, the Norwegian explorer of *Kon-Tiki* fame, describes a short expedition in 1982-83, looking for remains of pre-Muslim societies.

CONVERSION TO ISLAM

For many years Arab traders stopped at the Maldives en route to the Far East – their first record of the Maldive islands, which they called Dibajat, is from the 2nd century AD. Known as the 'Money Isles', the Maldives provided enormous quantities of cowry shells, an international currency of the early ages. It must have seemed a magical land to discover at the time – forget money growing on trees, in the Maldives it was washed up on the shore!

Abul Barakat Yoosuf Al Barbary, a North African, is credited with converting the Maldivians to Islam in 1153. Though little is really known about what happened, Barakat was a Hafiz, a scholar who knew the entire Koran by heart, who proselytised in Male' for some time before meeting with success. One of the converts was the sultan, followed by the

TIMELINE

1117	1153	1194
The first king of the Theemuge Dynasty, and the first king of the whole Maldives, Sri Mahabarana, is crowned, bringing together under one ruler the many fiefdoms that made up the country at the time.	Islam is officially adopted as the national religion, having been brought by Arab traders and taken up by the Maldives' previously Buddhist rulers. The first Friday Mosque is built in Male'.	The Isdhoo Loamaafaanu, a copperplate now believed to show the earliest recorded example of Maldivian script, is made. Among other things it details the execution of Buddhist monks in the south of the now Muslim nation.

royal family. After conversion the sultan sent missionaries to the atolls to convert them too and the Buddhist temples around the country were destroyed or neglected.

A series of six sultanic dynasties followed, 84 sultans and sultanas in all, although some did not belong to the line of succession. At one stage, when the Portuguese first arrived on the scene, there were actually two ruling dynasties, the Theemuge (or Malei) dynasty and the Hilali.

The Story of Mohamed Thakurufaanu, by Hussain Salahuddeen, tells the story of the Maldives' greatest hero, who liberated the people from the Portuguese.

THE PORTUGUESE

Early in the 16th century the Portuguese, who were already well established in Goa in western India, decided they wanted a greater share of the profitable trade routes of the Indian Ocean. They were given permission by the sultan to build a fort and a factory in Male', but it wasn't long before they wanted more from the Maldives.

In 1558, after a few unsuccessful attempts, Captain Andreas Andre led an invasion army and killed Sultan Ali VI. The Maldivians called the Portuguese captain 'Andiri Andirin' and he ruled Male' and much of the country for the next 15 years. According to some Maldivian beliefs, Andre was born in the Maldives and went to Goa as a young man, where he came to serve the Portuguese. (Apart from a few months of Malabar domination in Male' during the 18th century, this was the only time that another country has occupied the Maldives; some argue that the Portuguese never actually ruled the Maldives at all, but had merely established a trading post.)

A Description of the Maldive Islands for the Journal of the Royal Asiatic Society, by HCP Bell, the most renowned historian of the Maldives and former British commissioner in the Ceylon Civil Service, draws from his archaeological expeditions in 1920 and 1922.

According to popular belief, the Portuguese were cruel rulers, and ultimately decreed that Maldivians must convert to Christianity or be killed. There was ongoing resistance, especially from Mohammed Thakurufaanu, son of an influential family on Utheemu Island in the northern atoll of Haa Alif. Thakurufaanu, with the help of his two brothers and some friends, started a series of guerrilla raids, culminating in an attack on Male', in which all the Portuguese were slaughtered.

This victory is commemorated annually as National Day on the first day of the third month of the lunar year. There is a memorial centre on the island of Utheemu to Thakurufaanu, the Maldives' greatest hero, who went on to found the next sultanic dynasty, the Utheemu, which ruled for 120 years. Many reforms were introduced, including a new judicial system, a defence force and a coinage to replace the cowry currency.

PROTECTED INDEPENDENCE

The Portuguese attacked several more times, and the rajahs of Cannanore, South India (who had helped Thakurufaanu), also attempted to gain control. In the 17th century, the Maldives accepted the protection of the Dutch, who ruled Ceylon at the time. They also had a short-lived

1333	**1337**	**1558**
Ibn Battuta arrives in the Maldives for a nine-month stay, during which time he marries twice and leaves disappointed by the moral laxity of the locals.	The Friday Mosque in Male' is rebuilt by order of Sultan Ahmed Shihabuddin. The previous Friday Mosque, dating from 1153, had become run down.	The Portuguese begin their occupation of the Maldives, imposing an overseer of a warehouse in Male', and ruling the country from their stronghold in Goa. Attempts to impose Christianity on the local population prove unpopular.

defence treaty with the French, and maintained good relations with the British, especially after the British took possession of Ceylon in 1796. These relations enabled the Maldives to be free of external threats while maintaining internal autonomy. Nevertheless, it was the remoteness of the islands, the prevalence of malaria and the lack of good ports, naval stores or productive land that were probably the main reasons neither the Dutch nor the British established a colonial administration.

THE LEGEND OF THAKURUFAANU

As the man who led a successful revolution against foreign domination, and then as the leader of the newly liberated nation, Mohammed Thakurufaanu (sultan from 1573 to 1585) is the Maldives' national hero. Respectfully referred to as Bodu Thakurufaanu (*bodu* meaning 'big' or 'great'), he is to the Maldives what George Washington is to the USA. The story of his raid on the Portuguese headquarters in Male' is part of Maldivian folklore and incorporates many compelling details.

In his home atoll of Thiladhunmathee, Thakurufaanu's family was known and respected as sailors, traders and *kateebs* (island chiefs). The family gained the trust of Viyazoaru, the Portuguese ruler of the four northern atolls, and was given the responsibility of disseminating orders, collecting taxes and carrying tribute to the Portuguese base in Ceylon. Unbeknown to Viyazoaru, Thakurufaanu and his brothers used their position to foster anti-Portuguese sentiment, recruit sympathisers and gain intelligence on the Portuguese. It also afforded the opportunity to visit southern India, where Thakurufaanu obtained a pledge from the rajah of Cannanore to assist in an overthrow of the Portuguese rulers in the Maldives.

Back in Thiladhunmathee Atoll, Thakurufaanu and his brothers built a boat in which to conduct an attack on Male'. This sailing vessel, named *Kalhuoffummi*, has its own legendary status – it was said to be not only fast and beautiful, but to have almost magical qualities that enabled it to elude the Portuguese on guerrilla raids and reconnaissance missions.

For the final assault, they sailed south through the atolls by night, stopping by day to gather provisions and supporters. Approaching Male', they concealed themselves on a nearby island. They stole into the capital at night to make contact with supporters there and to assess the Portuguese defences. They were assisted in this by the local imam, who subtly changed the times of the morning prayer calls, tricking the Portuguese into sleeping late and giving Thakurufaanu extra time to escape after his night-time reconnaissance visits.

The attack on Male' was carefully planned and timed, and allegedly backed by supernatural forces – one story relates how a coconut tree mysteriously appeared in the Portuguese compound and provided cover for Thakurufaanu as he crept close and killed Andiri Andirin with a spear. In the ensuing battle the Maldivians, with help from a detachment of Cannanore soldiers, defeated and killed some 300 Portuguese. Most versions of the story have the Portuguese drinking heavily on their last night, making it a cautionary tale about the evils of alcohol.

The Thakurufaanu brothers then set about re-establishing a Maldivian administration under Islamic principles. Soon after, Bodu Thakurufaanu became the new sultan, with the title of Al Sultan-ul Ghazi Mohammed Thakurufaanu Al Auzam Siree Savahitha Maharadhun, first Sultan of the third dynasty of the Kingdom of the Maldives.

1573	1834	1887
The Portuguese are driven out from the Maldives following an attack on the Portuguese garrison led by national hero Mohammed Thakurufaanu. To this day, the event is celebrated as the country's National Day.	Captain Robert Moresby, the British maritime surveyor, begins his celebrated charting of the Maldives' waters, the first time the complex atolls, islands and reefs are mapped.	The Maldives becomes a self-governing British Protectorate after Borah Merchants, British citizens from India, became embroiled in local disagreements. The British stepped in, but the Maldivian sultans continued to rule.

In the 1860s Borah merchants from Bombay were invited to Male' to establish warehouses and shops, but it wasn't long before they acquired an almost exclusive monopoly on foreign trade. The Maldivians feared the Borahs would soon gain complete control of the islands, so Sultan Mohammed Mueenuddin II signed an agreement with the British in 1887 recognising the Maldives' statehood and formalising its status as a protectorate.

THE EARLY 20TH CENTURY

In 1932 the Maldives' first constitution was drawn up under Sultan Shamsuddin, marking the dawn of true Maldivian statehood. The sultan was to be elected by a 'council of advisers' made up of the Maldivian elite, rather than being a hereditary position. In 1934 Shamsuddin was deposed and Hasan Nurudin became sultan.

WWII brought great hardship to the Maldives. Maritime trade with Ceylon was severely reduced, leading to shortages of rice and other necessities – many died of illness or malnutrition. A new constitution was introduced in 1942, and Nurudin was persuaded to abdicate the following year. His replacement, the elderly Abdul Majeed Didi, retired to Ceylon leaving the control of the government in the hands of his prime minister, Mohammed Amin Didi, who nationalised the fish export industry, instituted a broad modernisation programme and introduced an unpopular ban on tobacco smoking.

When Ceylon gained independence in 1948, the Maldivians signed a defence pact with the British, which gave the latter control of the foreign affairs of the islands but not the right to interfere internally. In return, the Maldivians agreed to provide facilities for British defence forces, giving the waning British Empire a vital foothold in the Indian Ocean after the loss of India.

In 1953 the sultanate was abolished and a republic was proclaimed with Amin Didi as its first president, but he was overthrown within a year. The sultanate was returned, with Mohammed Farid Didi elected as the 94th sultan of the Maldives.

BRITISH BASES & SOUTHERN SECESSION

While Britain did not overtly interfere in the running of the country, it did secure permission to re-establish its wartime airfield on Gan in the southernmost atoll of the country, Addu. In 1956 the Royal Air Force began developing the base, employing hundreds of Maldivians and resettling local people on neighbouring islands. The British were informally granted a 100-year lease of Gan that required them to pay £2000 a year.

When Ibrahim Nasir was elected prime minister in 1957, he immediately called for a review of the agreement with the British on Gan, demanding that the lease be shortened and the annual payment increased. This was followed by an insurrection against the Maldivian government

The Maldive Islands: Monograph on the History, Archaeology & Epigraphy is HCP Bell's main work. The Ceylon Government Press published it in 1940, three years after his death. Original copies of the book are rare, reprints are available from tourist shops in Male'.

Norwegian explorer and ethnographer Thor Heyerdahl was fascinated by the Maldives and its pre-Islamic culture. Although he spent many years trying to uncover the secrets of the past, many of his conclusions were later rejected.

1932	1953	1959
The country writes its first constitution, curbing the sultan's powers.	The Maldives declares itself a republic within the British Commonwealth and dissolves the Sultanate. However, the Sultanate is restored shortly afterwards as debate rages on about how best to replace the institution.	The three southernmost atolls of the Maldives – Addu, Gnaviyani and Huvadhoo, declare their independence from the rest of the country founding the United Suvadive Republic.

by the inhabitants of the southern atolls of Addu and Huvadhoo, who objected to Nasir's demand that the British cease employing local labour. They decided to cut ties altogether and form an independent state in 1959, electing Abdulla Afif Didi president and believing that the so-called United Suvadive Republic would be recognised by the British.

In 1960 the Maldivian government officially granted the British the use of Gan and other facilities in Addu Atoll for 30 years (effective from December 1956) in return for the payment of £100,000 a year and a grant of £750,000 to finance specific development projects. Brokering a deal with the British on Gan effectively ruled the UK out of recognising the breakaway south and indeed Nasir eventually sent gunboats from Male' to quash the rebellion. Afif fled to the Seychelles, then a British colony, while other leaders were banished to various islands in the Maldives.

In 1965 Britain recognised the islands as a completely sovereign and independent state, and ceased to be responsible for their defence (although it retained the use of Gan and continued to pay rent until 1976). The Maldives was granted independence on 26 July 1965 and later became a member of the UN.

THE REPUBLIC

Following a referendum in 1968, the sultanate was again abolished, Sultan Majeed Didi retired to Ceylon and a new republic was inaugurated. Nasir was elected president, although as political parties remained illegal, he didn't face much opposition. In 1972 the Sri Lankan market for dried fish, the Maldives' biggest export, collapsed. The first tourist resorts opened that year, but the money generated didn't benefit many ordinary inhabitants of the country. Prices kept going up and there were revolts, plots and banishments as Nasir clung to power. In 1978, fearing for his life, Nasir stepped down and skipped across to Singapore, reputedly with US$4 million from the Maldivian national coffers.

A former university lecturer and Maldivian ambassador to the UN, Maumoon Abdul Gayoom, became president in Nasir's place. Hailed as a reformer, Gayoom's style of governing was initially much more open, and he immediately denounced Nasir's regime and banished several of the former president's associates. A 1980 attempted coup against Gayoom, involving mercenaries, was discovered and more banishment occurred. Despite Gayoom's reputation as a reformer, he made no move to institute democracy in the Maldives.

Gayoom was re-elected in 1983 and continued to promote education, health and industry, particularly tourism. He gave the tiny country a higher international profile with full membership in the Commonwealth and the South Asian Association for Regional Co-operation (SAARC). The focus of the country's economy remained the development of tourism, which continued throughout the 1980s.

1963	**1965**	**1968**
The United Suvadive Republic is forced to give up its independence bid, fostering wide resentment against the British, who many in the southern atolls believe betrayed them.	The Maldives finally gains full independence from the United Kingdom. The country does not opt to join the British Commonwealth, however, and remains outside the organisation until 1982.	The Maldives abolish the sultanate and declare themselves a republic again.

THE 1988 COUP

In September 1988, 51-year-old Gayoom began a third term as president, having won an election where he was the only candidate, again. Only a month later a group of disaffected Maldivian businessmen attempted a coup, employing about 90 Sri Lankan Tamil mercenaries. Half of these soldiers infiltrated Male' as visitors, while the rest landed by boat. The mercenaries took several key installations, but failed to capture the National Security Service (NSS) headquarters.

More than 1600 Indian paratroopers, immediately dispatched by the Indian prime minister, Rajiv Gandhi, ended further gains by the invaders who then fled by boat towards Sri Lanka. They took 27 hostages and left 14 people dead and 40 wounded. No tourists were affected – many didn't even know that a coup had been attempted. The mercenaries were caught by an Indian frigate 100km from the Sri Lankan coast. Most were returned to the Maldives for trial: several were sentenced to death, but reprieved and returned to Sri Lanka.

The coup attempt saw the standards of police and NSS behaviour decline. Many people in police captivity reportedly faced an increased use of torture and the NSS became a widely feared entity.

Non-Muslims may not be citizens of the Maldives, and when the new constitution was ratified in 2008 around 3,000 people lost their Maldivian passports.

GROWTH & DEVELOPMENT

In 1993 Gayoom was nominated for a fourth five-year term, and confirmed with an overwhelming referendum vote (there were no free elections again). While on paper the country continued to grow economically, through the now massive tourism industry and the stable fishing industry, much of this wealth was concentrated in the hands of a small group of people, and almost none of it trickled down to the people of the atolls.

At the same time, the Maldives experienced many of the problems of developing countries, notably rapid growth in the main city, the environmental effects of growth, regional disparities, youth unemployment and income inequality.

The 1998 El Niño event, which caused coral bleaching throughout the atolls, was detrimental for tourism and it signalled that global warming might threaten the existence of the Maldives. When Gayoom began a fifth term as president in 1998, the environment and sea-level rises were priorities for him.

The 1990s saw the Maldives develop hugely – the whole country became linked up with a modern telecommunications system, and mobile phones and the internet became widely available. By the end of the century 90% of Maldivians had electricity and basic hospitals, and higher secondary schools centres had been established in outer atolls. With Japanese assistance Male' was surrounded by an ingenious sea wall (which was to prove very useful just a few years later when the tsunami struck).

The Maldives is the smallest Muslim nation in the world, but also the third Muslim nation to institute a multi-party democratic political system.

1972	1976	1978
Kurumba Island, the Maldives' first holiday resort just a short distance from Male', opens, and a small trickle of intrepid travellers begin to arrive in search of the best beaches in the world.	The British Naval Base at Gan closes.	President Gayoom comes to power, ushering in three decades of massive development and growth in the tourism industry, but simultaneously seeing the stifling of dissent and the banning of political parties.

The official name for the country is the Republic of Maldives, or *Divehi Rajje ge Jumhuriyya*. Maldivians refer to their country as *Maale Dhivehi Raajje*, meaning 'The Island Kingdom under the authority of Male' – probably from where the word Maldives hails.

In 1997, to accommodate a growing population, work began on a new island near the capital, which is an extra metre or so above sea level.

THE EVAN NASEEM KILLING

When a 19-year-old inmate at Maafushi Prison in South Male' Atoll was beaten to death by guards in September 2003, a public outcry quickly followed. When Evan Naseem's family put their son's brutally tortured corpse on display Male' spontaneously erupted in rioting. The People's Majlis (Parliament), also known as the Citizen's Council, was stoned and police stations were burned by the mob. The NSS arrested and beat many rioters. In the same month President Gayoom was renominated as the sole presidential candidate for the referendum by the Majlis, a body made up not in small part of Gayoom family members and people appointed by the president.

Realising that something was up, Gayoom did make an example of the torturers who killed Evan Naseem, but stopped short of punishing or removing any senior ministers or Adam Zahir, the NSS chief of staff. Meanwhile, the Maldivian Democratic Party (MDP) was founded in Colombo in nearby Sri Lanka.

The Maldives is the flattest country in the world, with a highpoint of just 2.4 metres.

BLACK FRIDAY

Under pressure from colleagues, and in a move to outflank the growing reform movement, Gayoom launched his own reform programme in 2004. His proposals included having multiple candidates in the presidential election, a two-term limit for the president and the legalisation of political parties.

However, just a month later Gayoom banned political meetings of prodemocracy activists in Male' when they proved rather too popular. The events of Black Friday took place in Male' on 13 August 2004. Reformist and prodemocracy campaigners all gathered in the capital's main square, encouraged by the apparent lack of obstruction from the NSS. Former political prisoners and well-known reformists all attended with the apparent blessing of Gayoom, and held a successful meeting calling for reform. Then out of nowhere the NSS cleared the square, arresting and beating over a thousand people in the process. Women and children were beaten, and many were taken into solitary confinement, where they remained for months. The government claimed that the protesters had been rioting, but international opinion was against the measures taken.

There is no official total number of islands in the Maldives – seasonal sand bank shifts and the ever-changing nature of the country's geography mean that the number of islands is always changing. It's approximately 1200.

TSUNAMI

On the morning of 26 December 2004, the Indian Ocean tsunami devastated countries throughout the region. While it could have been much, much worse for the Maldives, whose vast, deep interatoll channels absorbed much of the strength of the wave, the result was still devastating,

1988	1998	2004
A coup d'état attempt by Sri Lankan mercenaries in Male' is quickly foiled with Indian assistance.	The El Niño weather system causes water temperatures to rise above 32C for two weeks, this killing off vital algae and bringing about coral bleaching still in evidence over a decade later.	The Indian Ocean tsunami wreaks havoc on the island chain, wiping out many towns and villages, leading to the abandonment of several islands and creating thousands of internally displaced people.

killing over 100 people. Twenty-one islands were destroyed, with over 11,000 people made homeless, many of whom continue today to exist as IDPs (internally displaced persons) on other islands. While large numbers of resorts were closed, they were rebuilt with incredible speed, nearly all being open again just a year later.

The long-term effects of the tsunami are still being felt by thousands in the Maldives, though this is not clear to most visitors, who rarely see the poorest islands in the country. New islands are being developed to house displaced people, but in general it was the very poorest who suffered the most and who are still feeling the effects today.

> Despite being a total size of 90,000sq km, the Maldives is 99% water, and has just 298 sq km of land, effectively making it smaller than Andorra.

DEMOCRACY ARRIVES

Gayoom surprised many observers by following through with his reform package and a new constitution was ratified in August 2008, which led to the country's first freely contested elections later that year.

The first round of voting gave Gayoom a healthy 40% of the vote, while Mohammed Nasheed's Democrats got just 25%. As no party got an overall majority a run-off was held on 29 October in which Nasheed, with the other candidates throwing their weight behind him, took 53.65% of the vote and became the country's first democratically elected leader.

One of Nasheed's first pronouncements as president was that his administration would not seek to prosecute any member of the former government, and in particular former president Gayoom. In the first few months of the new administration a radical reform and liberalisation agenda was set in motion, and pledges such as making the Maldives a carbon-neutral country within a decade were made, not to mention the announcement of a fund to buy land for the future of the Maldives in the event that the country is eventually lost to rising sea levels, a total ban on shark hunting, the privatisation of over 20 cumbersome state-run enterprises, and a plan for a national transportation network and the diversification of the tourism industry by the ending of the long-term policy of separating locals and travellers. With Maldivians now taking their new found democratic rights to heart, this is a very interesting time to be visiting the country and you can expect to hear vibrant debate and discussion wherever you go.

> For a detailed overview of Maldivian history see www.maldivesstory.com.mv.

2005	2007	2008
The People's Majlis, the Maldivian Parliament, votes to allow multi-party elections after a campaign for democracy that saw many activists beaten, imprisoned and harassed by the authorities.	A bomb in Sultan's Park in Male' explodes, injuring 12 tourists. Later the same year three men are sentenced to 15 years in jail for terrorism, admitting they were targeting non-Muslims as part of a jihad.	The first democratic election in the Maldives sees Mohammed Nasheed elected to the presidency, beating Maumoon Gayoom and beginning a new era in Maldivian politics.

The Culture

NATIONAL PSYCHE

Maldivians are devout Muslims. In some countries this might be considered incidental, but the national faith is the cornerstone of Maldivian identity and it is defended passionately at all levels of society. Officially 100% of the population are practising Sunni Muslims, and indeed, under the 2008 constitution, it's impossible to be a citizen of the Maldives if you are a non-Muslim. There's no scope for religious dissent, but there's also almost no desire *to* dissent.

This deep religious faith breeds a generally high level of conservatism, but that does not preclude the arrival of hundreds of thousands of non-Muslim tourists to the islands every year, coming to bathe semi-naked, drink lots of alcohol and often engage in premarital sex. It's definitely an unusual contradiction. Arguably, were the tourist industry not so carefully engineered to separate the tourists and local population, there would be far more cultural clashes and tension between devout Islam and Western liberalism. The new government has signalled that it's looking into integrating tourism more with daily Maldivian life – guest houses on inhabited islands are mooted, which will help to attract more independent travellers, although with more exposure to foreign culture, some counter, there's more scope for cultural pollution from non-Muslims.

A deep island mentality also permeates the country, so much so that people's first loyalty is to their own small island before their atoll or even the country as a whole. Not quite Asia, not quite Africa and not the Middle East, despite the cultural similarities, the Maldives has been slow to join the international community (it joined the Commonwealth and the South Asian Association for Regional Co-operation only in the 1980s) and remains a non-aligned nation with no particular enemies or allies.

The hardship implicit in survival on these relatively barren islands that are so remote has created a nation of hard workers. The work ethic runs throughout the country; historically a lazy Maldivian was a Maldivian who didn't eat.

Another much-ignored feature of the Maldivian people is their earthy humour and cheerfulness. Joking and laughter is a way of life and you'll notice this without even leaving your resort - take a few minutes to speak to the local staff and you'll soon witness this for yourself.

LIFESTYLE

The most obvious dichotomy in lifestyle in the Maldives is between people in the capital Male' and those 'in the atolls' - the term used by everyone to denote 'islanders' or anyone who lives outside the immediate area of bustling modernity that is Male'.

In Male' life is considerably easier and more comfortable than in the rest of the country on most fronts, with the obvious exception of space. Life in Male', one of the most densely populated places on earth, is only good for those who have decent-sized houses. With all the new developments on Hulhumale' island near the capital, there should be a gradual decrease in population and thus a slight easing of the population crush there in the next few years. The past two decades of extraordinary growth have created a massive economy in Male', although many residents of the city complain that while there are plenty of opportunities to earn and

---

The annual rate of population growth is about 3%.

The Maldivian caste system has effectively disappeared today. Traditionally the very lowest caste was that of the palm-toddy tappers *(raa-veri)*.

Life expectancy for a Maldivian is about 63 years for men and 65 years for women.

live well in the commercial and tourism sectors, there's a great lack of challenging, creative jobs if exporting fish and importing tourists are not your idea of fun. With limited education beyond high school and a lack of careers for the ambitious without good connections, it's no surprise that many young people in Male' dream of going abroad, at least to complete their education and training.

On the islands things are far more simple and laid-back, but people's lives aren't always as easy as those in Male'. In the atolls most people live in the extended family homestead (it's unusual to live alone or just as a couple in a way that it wouldn't be in Male'), and both men and women assume fairly traditional roles. While men go out to work (in general either as fishermen or on jobs that keep them away from home for long stretches at a time in the tourist or shipping industries), women are the homemakers, looking after the children, cooking and maintaining the household. Fish is traded for other necessities at the nearest big island. Attending the mosque is the main religious activity, and on smaller islands it's probably the main social and cultural activity as well.

> You can address Maldivians by their first or last name. Since so many men are called Mohammed, Hassan or Ali, the surname is more appropriate. In some cases an honorary title like Maniku or Didi is used to show respect.

The most important ritual in a man's life comes when he is circumcised at the age of six or seven. These are big celebrations that last for a week and are far more significant than marriages (not a big deal) and birthdays (not celebrated). Marriage is of course important, but it's not the massive celebration it is in most of the rest of Asia.

Rural life for the young can be fairly dull, although despite appearances even tiny fishing villages are surprisingly modern; most now have telephones, radio and TV. Nevertheless, many teenagers effectively go to boarding school, as provision for education outside population centres is

---

RESPONSIBLE TRAVEL

Maldivian resorts make it quite clear what guests should and shouldn't do. Guests must respect the environment (no damage to fish or coral) and they must respect Muslim sensibilities. Nudity is strictly forbidden and women must not go topless; bikinis and brief bathers are quite acceptable in resorts, although most prefer that you cover up in the bar, dining and reception areas. In Male' and on other inhabited islands, travellers should make an effort not to offend local standards. Men should never go bare-chested and women should avoid low-cut tops and tank tops. Long trousers or long skirts are preferable, but shorts are OK if they cover the thighs.

It's best to dress neatly and conservatively when dealing with officials and businesspeople. Maldivian professional men always wear long trousers, clean shoes (often slip-ons), a shirt and usually a tie. Women usually wear dresses below the knee that cover the shoulders and arms.

Those who spend time outside the resorts should be aware of a few more points:

- Lose the shoes – people take their shoes off before going inside a house or mosque. Maldivians can slip off their footwear without breaking step, but visitors may find it inconvenient. Slip-on shoes are easier than lace-ups, and flip-flops (thongs) are easier than sandals.

- Keep your cool – be patient and polite, especially in government offices, which can be painfully slow and frustrating.

- Payment etiquette – if you ask someone to lunch, that means you'll pay for it; and if someone else asks you, don't reach for the bill.

- Religion rules – Islam is the state religion, so be aware that prayer times take precedence over business and pleasure, and that Ramazan, a month of fasting, places great demands on local people. Visiting a mosque requires long trousers or a long skirt and no shoes. Never consume alcohol or pork outside resorts.

scant. There are a few preschools or kindergartens, where children start learning the Quran from about the age of three. There are government primary schools (madrasa) on every inhabited island, but some are very small and do not go past fifth grade. For grades six and seven, children may have to go to a middle school on a larger island. Atoll capitals have an Atoll Education Centre (AEC) with adult education and secondary schooling to grade 10 (16 years old).

Officially, 90% of students finish primary school, and the adult literacy rate is 98%. English is taught as a second language from grade one and is the usual language of instruction at higher secondary school – most Maldivians with a secondary education will speak excellent English.

The best students can continue to a free-of-charge higher secondary school, which teaches children to the age of 18 – there's one in Male', one in Hithadhoo, in the country's far south, and one in Kulhuduffushi, in the far north. Students coming to Male' to study generally take live-in domestic jobs, affecting their study time: girls are often expected to do a lot of housework.

The Maldives College of Higher Education, also in Male', has faculties of health, education, tourism-hospitality and engineering as well as one for Sharia'a law. For university studies, many young Maldivians go abroad, usually to Sri Lanka, India, Britain, Australia or Fiji, although the new government is planning on founding the country's first university in the near future.

There is a system of bonded labour under which people must work for the government at a meagre wage for a period that depends on the length of their education in government schools. For many this means a stint in the National Security Service or in a government office. They may pursue another occupation part-time to establish their career or to make ends meet. Many people in Male' have a second job or a business interest on the side.

ECONOMY

Fish and ships just about sum up the Maldivian economy beyond the tourist industry. Tourism accounts for 20% of GDP and up to 90% of government tax revenue. (Each traveller pays a US$8 'bed tax' per night they are in the Maldives – with more than 600,000 visitors usually spending at least a week in the country per year, you do the maths!)

Yet the Maldives, like luxury destinations around the world, has been feeling the pinch of the global economic turndown quite severely. During research for this guidebook in early 2009, ashen-faced reservation managers, particularly at the top end, were complaining of low residency and daily cancellations. Indeed, January 2009 saw a decline of 5% compared with tourist numbers in January 2008. Another matter of concern is the fact that the Maldives appears to have put many of its eggs in one diamond-encrusted basket – it seemed that every other cheap diving resort was being renovated into a five-star luxury property in 2009, precisely at a time when charging US$3000 a night for a room was starting to feel a little ludicrous. Yet the Russian billionaires are still coming, they're just, in the words of one five-star resort general manager, 'buying a little less vintage champagne'.

Elsewhere the previous government policies helped to mechanise the fishing fleet, introduce new packing techniques and develop new markets. Nevertheless, the fishing industry is vulnerable to international market fluctuations. Most adult males have some experience in fishing,

Cars remain the ultimate status symbol here, even in a country with virtually no roads. Some atoll chiefs have cars simply to show off, on their entirely sand-covered islands. At least it's environmentally friendly...

Check out www.presidency maldives.gov.mv for the latest information on what President Nasheed is up to.

ALL-PURPOSE, ALL-MALDIVIAN DHONI

The truck and bus of the Maldives is the sturdy dhoni, a vessel so ubiquitous that the word will soon become part of your vocabulary. Built in numerous shapes and sizes, the dhoni has been adapted for use as an ocean freighter, interatoll cruiser, local ferry, family fishing boat, excursion boat, dive boat, live-aboard yacht, delivery truck and mini fuel tanker. The traditional dhoni is thought to derive from the Arab dhow, but the design has been used and refined for so long in the Maldives that it is truly a local product.

Traditionally, dhonis have a tall, curved prow that stands up like a scimitar cutting through the sea breezes. Most Maldivians say this distinctive prow is purely decorative, but in shallow water a man will stand at the front, spotting the reefs and channels, signalling to the skipper and holding the prow for balance. It can interfere with boarding or loading, so it's often dispensed with on modern utility craft, or there is the removable prow-piece that slots into the front of the boat to look good, but lifts out of the way for loading. If you want to stand at the front of a dhoni, be aware that a removable prow-piece can be a slightly wobbly balancing post!

The flat stern is purely functional – it's where the skipper stands and steers, casually holding the tiller with his foot or between his legs. The stern platform is also used for fishing, and for one other thing – when a small dhoni makes a long trip, the 'head' is at the back. If nature calls, go right to the stern of the boat, face forward or backwards as your need and gender dictate, and rely on the skipper, passengers and crew to keep facing the front.

The details on a dhoni are a mix of modern and traditional. The rudder is attached with neat rope lashing, but nowadays the rope is always plastic, not coir (coconut fibre). The dhoni design required very little adaptation to take a diesel engine, and a motorised (ingeenu) dhoni has the same shallow draft as a sail-powered (riyalu) dhoni. The propeller is protected so it won't snag on mooring lines or get damaged on a shallow reef. Despite modern materials (cotton caulking instead of coir; red oxide paint as well as shark oil), a modern dhoni will still leak, just like a traditional one, so there is a bilge pump just in front of the skipper – it's a simple but effective gadget made from plastic plumbing pipes.

Most inhabited islands have a dhoni or two under construction or repair and you may see them on an excursion from a resort. The best dhoni builders are said to come from Raa Atoll and teams of them can be contracted to come to an island to make a new boat. Twelve workers, six on each side of the boat, can make a 14m hull in about 45 days, if their hosts keep them well fed. The keel is made from imported hardwood, while the hull planks are traditionally from coconut trees. A lot of the work is now done with power tools, but no plans are used.

and casual employment on fishing boats is something of an economic backstop. Men are unlikely to take on menial work for low pay when there is a prospect that they can get a few days or weeks of relatively well-paid work on a fishing boat, or dhoni (see the boxed text, above). The 2009 ban on all shark fishing has earned the Maldives valuable environmental credibility, but has unsurprisingly been unpopular with fishermen, many of whom hunted sharks in Maldivian waters for sale to China.

Trade and shipping (nearly all based in Male') is the third-biggest earner; nearly all food is imported and what little domestic agriculture there is accounts for less than 3% of GDP. Manufacturing and construction make up 15% of GDP: small boat yards, fish packing, clothing and a plastic pipe plant are modern enterprises, but mostly it's cottage industries producing coconut oil, coir (coconut-husk fibre) and coir products such as rope and matting. Some of the new industrial activities are on islands near Male' while others, such as fish-packing plants, are being established in the outer atolls. There is no income tax.

Keep informed about the developments of Hulhumale' island, the reclaimed land that will provide the future base for Male' and the government in the wake of rising sea levels, at www.hdc.com.mv.

POLITICS

A multi-party system was created by a unanimous vote of the People's Majlis (Parliament; also known as the Citizens' Council) in 2005, followed by the promulgation of a new constitution in 2008. Under the 2008 constitution, which enacts the separation of powers and provides for a bill of rights, the Maldives is a presidential republic, with the president both head of state and head of government.

The Maldivian president is directly elected by the people and is limited to two five-year terms in office. The People's Majlis is in Male', the capital island, and each of the 20 administrative atolls plus the island of Male' have two representatives each, elected for five-year terms. The president chooses the remaining eight parliamentary representatives, has the power to appoint or dismiss cabinet ministers, and appoints all judges. All citizens over 21 years of age can vote.

The main political parties operating in the Maldives are the ruling Maldivian Democratic Party (MDP), former President Maumoon Gayoom's Dhivehi Rayyithunge Party (DRP) and the Republican Party (Jumhooree Party).

> A plan for a national transport network has been announced by the new government, linking islands to each other by ferries and catamarans. If this goes ahead, the scope for individual travel will increase massively.

POPULATION

A third of the Maldives' estimated 300,000 population live on the tiny capital island of Male', where some 100,000 people are packed into a rectangle of land just a couple of kilometres across. The rest of the population is spread out on the atolls – there are hardly any other towns in the whole country. The second city is Hithadhoo on Addu Atoll, with a population of 9500, and beyond that there are very few settlements with more than 5000 inhabitants. The annual growth rate is estimated at 2.8%, meaning the Maldives is a young country, with a median age of 18 years. With no permanent migration, the Maldives is is ethnically almost homogenous.

It is thought that the original settlers of the Maldives were Dravidian and Sinhalese people who came from south India and Sri Lanka. There has also been a great deal of intermarriage and mixing with people from the Middle East and Africa.

> Officially only Muslims may become citizens of the Maldives. It is possible for foreigners to convert and later become Maldivian nationals, although this is extremely rare.

MEDIA

Until recently the media in the Maldives was exceptionally tame and did very little but repeat the government line on the issues of the day. Debate was stifled and the only possible means of dissent was online, which saw the rise of UK and Sri Lanka-based internet news sites such as the excellent *Minivan News* (www.minivannews.com) and the tabloid-style *Dhivehi Observer* (www.dhivehiobserver.com).

Things are rather different today, with a vibrant national debate being carried out in all media – although online is still the most popular. Daily newspapers are *Aufathis*, *Miadhu*, *Haveeru* and *Jazeera*, although they are inaccessible to most visitors as they are only printed in Dhivehi.

Television and radio stations are now crowded with debate and political programming too – the state-owned television channel TVM often hosting talk shows and discussion panels about the political situation in the country. For more on local media outlets, see p175.

> The Giravaaran people, who most believe were the first to settle in the Maldives, remain ethnically distinct from the rest of the population. However, they have left their native Giravaaru and now live in Male' since their number has decreased so dramatically. Their former home is now a resort.

RELIGION

Islam is the religion of the Maldives, and officially there are no other religious groups present. All Maldivians are Sunni Muslims. No other

---

IDOLATRY

Most countries prohibit the importation of things like narcotics and firearms, and most travellers understand such restrictions, but when you're forbidden to bring 'idols of worship' into the Maldives, what exactly does that mean? The Maldives is an Islamic nation, and it is sensitive about objects that may offend Muslim sensibilities. A small crucifix, worn as jewellery, is unlikely to be a problem, and many tourists arrive wearing one. A large crucifix with an obvious Christ figure nailed to it may well be prohibited. The same is true of images of Buddha – a small decorative one is probably OK, but a large and ostentatious one may not be.

Maldivian authorities are concerned about evangelists and the objects they might use to spread their beliefs. Inspectors would not really be looking for a Bible in someone's baggage, but if they found two or more Bibles they would almost certainly not allow them to be imported. It would be unwise to test the limits of idolatrous imports – like customs people everywhere, the Maldivian authorities take themselves very seriously.

---

religions or sects are permitted and it is impossible to become a citizen of the country unless you are a Sunni Muslim.

The Maldives observes a liberal form of Islam, like that practised in India and Indonesia. Maldivian women do not observe purdah, although many wear a headscarf. Children are taught the Arabic alphabet and learn to read and recite the Quran from a young age.

Most mosques are of simple, unadorned design, but some of the older mosques have intricate woodcarvings inside and elaborate carved grave stones outside. The Islamic Centre (p99) in Male' is especially imposing, with soaring ceilings and big carved wood panels and screens.

> The mother-goddess cult of pre-Muslim Maldivian tradition has survived centuries of Islam and remains a key belief of islanders.

The Prophet Mohammed

Mohammed was born in Mecca (now in Saudi Arabia) in AD 570 and had his first revelation from Allah in 610. He began to preach against idolatry and proved to be a powerful and persuasive speaker. His teachings appealed to the poorer levels of society and angered the wealthy merchant class.

In 622 Mohammed and his followers were forced to migrate to Medina, 300km to the north. This migration, known as the Hejira, marks the start of the Islamic Calendar: AD 622 became year 1 AH. By AD 630 Mohammed had gained enough followers to return and take Mecca.

Within two decades of Mohammed's death, most of Arabia had converted to Islam. The Prophet's followers spread the word, and the influence of the Islamic state soon extended from the Atlantic to the Indian Ocean, south into Africa and east to the Pacific.

The Five Pillars of Islam

Islam is the Arabic word for submission and underlies the duty of all Muslims to submit themselves to Allah.

Shahada, the profession of faith that 'there is no God but Allah, and Mohammed is his prophet', is the first of the Five Pillars of Islam: the tenets guiding Muslims in their daily life.

The second pillar, *salath*, is the call to prayer, and Islam decrees that Muslims must face Mecca and pray five times each day. In the Maldives, *salath* is also called *namadh*.

The third pillar is zakat, the act of giving alms to the needy. Some Islamic countries have turned this into an obligatory land tax that goes to help the poor.

> The word 'atoll' in English is generally accepted to come from the Dhivehi word *atolu*, the only known example of a Maldivian word being used in English.

The fourth pillar is the fast during the day for the month of Ramazan, the ninth month of the Islamic calendar.

The fifth pillar is the haj (pilgrimage) to Mecca, the holiest place in Islam. It is the duty of every able Muslim to make the haj at least once in their life.

Prayer Times

The initial prayer session is in the first hour before sunrise, the second around noon, the third in mid-afternoon around 3.30pm, the fourth at sunset and the final session in the early evening.

The call to prayer is delivered by the *mudhim* (muezzin). In former days, he climbed to the top of the minaret and shouted it out. Now the call is relayed by loudspeakers on the minaret and the *mudhim* even appears on TV. All TV stations cut out at prayer time, although only

---

WOMEN IN SOCIETY *Aishath Velezinee*

In the 14th century, long before the call for equality took momentum, the Maldives was ruled by women. Three queens reigned; one, Sultana Khadija, held the throne for 33 years from 1347 to 1379. The shift from monarchy to a constitutional republic barred women from the post of President, and this clause was only removed by the new 2008 constitution.

Traditional lifestyle, especially on the islands away from the capital, dictated gender-specific roles for women and men. Women tended to their children and the household duties during the day, and cooked fish in the evenings. Men spent the day fishing and then rested in the evenings. Modernisation and development changed the traditional way of life and conferred a double burden on many women - income generation plus domestic responsibilities. More opportunities and better education mean that more women are ready to join the workforce or take up income-generating activities at home. This has become a necessity rather than a choice for most women living in Male', as rising expenses and changing lifestyles demand a dual income to meet basic family expenses.

In Male' women work in all sectors, but mainly in teaching, nursing or administrative or secretarial positions. Less stereotypical jobs such as the police force also recruit women and offer equal opportunities. With no child-care facilities available, and little help from husbands on the domestic side, working mothers depend heavily on the efforts of other women in the extended family - grandmothers, aunts, sisters etc. While the movement of women from domestic roles to paid employment has been rapid, there is very little progress in getting men to pour their own water, let alone share in domestic work.

On the outer islands, with little opportunity for formal employment, women tend to be self-employed, but with little financial gain. Markets are limited by geography, demography and the lack of regular and reliable interisland transport. Women on islands close to the tourism zones grow fruits and vegetables for sale to resorts. They also weave coconut-leaf matting *(cadjan)* and make rope and other products from coir. On remoter islands women make dried fish, a product that can withstand the long boat journey to the market. At least a few women on each island are experts at sewing and most women grow their own fruit. Some island girls get an education and train as teachers and health workers, but most prefer to stay on Male', where there are wider career choices, rather than return home. Recent appointments of a few women to the posts of *atolu verin* (atoll chief) and *kateeb* (island chief), till now the realm of men alone, have opened new opportunities for educated women.

Marriage is seen as a must for all Maldivian women, and less than 1% of those over 30 have never married. Marriage and divorce have always been casual, giving a woman no security. Until a decade ago she could be divorced on the whim of her husband, without reason or compensation. Divorce carries no stigma, and early marriage, divorce and serial marriages are the norm. A woman retains her own name after marriage - this is sensible as she could be Mrs X, Mrs Y and Mrs Z in the space of a single year.

TVM (the national channel) cuts out for the entire duration - satellite channels just have their broadcasts interrupted to remind Muslims to go to the mosque.

Shops and offices close for 15 minutes after each call. Some people go to the mosque, some kneel where they are and others do not visibly participate. Mosques are busiest for the sunset prayers and at noon on Fridays.

Ramadan

Called Ramazan in the Maldives, this is the month of fasting, which begins at the time of a particular new moon and ends with the sighting of the next new moon. The Ramazan month gets a little earlier every year because it is based on a lunar calendar of twelve months, each with 28 days (see p172).

In 2009 a state pension for the over-65s was introduced for the first time in the Maldives. Men and women reaching this age now receive Rf2000 (US$156) per month.

In an effort to strengthen family and bring down the high divorce rate (which was once the highest in the world), the first-ever codified Family Law was introduced in 2001, raising the minimum age of marriage to 18 and making unilateral divorce illegal. Prenuptial contracts registered at the court can strengthen a woman's position within the marriage as she can stipulate her rights. Where once a man could divorce his wife merely by telling her that she was divorced, now both partners must go through the court to initiate divorce, and it is permitted only when all reconciliation attempts fail. While the divorce rate has gone down, questions remain as to whether fewer divorces mean a better life for women. Polygamy is legal, and men can have up to four wives at a time, although it is not common practice to have more than one wife.

Traditionally, a woman could choose a suitor and name a bride-price (rhan). The bride-price is paid by the husband to the wife, at the time of marriage or in instalments as mutually agreed, but must be paid in full if there's a divorce. Young women today quote higher bride-prices, reflecting higher expectations, and perhaps a scepticism about the fairytale happy-ever-after marriage. The wedding itself is a low-key affair, but is often followed by a large banquet for all family and friends, who can easily number in the hundreds.

Women in the Maldives can, and do, own land and property but women have a fraction of the property that men do. While inheritance generally follows Islamic Sharia'a law in the Maldives, land is divided according to civil law, whereby a daughter and son inherit equal shares of land.

There is little overt discrimination between the sexes. Although it's a fully Muslim society, women and men mingle freely and women enjoy personal liberty not experienced by women in most Muslim societies. However, Islam is used as a tool by some patriarchs to counter gender equality, even as they proclaim that Islam grants equality to women and men. Local discourse tends to say that the factors limiting gender equality are cultural rather than Islamic, and therefore it is possible to change them.

Movement of women is not officially restricted, but women's mobility is limited by factors such as domestic responsibilities and societal attitudes as to what is a woman's place. Home is where 'good girls' are. Although physical assaults against women are very unusual, women on streets and other public spaces can be harassed.

Most women in the Maldives go bareheaded, although many also wear a headscarf, a sign of commitment to Islam. The government has banned face coverings to limit the appearance of radical religious ideas. Gyms and fitness centres attract Maldivian women, as do hair and beauty salons. Formal functions require women to wear one of the officially sanctioned 'national dresses', which includes the traditional libaas (dress) and dhiguhedhun (traditional full-length dress with long sleeves and a wide collar) as well as a Malay-style skirt and blouse with libaas-style neck embroidery. For everyday wear, young women dress in T-shirts, tank tops, flimsy blouses, fashionable jeans, trousers and short skirts. The more self-conscious choose Indian-style shalwar kameez (loose blouses and trousers). Older women wear the traditional dhiguhedhun and libaas.

Aishath Velezinee is a Maldivian writer, researcher and women's rights advocate

During Ramazan Muslims should not eat, drink, smoke or have sex between sunrise and sunset. Exceptions to the eating and drinking rule are granted to young children, pregnant or menstruating women, and those who are travelling. It can be a difficult time for travel outside the resorts, as teashops and cafes are closed during the day, offices have shorter hours and people may be preoccupied with religious observances or the rigours of fasting. Visitors should avoid eating, drinking or smoking in public, or in the presence of those who are fasting. After a week or so, most Muslims adjust to the Ramazan routine and many say they enjoy it. There are feasts and parties long into the night, big breakfasts before dawn and long rests in the afternoon. Kuda Eid, the end of Ramazan, is a major celebration.

Rates of thalassaemia, a hereditary blood condition that makes regular blood transfusions necessary, is extremely high in the Maldives, with 18% of the population carrying the condition in some form.

Local Beliefs

On the islands people still fear jinnis, the evil spirits that come from the sea, land and sky. They are blamed for everything that can't be explained by religion or education.

To combat jinnis there are *fandhita*, which are the spells and potions provided by a local *hakim* (medicine man), who is often called upon when illness strikes, if a woman fails to conceive, or if the fishing catch is poor.

The hakim might cast a curing spell by writing phrases from the Quran on strips of paper and sticking or tying them to the patient or writing the sayings in ink on a plate, filling the plate with water to dissolve the ink, and making the patient drink the potion. Other concoctions include *isitri*, a love potion used in matchmaking, and its antidote *varitoli*, which is used to break up marriages.

To support the Society of Health Education (SHE), which works with victims of thalassaemia, visit www.she.org.mv.

SPORT

Soccer is the most popular sport and is played all year round. On most islands, the late-afternoon match among the young men is a daily ritual. There's a league competition in Male', played between club teams with names such as Valencia and Victory, and annual tournaments against teams from neighbouring countries. Matches are also held at the National Stadium (p106) in Male'.

Cricket is played in Male' for a few months, beginning in March. Volleyball is played indoors, on the beach and in the waterfront parks. The two venues for indoor sport are the Centre for Social Education, on the west side of Male', and a newer facility just east of the New Harbour, used for basketball (men and women), netball, volleyball and badminton.

The largest social problem in the Maldives today is drug addiction, which is common in both Male' and the atolls. 'Brown sugar', a poorly refined heroin derivative, is the narcotic most commonly abused. Prevention, education and treatment programmes are being introduced to combat the problem.

Traditional games include *bai bala*, where one team attempts to tag members of the other team inside a circle, and a tug-of-war, known as *wadhemun*. *Bashi* is a girls' game, played on something like a tennis court, where a girl stands facing away from the net and serves a tennis ball backwards, over her head. There is a team of girls on the other side who then try to catch it.

Thin mugoali (meaning 'three circles') is a game similar to baseball and has been played in the atolls for more than 400 years. The *mugoali* (bases) are made by rotating on one foot in the sand through 360 degrees, leaving a circle behind. You'll sometimes see *bashi* in Male' parks or on village islands in the late afternoon, but traditional games are becoming less popular as young people are opting for international sports.

The Maldives has participated in the Olympics since 1988, but have yet to win any medals. Unsurprisingly, the team has never taken part in the winter Olympics.

ARTS

Though performances of traditional music and dance are not everyday events, contemporary Dhivehi culture is strong and adaptive, despite foreign influences, which range from martial arts and Hindi movies to Shakira and Muslim fundamentalism.

Western and Indian fashions, pop music and videos are highly visible, but on public occasions and festivals the celebrations always have a Maldivian style. Four daily newspapers and several magazines are published in the national language and rock bands sing Dhivehi lyrics. It's remarkable that such a tiny population maintains such a distinctive culture.

Song & Dance

Bodu beru means 'big drum' and gives its name to the best-known form of traditional music and dance. It is what tourist resorts put on for a local culture night, and it can be quite sophisticated and compelling. Dancers begin with a slow, nonchalant swaying and swinging of the arms, and become more animated as the tempo increases, finishing in a rhythmic frenzy. In some versions the dancers enter a trance like state. There are four to six drummers in an ensemble and the sound has strong African influences.

This is also the entertainment at private parties, where a few guys will play the drums and everyone else dances - more and more frenetically as the night goes on.

Local rock bands often perform at resorts, where they do credible covers of old favourites as well as performing their own material. They may incorporate elements of *bodu beru* in their music, with lots of percussion and extended drum solos when they're in front of a local audience. Some popular contemporary bands are Seventh Floor, Mezzo and Zero Degree Atoll - CDs from these, and quite a few other bands, are sold in Male's music shops.

Literature

Despite the unique Maldivian script that dates from the 1600s, most Maldivian myths and stories are from an oral tradition and have only recently appeared in print. Many are stories of witchcraft and sorcery, while others are cautionary tales about the evils of vanity, lust and greed, and the sticky fates of those who transgressed. Some are decidedly weird and depressing, and don't make good bedtime reading for young children. In the early 1990s, Novelty Press published a small

The Maldives' biggest international ally is India, which has supported the new government and donated US$100m to the tiny island nation. Cynics point out that this generosity might have been because China is also wooing the Maldives as a friend, with an eye to building a submarine base in the country.

At the time of writing there were 98 established resort islands in the country. A further 63 will be allocated and developed between now and 2013.

SITTING IN THE MALDIVES

The Maldives has two unique pieces of furniture. One is the *undholi,* a wooden platform or a netting seat that's hung from a tree or triangular frame. Sometimes called a bed-boat, the *undholi* is a sofa, hammock and fan combination – swinging gently creates a cooling movement of air across the indolent occupant.

The *joli* is a static version – a net seat slung on a rectangular frame, usually made in sociable sets of three or four. They were once made of coir rope and wooden sticks, but steel pipes and plastic mesh are now almost universal – it's like sitting in a string shopping bag, but cool.

book called *Mysticism in the Maldives*, which is still available in some shops. The Hammond Innes thriller *The Strode Venturer* and Imogen Edwards-Jones' fun airport read *Beach Babylon* are about the only novels set in the Maldives.

Architecture

A traditional Maldivian village is notable for its neat and orderly layout, with wide streets in a regular, rectangular grid. Houses are made of concrete blocks or coral stone joined with mortar, and the walls line the sides of the streets. Many houses will have a shaded courtyard in front, enclosed by a chest-high wall fronting the street. This courtyard is an outdoor room, with *joli* and *undholi* seats (see the boxed text, p35), where families sit in the heat of the day or the cool of the evening. A more private courtyard behind, the *gifili*, has a well and serves as an open-air bathroom.

At intersections, the coral walls have rounded corners, which considerably soften the streetscape. These corners are apparently designed to facilitate turning vehicles, but they are like this even in small island villages that never see a vehicle. The same style is used in Male', where it does make turning easier for cars and trucks. On the upper floors of a modern building, the rounded corners are more for appearance than practicality, and seem to be a deliberate adaptation of a traditional feature.

The architecture of resorts is eclectic, imitative of anything from a Balinese *bale* to an African rondavel or an American motel. The most identifiably Maldivian feature is the open-air bathroom, a delightful feature that's popular with guests.

Visual Arts

There is no historical tradition of painting in the Maldives, but demand for local art (however fabricated) from the tourist industry has created a supply in the ultra-savvy Maldivian market, with more than a few locals selling paintings to visitors or creating beach scenes for hotel rooms.

The National Art Gallery in Male' (p100) puts on an exhibit of Maldivian art every few years. It combines photography, painting and some conceptual art, and is well worth a visit if it happens to coincide with your time in Male'. Some local names to look out for are Eagan Badeeu, Ahmed Naseer and Hassan Shameem.

Some islands were once famous for wood and stone carving – elaborate calligraphy and intricate intertwining patterns are a feature of many old mosques and gravestones. A little of this woodcarving is still done, mainly to decorate mosques. The facade of the Majlis building in Male' is decorated with intertwined carvings.

Crafts

MATS

Natural-fibre mats are woven on many islands, but the most famous are the ones known as *tundu kunaa*, made on the island of Gadhdhoo in Gaaf Dhaal Atoll. This may have been an endangered art form, but renewed interest thanks to the increase in tourism has arguably saved it from disappearing. A Danish researcher in the 1970s documented the weaving techniques and the plants used for fibre and dyes, and noted that a number of traditional designs had not been woven for 20 years. Collecting the materials and weaving a mat can take weeks, and the money that can be made selling the work is not much by modern Maldivian

Former Maldivian President Maumoon Gayoom now teaches at an Islamic College in Male' while also strongly criticising the new president's policies at every turn.

One populist act of President Nasheed has been to open up the former Presidential Palace in Male', Theemuge, to the general public. When the palace was opened in April 2009 large lines of curious Male' residents queued for hours to see how the former president lived.

standards. Some fine examples now decorate the reception areas of tourist resorts, and there's a growing appreciation of the work among local people and foreign collectors.

LACQUER WORK

Traditionally, lacquer work *(laajehun)* was for containers, bowls and trays used for gifts to the sultan – some fine examples can be seen in the National Museum (p98) in Male'. Different wood is used to make boxes, bowls, vases and other turned objects. Traditionally the lathe is hand-powered by a cord pulled round a spindle. Several layers of lacquer are applied in different colours. They then harden, and the design is incised with sharp tools, exposing the bright colours of the underlying layers.

LOCAL VOICE: EAGAN MOHAMED BADEEU

Eagan talks about living and working as an artist in Male'.

What can visitors expect from the Maldivian art scene? Souvenirs, such as the traditional Maldivian lacquered vases, jewellery and other craftwork, do still tend to dominate the art scene, but in fact most of this is imported and little is locally made. Beyond the touristy stuff there is an emerging art scene, which was boosted by the founding of the National Art Gallery in Male' in 2005 (p100), currently the only space where Maldivian artists can show their work. Most painted themes portray the natural beauty of the islands, though more contemporary and conceptual art styles are also becoming popular.

Is there a big artistic tradition in the Maldives? The Maldives has a rich culture and tradition of craftsmanship, especially for stone carving and lacquer work – the Old Friday Mosque in Male', for example, is a masterpiece of both, with the complicated floral and symmetrical patterns showing us how creative these craftsmen were. Our ancestors used organic dyes to colour the traditional *feyli* (Maldivian sarong) and *tundu kunaa* (reed mats), but there is no evidence of paintings in our tradition before the early 20th century.

You paint a lot of traditional Maldivian scenes. Are you worried that some of these traditions will be lost in the future? Yes, for me it is sad to see the dredged concrete harbours taking over from the timber jetties of our islands. Thirty years ago I remember young people sailing small dhonis for fun, learning how to use the ocean currents and the monsoon winds to navigate. However, today a young Maldivian is more likely to circle the island on a motorcycle than in a dhoni! Most of our traditions will be lost in the future and so it's up to us to keep traditions passed on by our forefathers alive for the next generation.

You must have travelled a lot in your country; do you have a favourite part of the Maldives? My favourite part of the country is Haa Dhaal Atoll in the north Maldives. I particularly love the island of Hanimaadhoo, which has a charming old village and a thick palm and banyan tree forest. Most of all, the lovely people there are very friendly. The island of Kulhuduffushi, the capital of Haa Dhaal, is another favourite of mine. The islanders are famous for celebrating Eid by performing lots of traditional dances, and people travel there to see them.

What is your favourite thing about Maldivian village life? I like to sit in a *holhuashi* (small beach hut) and chat with the island folk. On any island the holhuashi is where the village men gather to talk politics, play cards and chess. For me the most interesting time of the day is when the fishermen return after the day's catch. People gather on the beach to clean and buy the fish before the village women prepare a delicious *garudia* (fish broth) with rice, lime and chillies.

Does life vary strongly between the rural areas in Maldives and the bigger towns? Which do you prefer? Of course – Male' is now the world's most densely populated island, with all the problems of any big city, while rural islands are quiet, spacious and clean. Despite this, many families blindly migrate from their islands to Male'. If it were possible I would do the opposite as I'd love to live in the atolls – this is actually the dream of many people living in the capital!

The new government has announced plans to properly excavate the country's large number of pre-Islamic Buddhist sites in a bit to attract travellers interested in more than just beaches and diving.

Designs are usually floral motifs in yellow with red trim on a black background (most likely based on designs of Chinese ceramics). Production of lacquer work is a viable cottage industry in Baa Atoll, particularly on the islands of Eydhafushi and Thulhaadhoo.

JEWELLERY

Ribudhoo Island in Dhaalu (South Nilandhoo Atoll) is famous for making gold jewellery, and Hulhudheli, in the same atoll, for silver jewellery. According to local belief, a royal jeweller brought the goldsmithing skills to the island centuries ago, having been banished to Ribudhoo by a sultan. It's also said that the islanders plundered a shipwreck in the 1700s, and reworked the gold jewellery they found to disguise its origins.

Food & Drink

Your culinary experience in the Maldives could be, depending on your resort, anything from *haute cuisine* ordered from a menu you've discussed with the chef in advance to bangers and mash at the all-you-can-eat buffet in the communal dining room. What it's unlikely to be in either case is particularly Maldivian, given the dislocation from local life experienced in resorts. However, anyone staying in Male' or visiting inhabited islands should take advantage of this opportunity to try real Maldivian food (rather than the somewhat fanciful fare produced on 'Maldivian' cuisine nights in resorts, which often owes more to Indian and Sri Lankan cooking than anything local). Maldivian cuisine is unsurprisingly simple and testament to a nation's historic survival on a relatively small, but bountiful, amount of locally occurring ingredients.

STAPLES & SPECIALITIES

All that grows in the Maldives are coconuts, mangoes, papayas and pineapples; the only other locally occurring product is fish, which explains the simplicity of Maldivian cuisine historically.

However, as trade with the Indian subcontinent, Africa, Arabia and the Far East have always brought influences of a more exciting nature, the result is far less bland than it could be. That said, don't expect to see a Maldivian takeaway open up on a street near you any time soon.

The Indian influence is clear in local cuisine above all; Maldivian food is often hot and spicy. If you're going to eat local food, prepare your palate for spicy fish curry, fish soup, fish patties and variations thereof. A favourite Maldivian breakfast is *mas huni*, a healthy mixture of tuna, onion, coconut and chilli, eaten cold with *roshi* (unleavened bread, like an Indian chapati) and tea.

For snacks and light meals, Maldivians like *hedhikaa*, a selection of little finger foods. In homes the *hedhikaa* are placed on the table, and everyone helps themselves. In teashops this is called 'short eats' – a choice of things like *fihunu mas* (fish pieces with chilli coating), *gulha* (fried dough balls filled with fish and spices), *keemia* (fried fish rolls in batter) and *kuli boakiba* (spicy fish cakes). There are also samosa-like triangles of curried vegetables, and even small pizza squares are appearing in teashops now. Sweets include little bowls of *bondi bai* (rice pudding), tiny bananas and *zileybee* (coloured coils of sugared, fried batter). Generally, anything small and brown will be savoury and contain fish, and anything light or brightly coloured will be sweet.

A main meal will include rice or *roshi* or both, plus soups, curries, vegetables, pickles and spicy sauces. In a teashop, a substantial meal with rice and *roshi* is called 'long eats'. The most typical dish is *garudia*, a soup

Don't be fooled by beer in Male' – it's all nonalcoholic, even if it doesn't look it! For those gasping for the real thing, you'll need to cross the lagoon to the airport island where alcoholic beer is widely available.

DOS & DON'TS

- Always eat with your right hand; your left hand is considered unclean.

- Do ask for a spoon if you aren't comfortable eating with your bare hands Maldivian style; this won't offend.

- Remember that during Ramazan it's not acceptable to eat in public during daylight hours outside of resorts.

TRAVEL YOUR TASTEBUDS

If you are feeling like trying something both exotic and dear to the Maldivian people, go for *miruhulee boava* (octopus tentacles). This is not commonly found, but is often prepared in the atolls as a speciality, should you be lucky enough to visit an inhabited island as a guest. The tentacles are stripped and cleaned and braised in a sauce of curry leaves, cloves, garlic, chilli, onion, pepper and coconut oil – delicious.

---

made from dried and smoked fish, often eaten with rice, lime and chilli. The soup is poured over rice, mixed up by hand and eaten with the fingers. Another common meal is *mas riha*, a fish curry eaten with rice or *roshi* – the *roshi* is torn into strips, mixed on the plate with the curry and condiments, and eaten with the fingers. A cup of tea accompanies the meal, and is usually drunk black and sweet.

The Maldivian equivalent of the after-dinner mint is the areca nut, chewed after a meal or snack. The little oval nuts are sliced into thin sections, some cloves and lime paste are added, the whole lot is wrapped in an areca leaf, and the wad is chewed whole. It's definitely an acquired taste.

DRINKS

The only naturally occurring fresh water in the Maldives is rainwater, which is stored in natural underground aquifers beneath each island. This makes getting water quite a feat, and water conservation has always been extremely important in Maldivian culture, to the extent that the Maldives Tourism Law states that no water resources may be diverted from an inhabited island to supply a resort. All resorts have their own desalinating plants to keep visitors supplied with enough water for their (by local standards incredibly wasteful) water needs.

In resorts, consider the sheer carbon costs of only drinking imported Evian – even if you can afford to at $7 a bottle – and go for desalinated water, which is perfectly good to drink, if perhaps something of an acquired taste initially.

The main drinks other than rainwater are imported tea and toddy tapped from the crown of the palm trunk at the point where the coconuts grow. Every village has its toddy man *(raa veri)*. The *raa* is sweet and delicious if you can get over the pungent smell. It can be drunk immediately after it is tapped from the tree, or left to become a little alcoholic as the sugar ferments.

Fermented *raa* is of course the closest most Maldivians ever get to alcohol; the Maldives is strictly dry outside of resorts (and Maldivian staff cannot drink alcohol even there). Despite this, nonalcoholic beer is very popular in Male'. Soft drinks, including the only Coca-Cola made from salt water anywhere in the world, are available all over the country at prices much lower than in resorts. Outside resorts the range of drinks is very limited. Teashops will always serve *bor feng* (drinking water) and of course *sai* (tea). Unless you ask otherwise, tea comes black, with *hakuru* (sugar). *Kiru* (milk) isn't a common drink, and is usually made up from powder as there are no cows in the Maldives.

WHERE TO EAT & DRINK

In budget resorts you won't usually have any choice – most cheaper resorts have just one restaurant, while midrange places typically have two or more to afford some choice, and top-end resorts often boast three or

---

Wine is available in resorts, but only in the better ones. Expect to pay extraordinary mark-ups; you'll do well to find anything OK for under US$50. Sadly, it's illegal to bring wine into the country, so don't waste your time carrying a nice bottle or two to enjoy in your resort!

more. Buffets (always for breakfast, often for lunch and dinner too) allow for lots of different cuisines and plenty of choice. In Male', where there's a much broader choice, the most obvious place for authentic Maldivian 'short eats' is in any teashop in the town (see p105). Small towns and villages elsewhere will also have teashops and are a great way to sample real Maldivian food.

VEGETARIANS & VEGANS

Vegetarians will have no problem in resorts (although if there's only a set meal rather than a buffet spread, veggies will often be stuck with an unimaginative pasta dish or ratatouille at cheaper resorts). In general, resorts are well prepared for all types of diet, and in better resorts the chef may cook you a dish by request, if what's on offer isn't appealing. Vegans, again, should fare reasonably well – soya milk is on offer in most resorts and the buffet allows each diner to pick and mix. Outside resorts and Male' things won't be so easy – fish dominates menus in the islands, but people will make an enormous effort to accommodate your wishes and *something* will always be found.

Bis hulavuu is a popular snack – a pastry made from eggs, sugar and ghee and served cold. You may well be invited to try some if you visit an inhabited island.

EATING WITH KIDS

There are very often kids' sections to menus and buffets in resorts, giving youngsters a choice of slightly less-refined foods ranging from spaghetti to fish fingers and chicken nuggets. Even if there's nothing dedicated to the kids' tastes, resort buffets are usually diverse enough to cater to even the fussiest eaters. Baby-food products are not on sale in resorts, so bring whatever junior will need for the trip.

HABITS & CUSTOMS

There's not a huge amount of etiquette to worry about if you eat in Male' or resorts. If you're lucky enough to be entertained in a local house, you should obey some basic rules, but again, the Maldivians are very relaxed and as long as you show respect and enjoyment, they'll be very glad to have you eating with them.

When going to eat, wait to be shown where to sit and wait for the *kateeb* (island chief) or the male head of the household to sit down before you do. Take a little of everything offered and do so only with your right hand, as the left hand is considered unclean by Muslims. Do ask for cutlery if you find it hard to roll your food into little balls like the Maldivians do; this is quite normal for foreigners. Thanks should not be overdone, as this can suggest a person was not happy to do whatever it was in the first place, although expressing gratitude to the head of the household, the *kateeb* and the cook will always be welcome.

Kavaabu are small deep fried dough balls with tuna, mashed potato, pepper and lime – a very popular 'short eat'.

EAT YOUR WORDS

Most people in resorts will speak rudimentary English, although if you are lucky enough to visit an inhabited island and to be a guest in a local's house then it's likely they won't speak a word.

I'm a vegetarian	*aharen ehves haavatheh ge maheh nukan*
What is the local speciality?	*dhivehi aanmu keumakee kobaa?*
What is this?	*mee ko-on cheh?*
The meal was delicious	*keun varah meeru*
Thank you for your hospitality	*be-heh-ti gaai kamah shukuriyya*

Food Glossary

Any substantial meal, with rice and *roshi*, is called 'long eats', and might include the following:

bai	rice
bis	egg
garudia	the staple diet of fish soup, often taken with rice, lime and chilli
kandukukulhu	a special tuna curry
mas	fried fish; usually refers to skipjack tuna or bonito
mas huni & hana kuri mas	dried, tinned, fried or cold fish mixed with coconut, onion, chilli and spices
mas riha	fish curry
modunu	a simple salad
paan	bread
rihakuru	garudia boiled down to a salty sauce or paste
roshi	flat, unleavened bread
valo mas	smoked fish
hiki mas	sundried fish

'Short eats' *(hedhikaa)* is the selection of little sweet and savoury items displayed on the counter of a local teashop:

gulas	fish ball; deep-fried in flour and rice batter
kuli boakiba	spicy fish cake
bondi bai	rice pudding; sometimes with currants
kastad	sweet custard
foni boakiba	gelatin cakes and puddings

Most fruit is imported, but the following are grown locally:

kurumba	coconut, especially a young or new coconut
donkeo	little bananas
bambukeyo	breadfruit
bambukeyo hiti	breadfruit used in curries
bambukeyo bondibai	breadfruit used in desserts

Maldivians love their coffee and you can get very good quality espresso, latte or cappuccino anywhere in Male'.

Environment

Along with Tuvalu, Bangladesh and parts of the Netherlands, the Maldives has the misfortune to be one of the lowest-lying countries in the world at a time in history when sea levels are rising. Its highest natural point – 2.4m – is the lowest in any country in the world. While the political will to get an international agreement on how best to combat climate change may finally be here, the Maldives has long been making contingency plans in the very likely event that whatever the international community does will be too little, too late.

These contingency plans range from an already well-established project to reclaim land on a reef near Male' to create a new island 2m above sea level, to the recent announcement by President Nasheed that the Maldives will set aside a portion of its annual billion-dollar tourism revenue for a 'sovereign wealth fund' that will be used to purchase a new homeland for the Maldivians if rising sea levels do indeed engulf the country in decades to come. Both options are fairly bleak ones – the prospect of moving to the new residential island of Hulhumale' is not one relished by most Maldivians, who are attached to their home islands and traditional way of life, but the prospect of the entire country moving to India, Sri Lanka or even Australia is an even more sobering one.

Perhaps because of its perilous situation, the Maldives has become one of the most environmentally progressive countries in the world. The new government has pledged that the country will be carbon neutral within a decade, has imposed the first total ban on shark hunting anywhere in the world and is making ecotourism a cornerstone of its tourism strategy.

Bodu raalhu (big wave) is a relatively regular event in the Maldives, when the sea sweeps over the islands, causing damage and sometimes even loss of life.

THE LAND

Where is the Maldives? That's almost always the first question people ask when you tell them about going on holiday here. This long group of 26 atolls is split up into approximately 1200 islands, spread out 'like a string of pearls' (copyright all guidebooks ever published) due south of India and west of Sri Lanka, deep in the Indian Ocean.

Sometimes confused with Mauritius, Martinique or Madagascar, or simply an unknown quantity, the Maldives is a tiny country spread out

---

RESPONSIBLE TRAVEL IN THE MALDIVES

- Drink water desalinated at your resort rather than imported mineral water.
- Take all batteries and plastic home with you, as the Maldives does not have facilities to dispose of them.
- Offset your air travel by using companies such as www.climatecare.org.
- Minimise the use of air-conditioning.
- Keep the use of running water in your room to a minimum – water is still expensive to desalinate and uses fossil fuel to do so.
- When diving or snorkelling do not touch, feed or otherwise interfere with the fish and coral.
- Ask for your towels not to be rewashed every day.
- Don't purchase turtle-shell products.

AN ALTERNATIVE GEOGRAPHY

While the Maldives has appeared in the *Guinness Book of Records* as the world's flattest country, with no natural land higher than 2.4m above sea level, it's also one of the most mountainous countries in the world. Its people live on peaks above a plateau that extends 2000km from the Lakshadweep Islands near India to the Chagos Islands, well south of the equator. The plateau is over 5000m high and rises steeply between the Arabian Basin in the northwest and the Cocos-Keeling Basin in the southeast. Mountain ranges rise above the plateau, and the upper slopes and valleys are incredibly fertile, beautiful and rich with plant and animal life. The entire plateau is submerged beneath the Indian Ocean and only scattered, flat-topped peaks are visible at the surface. These peaks are capped not with snow, but with coconut palms.

---

over a large area – 99% of its 90,000 sq km is the Indian Ocean, dry land coming to a total area that is less than that of Andorra.

It's actually hard to give a definitive number for the islands that make up the country. Some 'islands' exist at low tide and disappear at high tide, while others are just sandbanks with no foliage, potentially washed away by the next big storm. Officially, it's a matter of vegetation – an island means a vegetated land area, but even this is not definitive. Some sandbanks sprout a small patch of scrub while others feature a single coconut palm, like the desert island of the comic-strip castaway.

The geological formation of the Maldives is fascinating and unique. The country is perched on the top of the enormous Laccadives-Chagos ridge, which cuts a swath across the Indian Ocean from India to Madagascar. The ridge, a meeting point of two giant tectonic plates, is where basalt magma spews up through the earth's crust, creating new rock. These magma eruptions created the Deccan Plateau, on which the Maldives sits. Originally the magma production created huge volcanoes that towered above the sea. While these have subsequently sunk back into the water as the ocean floor settled, the coral formations that grew up around these vast volcanoes became the Maldives, and this explains their idiosyncratic formation into vast round atolls.

Maldivian turtles are protected, but they are still caught illegally. The charity Ecocare Maldives has campaigned to raise awareness of the turtles' plight. See www.ecocare.mv.

Today then, the national territory officially comprises 1190 coral islands and innumerable reefs forming 26 atolls that are the natural geographic regions of the country – the English word 'atoll' actually derives from the Maldivian word *atolu*. The natural atolls are divided up into 21 administrative districts, whose easy-to-pronounce code names are the ones we use to divide up the country by region in this book (see p45).

WILDLIFE

Stand still on a Maldivian beach for a minute or two and you'll see a surprising amount of life. From the hermit crabs scurrying across the sands to the instantly recognisable whooping of the crows in the palm trees, from the juvenile sharks that chase schools of little fish through the shallows to the majestic flying foxes that swoop over the islands during the late afternoon, the Maldives is a fun place for nature lovers. And that's before you get to the amazing variety of life down on the reef. The best thing about wildlife in the Maldives is that it's universally safe. Who said this wasn't paradise?

Animals

One of the most unforgettable sights in the Maldives is giant fruit bats flying over the islands to roost in trees at dusk. Their size and numbers can make it quite a spectacle. Colourful lizards and geckos are very common and there is the occasional rat, usually euphemistically dismissed as a 'palm squirrel' or a 'Maldivian hamster' by resort staff keen to avoid cries of vermin.

The mosquito population varies from island to island but it's generally not a big problem. Nearly all the resorts spray pesticides daily to get rid of those that are about. There are ants, centipedes, scorpions and cockroaches, but they're no threat to anyone.

Local land birds include crows (many of which are shot by resorts on regular culls), the white-breasted water hen and the Indian mynah. There are migratory birds, such as harriers and falcons, but waders like plover, snipe, curlew and sandpiper are more common. Thirteen species of heron can be seen in the shallows (nearly every resort has one or two in residence) and there are terns, seagulls and two species of noddy.

Maldives: Un mur contre l'océan is a documentary by Patrick Fléouter. Investigating the construction of sea defences around Male', it ponders the future of the rest of the population.

ENDANGERED SPECIES

Most turtle species are endangered worldwide. Four species nest in the Maldives: green, olive ridley, hawksbill and loggerhead. Leatherback turtles visit Maldivian waters, but are not known to nest. Turtle numbers have declined in the Maldives, as elsewhere, but they can still be seen by divers at many sites. The catching of turtles and the sale or export of turtle-shell products is now totally prohibited.

Turtles are migratory and the population can be depleted by events many miles from their home beach, such as accidental capture in fishing

THOSE UNPRONOUNCEABLE ATOLLS

Confusingly enough, the 26 atolls of the Maldives are divided for all official purposes into 21 administrative districts, which are named by the letters of the Thaana alphabet and as such are a lot easier to pronounce. Would you rather talk about South Miladhunmadulu Atoll or Noonu? Thought so. However, it's not that simple, as the traditional atoll names are still universally used for North and South Male' Atolls, North and South Ari Atoll and Addu Atoll in the far south, so we also use these instead of the more obscure names Kaafu, Alif and Seenu. The following table gives both traditional and administrative names for most parts of the country; those marked with an asterisk are the ones used in this book.

Administrative name	Atoll name
Alif	Ari Atoll*
Baa*	South Maalhosmadulu Atoll
Dhaalu*	South Nilandhe Atoll
Faafu*	North Nilandhe Atoll
Gaaf Alif*	North Huvadhoo Atoll
Gaaf Dhaal*	South Huvadhoo Atoll
Gnaviyani*	Fuvahmulah Atoll
Haa Alif*	North Thiladhunmathee Atoll
Haa Dhaal*	South Thiladhunmathee Atoll & Maamakunudhoo Atoll
Kaafu	Male' Atoll*
Laamu*	Hadhdunmathee Atoll
Lhaviyani*	Faadhippolhu Atoll
Meemu*	Mulaku Atoll
Noonu*	South Miladhunmadulu Atoll
Raa*	North Maalhosmadulu Atoll
Seenu	Addu Atoll*
Shaviyani*	North Miladhunmadulu Atoll
Thaa*	Kolhumadulu Atoll
Vaavu*	Felidhe Atoll

nets, depletion of sea-grass areas and toxic pollutants. Widespread collection of eggs and the loss of nesting sites are problems that need to be addressed. The consequences do not show up in the adult turtle population for 10 to 20 years.

Turtle eggs are a traditional food and used in *velaa folhi,* a special Maldivian dish, which is still legally made today. Development of resorts has reduced the availability of nesting sites. Artificial lights confuse hatchling turtles, which are instinctively guided into the water by the position of the moon. Beach chairs and boats can also interfere with egg laying and with hatchlings. Some attempts are being made to artificially improve the survival chances of hatchlings by protecting them in hatching ponds.

Plants

Most islands have poor, sandy soil, and vegetation ranges from thick to sparse to none at all. The vegetated islands have mangroves, breadfruit trees, banyans, bamboo, pandanus, banana, heliotrope, caltrop, hibiscus, tropical vines and numerous coconut palms. Larger, wetter islands have small areas of rainforest.

Sweet potatoes, yams, taro, millet and watermelon are grown in the Maldives. The most fertile island is Fuvahmulah in the extreme south, which supports a wider variety of crops, including mangoes and pineapples. Lemons and limes once grew all over the islands, but a fungal disease killed them off, and virtually all citrus fruit is now imported.

Marine Life

Seaweeds and hard coralline algae grow on the reefs, but are continuously eaten by various herbivores. As well as the many types of coral, there are various shells, starfish, crustaceans and worms inhabiting the reef. There are more than 700 species of fish in the Indian Ocean, and these can be divided into two types: reef fish, which live inside the atoll lagoons, on and around coral-reef structures; and pelagics, which live in the open sea, but may come close to the atolls or into channels for food. These include some large animals, such as turtles and cetaceans, which are very popular with divers.

CORAL

These are coelenterates, a class of animal that also includes sea anemones and jellyfish. A coral growth is made up of individual polyps – tiny tube-like fleshy cylinders, which look very much like anemones. The top of the cylinder is open and ringed by waving tentacles (nematocysts), which sting and draw any passing prey inside. Coral polyps secrete a calcium-carbonate deposit around their base, and this cup-shaped skeletal structure is what forms a coral reef – new coral grows on old dead coral and the reef gradually builds up.

Most reef building is done by hermatypic corals, whose outer tissues are infused with zooxanthellae algae, which photosynthesise to make food from carbon dioxide and sunlight. The zooxanthellae is the main food source for the coral, while the coral surface provides a safe home for the zooxanthellae – they live in a symbiotic relationship, each dependent on the other. The zooxanthellae give coral its colour, so when a piece of coral is removed from the water, the zooxanthellae soon die and the coral becomes white. If the water temperature rises, the coral expels the algae, and the coral loses its colour in a process called 'coral bleaching'.

Polyps reproduce by splitting to form a colony of genetically identical polyps – each colony starts life as just a single polyp. Although each polyp catches and digests its own food, the nutrition then passes between the polyps to the whole colony. Most coral polyps only feed at night; during the day they withdraw into their hard limestone skeleton, so it is only after dark that a coral reef can be seen in its full, colourful glory.

HARD CORALS

These Acropora species take many forms. One of the most common and easiest to recognise is the staghorn coral, which grows by budding off new branches from the tips. Brain corals are huge and round with a surface looking very much like a human brain. They grow by adding new base levels of skeletal matter then expanding outwards. Flat or sheet corals, like plate coral or table coral, expand at their outer edges. Some corals take different shapes depending on their immediate environment.

RISE & RISE OF THE ATOLLS

A coral reef or garden is not, as many people believe, formed of multicoloured marine plants. It is a living colony of coral polyps – tiny, tentacled creatures that feed on plankton. Coral polyps are invertebrates with sac-like bodies and calcareous or horny skeletons. After extracting calcium deposits from the water around them, the polyps excrete tiny, cup-shaped, limestone skeletons. These little guys can make mountains.

A coral reef is the rock-like aggregation of millions of these polyp skeletons. Only the outer layer of coral is alive. As polyps reproduce and die, the new polyps attach themselves in successive layers to the skeletons already in place. Coral grows best in clear, shallow water, and especially where waves and currents from the open sea bring extra oxygen and nutrients.

Charles Darwin put forward the first scientific theory of atoll formation based on observations of atolls and islands in the Pacific. He envisaged a process where coral builds up around the shores of a volcanic island to produce a fringing reef. Then the island sinks slowly into the sea while the coral grows upwards at about the same rate. This forms a barrier reef, separated from the shore of the sinking island by a ring-shaped lagoon. By the time the island is completely submerged, the coral growth has become the base for an atoll, circling the place where the volcanic peak used to be.

This theory doesn't quite fit the Maldives, though. Unlike the isolated Pacific atolls, Maldivian atolls all sit on top of the same long, underwater plateau, around 300m to 500m under the surface of the sea. This plateau is a layer of accumulated coral-stone over 2000m thick. Under this is the 'volcanic basement', a 2000km-long ridge of basalt that was formed over 50 million years ago.

The build-up of coral over this ridge is as much to do with sea-level changes as it is with the plateau subsiding. When sea levels rise the coral grows upwards to stay near the sea surface, as in the Darwin model, but there were at least two periods when the sea level actually dropped significantly – by as much as 120m. At these times much of the accumulated coral plateau would have been exposed, subjected to weathering, and 'karstified' – eroded into steep-sided, flat-topped columns. When sea levels rose again, new coral grew on the tops of the karst mountains and formed the bases of the individual Maldivian atolls.

Coral grows best on the edges of an atoll, where it is well supplied with nutrients from the open sea. A fringing reef forms around an enclosed lagoon, growing higher as the sea level rises. Rubble from broken coral accumulates in the lagoon, so the level of the lagoon floor also rises, and smaller reefs can rise within it. Sand and debris accumulate on the higher parts of the reef, creating sandbars on which vegetation can eventually take root. The classic atoll shape is oval, with the widest reefs and most of the islands around the outer edges.

Test drilling and seismic research has revealed the complex layers of coral growth that underlie the Maldives. The evidence shows that coral growth can match the fastest sea-level rises on record, some 125m in only 10,000 years – about 1.25cm per year. In geological terms, that's really fast.

SOFT CORALS

These are made up of individual polyps, but do not form a hard limestone skeleton. Lacking the skeleton that protects hard coral, it would seem likely that soft coral would fall prey to fish, but they seem to remain relatively immune either due to toxic substances in their tissues or to the presence of sharp limestone needles. Soft corals can move around and will sometimes engulf and kill off a hard coral. Attractive varieties include fan corals and whips. Soft corals thrive on reef edges washed by strong currents.

REEF FISH

Hundreds of fish species can be spotted by anyone with a mask and snorkel. They're easy to see and enjoy, but people with a naturalist bent should buy one of the field guides to reef fish, or check the attractive posters, which are often displayed in dive schools. You're sure to see several types of butterflyfish, angelfish, parrotfish, rock cod, unicornfish, trumpetfish, bluestripe snapper, Moorish idol and oriental sweetlips. For more on fish, see p86.

The Maldives has a very small proportion of arable land – just 13% – meaning that fish and imported foods make up the bulk of most people's diets.

SHARKS

It's not a feat to see a shark in the Maldives, even if you don't get in the water; juvenile reef sharks love to swim about in the warm water of the shallow lagoon right next to the beach and eat fish all day long. They're tiny – most never grow beyond 50cm long – but are fully formed sharks, so can scare some people! They don't bite, although feeding or provoking them still isn't a good idea.

Get out into the deeper water and sharks are visible, but you'll have to go looking for them. The white-tip reef shark is a small, nonaggressive, territorial shark, rarely more than 1.5m long and often seen over areas of coral or off reef edges. Grey reef sharks are also timid, shallow-water dwellers and often grow to over 2m in length.

CORAL BLEACHING – DEATH ON THE REEF

In March 1998, the waters of the Maldives experienced a temporary rise in temperature associated with the El Niño effect. For a period of about two weeks, surface-water temperatures were above 32°C, resulting in the loss of the symbiotic algae that lives within the coral polyps. The loss of the zooxanthellae algae causes the coral to lose its colour ('coral bleaching'), and if this algae does not return, the coral polyps die. Coral bleaching has occurred, with varying degrees of severity, in shallow waters throughout the Maldives archipelago. When the coral dies, the underlying calcium carbonate is exposed and becomes more brittle, so many of the more delicate branch and table structures have been broken up by wave action. Mainly hard corals were affected – soft corals and sea fans are less dependent on zooxanthellae algae, are less affected by the sea temperature changes and recover more quickly from damage.

Some corals, particularly in deeper water, recovered almost immediately as the symbiotic algae returned. In a few places the coral was not damaged at all. In most areas, however, virtually all the old hard corals died and it will take years, perhaps decades, for them to recover. Some of the biggest table corals may have been hundreds of years old. Marine biologists are watching this recolonisation process with interest (see p85).

The Maldives' dive industry has adapted to the changed environment, seeking places where the regrowth is fastest and where there are lots of attractive soft corals. There's still a vast number and variety of reef fish to see, and spotting pelagic species, especially mantas and whale sharks, is a major attraction. Some long-time divers have become more interested in the very small marine life, and in macrophotography.

Other species are more open-sea dwellers, but do come into atolls and especially to channel entrances where food is plentiful. These include the strange-looking hammerhead shark and the whale shark, the world's largest fish species, which is a harmless plankton eater. Sharks do not pose any danger to divers in the Maldives – there's simply too much else for them to eat.

In 2009 the Maldivian government outlawed the hunting of sharks, making the Maldives the world's first shark sanctuary. Seeing one of these graceful creatures up close on a reef is undoubtedly a highlight of any visit.

WHALES & DOLPHINS

Whales dwell in the open sea, and so are not found in the atolls. Species seen in the Maldives include beaked, blue, Bryde's dwarf, false killer, melon-headed, sperm and pilot whales. You'll need to go on a specialised whale-watching trip to see them, however (see p59).

Dolphins are extremely common throughout the Maldives, and you're very likely to see them, albeit fleetingly. These fun-loving, curious creatures often swim alongside speedboats and dhonis, and also swim off the side of reefs looking for food. Most resorts offer dolphin cruises, which allow you to see large schools up close. Species known to swim in Maldivian waters include bottlenose, Fraser's, Risso's, spotted, striped and spinner dolphins.

STINGRAYS & MANTA RAYS

Some of the most dramatic creatures in the ocean, rays are cartilaginous fish – like flattened sharks. Ray feeding is a popular activity at many resorts and it's quite something to see these muscular, alienesque creatures jump out of the water and chow down on raw steak. Stingrays are sea-bottom feeders, and equipped with crushing teeth to grind the molluscs and crustaceans they sift out of the sand. They are occasionally found in the shallows, often lying motionless on the sandy bottom of lagoons. A barbed and poisonous spine on top of the tail can swing up and forward, and will deliver a very painful injury to anyone who stands on one, but you're unlikely to get close to it as the sound of you approaching will probably frighten it away first.

Manta rays are among the largest fish found in the Maldives and a firm favourite of divers. They tend to swim along near the surface and pass overhead as a large shadow. They are quite harmless and, in some places, seem quite relaxed about divers approaching them closely. Manta rays are sometimes seen to leap completely out of the water, landing back with a tremendous splash. The eagle ray is closely related to the manta, and is often spotted by divers.

NATIONAL PARKS

There are 25 Protected Marine Areas in the Maldives, usually popular diving sites where fishing of any kind is banned. These are excellent, as they have created enclaves of huge marine life that's guaranteed a safe future. While there are no specially designated island reserves in the Maldives, there are a large number of uninhabited islands and permission from the government is needed to develop or live there. With some of the tightest development restrictions in the world, the Maldives' future as pristine wilderness in many parts is assured.

The depletion of freshwater aquifers is one of the Maldives' biggest environmental problems. As all fresh water comes from rainwater collected below ground and from desalination, water conservation is extremely important.

ENVIRONMENTAL ISSUES

As a small island nation in a big ocean, the Maldives had a way of life that was ecologically sustainable for centuries, but certainly not self-sufficient. The comparatively small population survived by harvesting the vast resources of the sea and obtaining the other necessities of life through trade. The impact on the limited resources of their islands was probably minimal.

Now the Maldives' interrelationship with the rest of the world is greater than ever, and it has a high rate of growth supported by two main industries:

WATER, WATER, EVERYWHERE

Ensuring a supply of fresh water has always been imperative for small island communities. Rainwater quickly soaks into the sandy island soil and usually forms an underground reservoir of fresh water, held in place by a circle of salt water from the surrounding sea. Wells can be dug to extract the fresh ground water, but if water is pumped out faster than rainfall replenishes the supply, then salty water infiltrates from around the island and the well water becomes brackish. Decaying organic matter and septic tanks can also contaminate the ground water, giving it an unpleasant sulphurous smell.

One way to increase the fresh-water supply is to catch and store rainwater from rooftops. This wasn't feasible on islands that had only small buildings with roofs of palm thatch, but economic development and the use of corrugated iron has changed all that. Nearly every inhabited island now has a government-supported primary school, which is often the biggest, newest building on the island. The other sizable building is likely to be the mosque, which is a focus of community pride. Along with education and spiritual sustenance, many Maldivians now also get their drinking water from the local school or the mosque.

Expanding tourist resorts required more water than was available from wells or rooftops and, as resorts grew larger, the tourists' showers became saltier. Also, the ground water became too salty to irrigate the exotic gardens that every tourist expects on a tropical island. The solution was the desalination of sea water using 'reverse osmosis' – a combination of membrane technology and brute force.

Now every resort has a desalination plant, with racks of metal cylinders, each containing an inner cylinder made of a polymer membrane. Sea water is pumped into the inner cylinder at high pressure and the membrane allows pure water to pass through into the outer cylinder from which it is piped away. Normally, when a membrane separates fresh water from salt water, both salt and water will pass through the membrane in opposite directions to equalise the saltiness on either side – this process is called osmosis. Under pressure, the special polymer membrane allows the natural process of osmosis to be reversed.

Small, reliable desalination plants have been a boon for the resorts, providing abundant fresh water for bathrooms, kitchens, gardens and, increasingly, for swimming pools. Of course, it's expensive, as the plants use lots of diesel fuel for their powerful pumps and the polymer membranes need to be replaced regularly. Many resorts ask their guests to be moderate in their water use, while a few are finding ways to recycle bath and laundry water onto garden beds. Most have dual water supplies, so that brackish ground water is used to flush the toilet while desalinated sea water is provided in the shower and the hand basin.

Is desalinated water good enough to drink? If a desalination plant is working properly, it should produce, in effect, 100% pure distilled water. The island of Thulusdhoo, in North Male' Atoll, has the only factory in the world where Coca-Cola is made out of sea water. In most resorts, the water from the bathroom tap tastes just fine, but management advises guests not to drink it. One story is that the water is too pure and lacks the trace minerals essential for good health. Another is that the water is purified in the plant, but in the pipes it can pick up bacteria, which may cause diarrhoea. Usually, the resort and hotel management will suggest that guests buy mineral water from the bar, shop or restaurant, where it will cost between US$3 and US$7 for 1.5L. This water is bottled in the Maldives using purified, desalinated water.

fishing and tourism. Both industries depend on the preservation of the environment, and there are strict regulations to ensure sustainability. To a great extent the Maldives avoids environmental problems by importing so many of its needs. This is of course far less a case of being environmentally friendly than just moving the environmental problems elsewhere.

Bluepeace (www.bluepeacemaldives.org) is an organisation campaigning to protect the Maldives' unique environment (see p52). Their comprehensive website and blog is a great place to start for anyone interested in the ecology of the Maldives.

Global Warming

There are no prizes for guessing what the country's long-term environmental concern is. With waters rising faster than previously believed, low-lying islands are set to start disappearing in the next few decades.

In the long term it's simply not an option to protect low-lying islands with breakwaters, and if the sea continues to rise as predicted then there is no long-term future for much of the country. While a wait-and-see attitude appears to be that adopted by most, there are clear efforts being made to support human life in the Maldives now that the water has risen by 1m – most importantly the land reclamation project that has created 2m-high Hulhumale' island (see p109) next to the airport, and one day will house around half the country's population.

If the day does indeed come when waters engulf the entire country, then the government's newly created 'sovereign wealth fund' will be used to buy land elsewhere in the world for at least some, if not all, of the Maldivian population. India and Sri Lanka are most likely destinations due to proximity and similarities in culture, climate and cuisine, but Australia is also frequently mooted given its large amount of free space.

Fisheries

Net fishing and trawling is prohibited in Maldivian waters, which include an 'exclusive economic zone' extending for 320km beyond the atolls. All fishing is by pole and line, with over 75% of the catch being skipjack or yellowfin tuna. The no-nets policy helps to prevent over-fishing and protects other marine species, such as dolphins, from being inadvertently caught in nets.

The local tuna population appears to be holding up despite increased catches, and Maldivian fisheries are patrolled to prevent poaching. But the tuna are migratory, and can be caught without limit in international waters using drift nets and long-line techniques.

Tourism

Tourism development is strictly regulated and resorts are established only on uninhabited islands that the government makes available. Overwhelmingly, the regulations have been effective in minimising the impact on the environment – the World Tourism Organization has cited the Maldives as a model for sustainable tourism development.

Construction and operation of the resorts does use resources, but the vast majority of these are imported. Large amounts of diesel fuel are used to generate electricity and desalinate water. The demand for hot running water and air-conditioning has raised the overall energy cost per guest.

Extraordinarily, most resorts simply pump sewage out into the sea. While 20% of the resorts do treat their own sewage and dispose of it responsibly, the vast majority do not. New resorts are now required to do so by law, but the older resorts can still get away with such negligent behaviour.

The approximately 1200 islands that make up the Maldives account for less than 1% of the country's area – the other 99% is water.

Beach erosion is another constant problem facing most islands in the Maldives. Changing currents and rising sea levels mean that beaches shrink and grow, often unpredictably.

LOCAL VOICE – ALI RILWAN OF BLUEPEACE

Meeting Ali Rilwan is as much an ordeal of keeping up as it is an illuminating insight into the environmental problems faced by the Maldives. Rilwan has barely inhaled since we met and is rattling through the most pressing ecological issues of the day while the rest of the crowd around our table at the Sea House in Male' drink coffee and chat to their friends against the backdrop of the city's busy harbour.

'We're concerned about all the nature reserves that have been created but aren't being enforced – the government now needs to find a mechanism to police the rules. For example, Hithadhoo island in Gaaf Alif atoll is protected but has no warden to prevent poachers stealing the frigate bird eggs…' Rilwan's organisation, Bluepeace, has been challenging the government on environmental policy since 1989 when the volunteer pressure group was founded. These challenges saw Rilwan jailed and repeatedly harassed under the Gayoom regime, though he doesn't seem to have much time to celebrate the recent introduction of democracy and the election of Mohammed Nasheed. 'Not when 80% of resorts in the country do not treat their sewage and simply pump it out to sea. Look at Male' – a city of 100,000 people – its waste is also just pumped out directly into the sea as well. The word for beach in Divehi is *godudhoh*, or 'rubbish dump', but this was never a problem until the late 20th century…'

'We want to see the government start to release resorts to those who will truly take responsibility for them, not just to the highest bidder. One island we're particularly against developing is Hudhufushi in Lhaviyani Atoll, which is a very important stingray and shark breeding ground. Yet a resort is being built there at the moment…'

With such big policy matters at the top of the agenda, what can tourists do to help, I wonder? 'Take back your batteries. This tiny thing makes a big difference in a country where there are no facilities to dispose of them; bring your own plastic water bottle, use it here and take it back with you and talk to resort staff and ask them about their environmental policies and challenge them to do better!'

Bluepeace (www.bluepeacemaldives.org) is a non-profit NGO based in Male'. You can support them by offering your time as a volunteer or by being a donor in kind.

Efficient incinerators must be installed to get rid of garbage that can't be composted, but many resorts request that visitors take home plastic bottles, used batteries and other items that may present a disposal problem.

When the first resorts were developed, jetties and breakwaters were built and boat channels cut through reefs, without much understanding of the immediate environmental consequences. In some cases natural erosion and deposition patterns were disrupted, with unexpected results. More structures were built to limit the damage and sand was pumped up to restore the beach. This was expensive and it marred the natural appearance of the island, and now developers are more careful about altering coasts and reefs. Environmental studies are required before major works can be undertaken.

Choosing a Resort

Don't worry about being swayed by the judicious use of Photoshop in brochures – almost every resort in the Maldives will get you a superb beach, amazing weather and turquoise waters overlooked by majestic palms. Indeed, some visitors jokingly complain that any photograph they take just looks like one lifted from a promotional pamphlet, so uniform is the perfection.

It's what nestles among the trees beyond the beach that should most concern you, and we're not talking about creepy crawlies here. The standard of facilities and variety of accommodation in Maldivian resorts is enormous – from budget and extremely average accommodation to the best of everything if you can afford to pay through the nose for it. Therefore your choice of resort is absolutely key to getting the holiday you want. Take plenty of time and weigh up as many options as possible before settling for the resort or resorts you'll book into. This chapter will help you navigate the various factors to take into consideration when selecting a resort, as well as listing some of our favourites in the country.

George Corbin is credited with kick-starting the Maldives tourist industry. In 1971 he brought a small group of Europeans to the country despite there being no hotels.

ATMOSPHERE

What is surprising is that every resort has a fairly distinct atmosphere. Not totally unique in all cases – but it's incredible how quickly you can tell if you're visiting a honeymooners' paradise, a diving mecca or a family bucket-and-spade affair. This is the one thing that's totally impossible to judge from a website or brochure, so the most important decision to make before choosing a resort is the type of holiday you want, and the atmosphere most conducive to providing it. Honeymooners who find themselves surrounded by package tour groups and screaming children may quickly come to regret booking into the first resort whose website they looked at. Similarly, divers and surfers may find the almost total social-life vacuum in a honeymoon resort a little claustrophobic after a week.

Back to Nature

If you've ever fancied the whole Robinson Crusoe experience, or the slightly less lonely Swiss Family Robinson getaway, the Maldives is way ahead of you, having built much of its tourism industry on precisely this desert island ideal; many places also provide a butler, gourmet restaurant and a fleet of staff who cater to your every whim, making it somewhat more fun than being a real castaway. These resorts tend to be very well designed, use imported woods and natural fibres, have little or no air-conditioning and often open-air rooms with no window panes. The simplicity of such places (even at the top end, though it's also mixed with supreme style and comfort), not to mention their peacefulness and relaxed feel, is what attracts people.

High Style

Maldives is surfing the current wave of the luxury and boutique-hotel craze without working up a sweat at all. Indeed, few countries in the world have such a wealth of choice in this market. All major luxury hotel brands have or are hoping to establish a presence here, and at times things can look like a never-ending glossy *Condé Nast Traveller* editorial. As well as our personal favourites, at the time of writing there were a host of new

TOP FIVE BACK-TO-NATURE RESORTS

Nika Island (p138)

Makunudu Island (p119)

Soneva Fushi (p151)

Rihiveli Beach Resort (p128)

Banyan Tree Madivaru (p141)

TOP FIVE HIGH-STYLE RESORTS

One & Only Reethi Rah (p123)

Banyan Tree Madivaru (p141)

Island Hideaway (p145)

Conrad Maldives Rangali Island (p139)

Four Seasons Landaa Giraavaru (p152)

properties in the pipeline by such brand names as Raffles, Ritz-Carlton and Shangri-La, and these are likely to be in the same league.

The pampering on offer here is almost legendary. You'll have your own *thakuru* (personal butler), who will look after you during your stay, you'll nearly always have a sumptuous architect-designed villa stuffed full of beautifully designed furniture and fabrics, a vast, decadent bathroom (often open air) and a private open-air area (in a water villa this is usually a sun deck with a direct staircase into the sea). Some of our very favourite resorts in this category include private pools – OK, not big enough to do lengths in, but still a wonderful way to cool off or wash the salt off yourself after a dip in the sea.

Food in these resorts is almost universally top notch. There will be a huge choice of cuisine, with European, Asian and Japanese specialist chefs employed to come up with an amazing array of dishes day and night. Social life will be quiet, and will usually revolve around one of the bars. Most of the market here are honeymooners, couples and families, but kids will certainly not run riot (most resorts impose a limit on numbers of children) and even if they do, there will be enough space to get away from them. Despite the general feel being romantic and stylish, activities will not be ignored – everything from diving to water sports and excursions will be well catered for. Essentially, if you can afford this level of accommodation, you are guaranteed an amazing time, whatever your interests.

Over-Water Villas

TOP FIVE WATER VILLAS

Soneva Gili (p123)

One & Only Reethi Rah (p123)

Huvafen Fushi (p124)

W Retreat & Spa (p140)

Coco Palm Boduhithi (p122)

The over-water villa was introduced to the Maldives in the 1970s from Tahiti and has slowly become the ultimate status symbol and a feature at almost every resort – with the exception of the low budget and some ecologically conscious back-to-nature style resorts. The variation in water villas is immense – at the cheaper end (Paradise Island, Summer Island Village) they are little more than cheap-looking modern structures that happen to be built on stilts over the water. However, where design has been considered, they can be fabulous experiences, built with sunset watching, privacy and sea access direct from the bedroom in mind. The massive, almost entirely open-air villas at Soneva Gili are frankly impossible to beat, although the super-sleek Lagoon and Ocean Villas at Huvafen Fushi run a very close second, largely as they all have their own infinity pools. Other favourites include Four Seasons Landaa Giraavaru, Island Hideaway, Cocoa Island, W Retreat & Spa, Coco Palm Boduhithi and Nika Island. Essentially you get what you pay for, so it's probably false economy to go for the very cheapest available. Prices have been driven down though, and midrange resorts nearly all have very high-quality water villas. Some good midrange options include Olhuveli Beach & Spa, Sheraton Maldives Full Moon Resort & Spa and Chaaya Lagoon Hakuraa Huraa.

Romance

TOP FIVE ROMANTIC RESORTS

Makunudu Island (p119)

Mirihi (p139)

Soneva Gili (p123)

Baros (p121)

Cocoa Island (p129)

Romance is big business in the Maldives, where more than a few visitors are on their honeymoon, renewing their vows or just having an indulgent break with their significant other. Almost anywhere is romantic; although again, the more budget the resort, the more families and big charter groups you'll get, and the intimacy of the romantic experience can be diminished if it's peace, quiet and candlelit dinners you're after. Romance does not necessarily mean huge cost. It's hard to think of anywhere more lovely than little Makunudu Island, for example, where there's no TV or loud music, just gorgeously simple and traditional houses dotted along the beach, and vegetation thick with trees planted by past honeymooners. However, the usual Maldivian maxim of getting what you pay for is still true here – the very most lovely, romantic resorts are certainly not the cheap ones.

Be aware that at present you cannot actually get married in the Maldives, although this may well change in the near future. However, if you really want to, you can organise non-legally binding services and effectively have your wedding here even if the legal formalities are completed elsewhere. Nearly all midrange and top-end resorts can organise such ceremonies, so check websites for details and special packages. See p173 for more about marriage ceremonies.

Diving

All resorts have their own diving school, and all are run to extremely professional standards as required by Maldivian law. Every resort has access to good diving, although nearly all diving is from boats – even if the house reef is excellent, any diver will tell you that variety is what they look for. It's very hard to say that one resort has better diving than another, when in fact all the sites are shared, but there are a few resorts that have obvious advantages, such as the Equator Village, where coral was not affected by the bleaching in 1998; Helengeli, from where some 40 dive sites can be reached, giving a huge choice; or a number of resorts in and around Ari Atoll, where the dive sites are excellent, including the Kuramathi resorts for hammerhead sightings, Chaaya Reef Ellaidhoo and Adaaran Club Bathala.

Ecotourism

Ecotourism can so often be a gimmick that it's important to separate the wheat from the chaff when selecting a place that claims to be approaching tourism in a unique way, both in terms of sustainability and education. Despite the lip service paid by many resorts, there are actually relatively few that have genuine ecotourism credentials. These include educational programmes, sustainable development, environmentally friendly building practices, minimal use of air-conditioning and electricity in general and a resort ethos that fosters environmental awareness and care (ie not only offering you Evian when you ask for water – an accusation that can be laid at the door of many resorts – but water that has been desalinated on site as well). The resorts we recommend in this category are leading the way in the use of materials, their interaction with the local ecosystem and the activities they offer guests. Those that are serious about their commitment to ecotourism include the two Soneva properties, Rihiveli Beach Resort, both Banyan Tree and Angsana properties, Coco Palm Boduhithi and Nika Island.

ACTIVITIES

Few people will want to spend an entire holiday sunbathing and swimming (although some do!), and so all resorts are careful to provide a programme of excursions and activities for guests. Bear in mind that this is the only way you'll be able to leave the island during your stay, public transport being nonexistent and opportunities for sightseeing almost as scarce. It's therefore important to give some thought to what you'd like to do other than sun-worship, and check that the resort you're interested in can cater sufficiently to your interest.

While all resorts have a diving centre, the uniformity ends there; you'll have to check and see if the resort you're planning to visit has a water

---

TOP FIVE DIVING RESORTS

Helengeli (p115)

Adaaran Club Bathala (p135)

Equator Village (p167)

Chaaya Reef Ellaidhoo (p135)

Kuramathi (p133)

TOP FIVE STYLISH MIDRANGE RESORTS

These resorts will offer great style and attractive resorts at relatively affordable prices

Olhuveli Beach & Spa (p128)

Kandooma (p127)

Kurumba Maldives (p120)

J Resort Kudarah (p138)

Cinnamon Island Resort & Spa (p145)

sports centre or its own spa, organises guided snorkelling, lays on marine biology lectures and morning yoga sessions or has a resident tennis pro. For example, the only resort to offer a golf course is Kuredu Island Resort in Lhaviyani, although there are plans to build a second course on one of the islands in the new wave of resort development. Other unique features are Soneva Fushi's observatory, Island Hideaway's marina and Huvafen Fushi's underwater spa.

Island Hideaway (p145) and Beach House at Manafaru (p146) offer a nearby landing strip for those coming by private jet. The less fortunate must use Maldivian flights from Male'.

Day Trips

Day trips from your resort are one of the very few ways you'll be able to see something of the Maldives. Even if you are a fully independent traveller (FIT) this is still a good way to see otherwise inaccessible islands of the Maldives. Most commonly offered are day trips to the charming capital Male' from resorts in North and South Male' Atolls. There's enough to see for a few hours plus plenty of shopping to merit this trip and it's a great way to get a feel for Maldivian people – you'll find the terrifyingly polite resort staff replaced by a friendly and funny city populace.

Another popular excursion is a trip to an inhabited island. These are a poor substitute for individual exploration of the country, but until that becomes possible this is as close as most people will be able to get to seeing a small island community, traditional housing, craftwork and lifestyle. The trip inevitably feels rather contrived, but can still be immensely enjoyable depending on how friendly the locals are and how many people are around (with children often in school or studying in Male', and menfolk away for work, some islands feel more like ghost towns than centres of population). The fewer people in your group the better. From a few resorts such as Equator Village, Kandooma and J Resort Handhufushi, you can easily access Maldivian towns alone by bicycle or, in Kandooma's case, by wading across the lagoon at low tide. In all cases you're likely to have a far more interesting and authentic experience if you explore alone, although be aware that the resort guides will know all the locals and can be helpful in making contacts and telling you in detail about local life.

Banyan Tree (p141) and Angsana Ihuru (p121) won huge acclaim when they helped neighbouring inhabited island Naalaafushi rebuild after the tsunami in partnership with the United Nations Development Programme.

Fishing

Just about any resort will do sunset, sunrise or night-fishing trips, but they are a more authentically Maldivian experience at small, locally run resorts like Asdu Sun Island and Thulhagiri. Most resorts near Male' can arrange a big-game fishing trip, including Bandos, Baros, Club Faru, Sheraton Maldives Full Moon Resort & Spa, Kurumba Maldives and Cocoa Island. These work out more economically if there are several participants, as costs are high: from $450 for a half-day trip for up to four people. Large boats, fully equipped with radar technology, are used to catch dorado, tuna, marlin, barracuda, jackfish and sharks.

Snorkelling & Diving

The underwater world is definitely one of the best reasons to come to the Maldives. All resorts cater for divers and snorkellers, and most organise twice- or thrice-daily diving excursions and usually at least one snorkelling trip a day. If you're keen on either, it'll always be cheaper to bring your own equipment, including snorkel, mask and fins, plus buoyancy control device (BCD) and dive computer, if you're a diver. Dive schools vary enormously in quality and helpfulness, but all are of an exceptionally high safety standard, as regulated by strict Maldivian laws. Resorts themselves are not so important for divers – it's their location and the

RESORT BASICS

You'll be met at the airport by your resort representative, who will usually take your ticket and/or passport from you, something that is quite normal here despite feeling rather odd to the seasoned traveller.

Unless you're arriving after dark you'll soon be transferred to your resort – either by a waiting dhoni, speedboat, airplane or seaplane from the nearby lagoon airport. You may have to wait for other passengers to get through customs, but it shouldn't be too long if your resort is on the ball. You can use US dollars or euros at the airport cafe, and change some cash into rufiya at the bank.

Travellers arriving after dark will have to spend a night at the airport hotel or at a hotel in Male', as neither boat nor seaplane transfers are carried out after sunset for obvious reasons.

On arrival at the resort you'll be given a drink, asked to fill out a registration form and taken to your room. Resort staff will bring your luggage separately.

Room Types

Some resorts have just one type of room, which confusingly may be called 'Superior', 'Deluxe', or 'Super Deluxe'. Most bigger, newer resorts have several types of room, ranging from the cheapest 'Superior Garden Villas' to the 'Deluxe Over-Water Suites'. A 'Garden Villa' will not have a beach frontage, and a 'Water Villa' will be on stilts over the lagoon – and twice the cost.

More expensive rooms tend to be bigger, newer, better finished, and can have a bathtub as well as a shower, a minibar instead of an empty fridge, tea- and coffee-making facilities (even an espresso machine), a CD sound system, and maybe even a Jacuzzi. Smaller over-water accommodation is called a 'water bungalow', although the delineation of the terms water bungalow and water villa is fluid and largely interchangeable.

Single Supplements & Extra Beds

This book gives room rates for single/double occupancy when they differ, but most package-deal prices are quoted on a per-person basis, assuming double occupancy. Solo travellers have to pay a 'single-person supplement' for the privilege of having a room all to themselves.

Extra people can usually share a room, but there's a charge for the extra bed, which varies enormously resort to resort, as well as additional costs for meals. In a package-tour price list, this appears as a supplement for children sharing the same room as parents, or for extra adults sharing a room.

For children two years and younger, usually just the US$8 bed tax is payable. From two to 12 years, the child supplement with full board will be from US$15 to US$30 in most budget to midrange resorts, but much more in expensive resorts. Transfers from the airport are normally charged at half the adult rate. A more expensive option is to get two adjacent rooms, ideally with a connecting door. You might get a discount on the second room.

Pricing Periods

Pricing patterns vary with the resort and the demands of its main market – some are incredibly detailed and complex with a different rate every week. The basic pattern is that Christmas-New Year is the peak season, with very high prices, minimum-stay requirements and surcharges for Christmas dinner and New Year's Eve. Early January to late March is high season, when many Europeans take a winter holiday. The weeks around Easter may attract even higher rates (but not as high as Christmas). From Easter to about mid-July is low season (and the wettest part of the year). July, August and September is another high season, for the European summer holidays. Mid-September to early December is low season again.

Specific markets can have their own times of high demand, such as the August holiday week for Italians, Chinese New Year in the Asian market or the end of Ramadan for some Middle Eastern guests.

ease of access to dive sights nearby. Most resorts have at least 10 sites nearby and visit them in rotation. If there's a particular dive site you want to visit, you should contact the dive school at the resort and check it'll be running a trip there during your stay. See p67 for more about snorkelling and diving.

Spa Treatments

As a destination for relaxation, the Maldives has also become well known for offering a huge array of treatments in purpose-built spas. These include all types of massage, beauty treatments, Ayurvedic (Indian herbal) medicine, acupuncture and even traditional Maldivian treatments. Almost all midrange and top-end resorts have a spa, and even some of the budget options are now building them. The best are sometimes booked up months in advance, so it can pay to plan ahead if you're interested in certain treatments. With staff often from Bali, Thailand, India and Sri Lanka, you're in safe (if expensive) hands. You can check most resort websites for a full treatment list, but resorts particularly well known for their spas include Soneva Fushi, Soneva Gili, Cocoa Island, Sheraton Maldives Full Moon Resort & Spa, Banyan Tree, One & Only Reethi Rah and W Retreat & Spa. The underwater spa at Huvafen Fushi is the first of its kind in the world and is truly unique; you can be massaged while watching the fish swimming around the glass walls of the room. Resorts well known for Ayurvedic therapy include Adaaran Select Meedhupparu, Taj Exotica, Four Seasons Landaa Giraavaru and Olhuveli Beach & Spa.

> The twin-otter seaplanes used to transfer guests to resorts are all built in Canada and have to be flown around the world, a 16,700km journey that is still more economical than stripping the plane down and shipping it.

Surfing

The best resorts for surfing are Chaaya Island Dhonveli and Adaaran Select Hudhuran Fushi, which are both blessed with their own surf breaks and are very popular with surfers during the season. The popularity of surfing is tangibly on the increase in the Maldives, with surfer arrivals going up massively in the past few years. However, it's really only these two resorts that are perfectly located near good breaks, although nearby resorts, such as Four Seasons Kuda Huraa, Paradise Island and Club Med Kani, can organise boat trips. Another fantastic option to avoid the crowds and explore a pristine region of the country is to join a 'surfari'. See p89 for details on surfing in the Maldives.

Water Sports

Second only to diving schools, most resorts have a water sports centre (but not all, so check before booking). These vary enormously – some offer the most basic array of canoes and windsurfing, while others run the gauntlet from water skiing to kite-boarding and wakeboarding. The best resorts for sailing and windsurfing have a wide lagoon that's not too shallow, and lots of equipment to choose from.

Resorts with particularly strong water sports facilities include Kuredu Island Resort, Adaaran Select Hudhuran Fushi, Chaaya Island Dhonveli, Alimatha Aquatic, Bandos, the three Kuramathi resorts, Kanuhura, Meeru, Summer Island Village, Club Faru, Club Med Kani, Vilu Reef, Olhuveli and Reethi Beach.

You'll find jet skis and other not-so-cheap thrills at Kuredu Island Resort, Kanuhura, Chaaya Island Dhonveli, Chaaya Reef Ellaidhoo, Conrad Maldives Rangali Island, Reethi Beach, Fun Island, Holiday Island,Vilu Reef, Paradise Island, W Retreat & Spa, both Four Seasons resorts and Royal Island, among many others.

Wildlife Watching

Most resorts offer dolphin cruises, and although there's no guarantee you'll see anything, dolphins are a common sight in the Maldives, so you're always in with a good chance. Depending on favoured dolphin-feeding grounds near your resort, the cruises can last from one to three hours and are usually by dhoni. These are often billed as 'champagne sunset dolphin cruises', and you can enjoy a glass of fizz while watching a lovely sunset even if flipper doesn't show up.

Whale watching is rarely available – as the whales don't swim within the atolls themselves, any whale watching boat has to first get out to the open ocean. Be aware that the Whale Submarine (p100) in Male' is something of a misnomer; it's a submarine that visits a reef nearby – there are no whales to be seen here.

FOOD & DRINK

A miniature revolution in fine cuisine has occurred in the past few years in the Maldives. Once even the top-end hotels had decidedly average offerings at meal times, but now things are quite different, with luxury hotels offering a huge choice from an ever-growing number of eateries, allowing guests to eat somewhere different every day for several days.

However, the buffet, the standard lunch and dinner option, is still in evidence, and extremely variable it can be too – the usual Maldivian maxim that you get what you pay for is especially true here.

Alcohol is also becoming more of a feature at resorts – many have spent years building up wine cellars to rival any French restaurant, and as you'd expect these are not cheap. Reethi Rah claims to have over 8000 bottles of wine in its cellar, while Huvafen Fushi's wine cellar is a work of art itself, buried deep below the island and hired out for private dinners at great expense.

However, in all cases alcohol is expensive and with a few luxury exceptions, limited in range. In lesser resorts beers available will not thrill connoisseurs – although Kirin and Tiger are commonly seen amid the Heineken and Carling. All-inclusive packages cover certain designated drinks, usually the cheapest non-brand-name beer going, a house red and white wine and non-brand-name spirits. People on these tours can usually be found drinking, perhaps to justify the price of the package.

MEALS

Typically, breakfast will include a choice of cereals, fresh fruit, fruit juice from cans or concentrate, instant or real coffee, tea, bread rolls, toast, omelettes or fried eggs done as you like, sausages, bacon, baked beans, and often a curry and rice. At more upmarket resorts you could also have muesli, yoghurt, more fresh fruits, fresh-squeezed fruit juice, brewed coffee, better bread, croissants and real ham. You get what you pay for, remember.

For lunch, most resorts manage soup and a simple salad, pasta, rice, noodles, and at least one each of fish, beef and chicken dishes, often prepared as curry, casserole or stew, with fruit and dessert to finish. Better resorts offer more varied salad vegetables, pasta freshly tossed with a choice of sauces, Hokkien noodles, freshly fried fish fillets and more creative chicken and beef dishes.

Dinner will usually have the biggest selection, and may be a 'theme night' specialising in regional cuisines such as Italian, Asian, Indian or Maldivian (usually meaning fanciful versions of local dishes, not authentic for the most part). Most resorts will have soup, salad and a

Kuredu (p153) is the only resort to offer a golf course – a real luxury in a country where land is at a premium!

dozen or so hot dishes, with at least two each of fish, beef and chicken. A few dishes will be vegetarian – ratatouille, vegetable curry, *pasta alla fungi* or potatoes Provençale. There'll be a pasta dish or three, possibly a lasagne, and stir-fried noodles, as well as plain rice, saffron rice, fried

MALDIVES RESORT RATINGS

Each resort is given a number out of three for how it scores on each front, three being the very highest standard in its field. A zero means that the resort has absolutely nothing worth mentioning on a subject; for example if it doesn't accept kids, it gets a zero for children's activities.

A = Beach
B = Romance
C = Social Life
D = Pampering
E = Children's Activities

F = Food
G = Design
H = Diving
I = Snorkelling
J = Water Sports

Resort	A	B	C	D	E	F	G	H	I	J
Adaaran Club Bathala	3	2	2	1	2	2	1	3	3	3
Adaaran Club Rannalhi	3	2	3	1	3	2	1	3	3	2
Adaaran Select Hudhuran Fushi	2	2	2	2	2	2	2	3	3	3
Adaaran Select Meedhupparu	3	2	2	2	2	2	1	3	2	3
Alimatha Aquatic	3	2	2	1	1	2	2	3	3	3
Anantara Dhigu & Veli	3	2	2	2	3	1	2	3	3	3
Angaga	3	2	2	1	2	2	2	3	3	2
Angsana Ihuru	3	3	1	2	0	3	3	3	3	3
Angsana Velavaru	3	3	1	3	1	3	3	3	3	3
Asdu Sun Island	2	1	2	1	1	1	1	3	3	2
Athuruga	3	2	3	1	2	2	2	3	3	2
Bandos Island Resort	2	1	3	1	3	2	1	2	3	3
Banyan Tree Madivaru	3	3	0	3	1	3	3	3	3	2
Banyan Tree Vabbinfaru	3	3	1	3	1	3	3	3	3	2
Baros	3	3	1	3	1	3	3	3	2	3
Beach House at Manafaru	3	2	1	2	2	3	3	2	3	3
Biyadhoo	2	1	2	1	1	2	1	3	3	3
Chaaya Island Dhonveli	3	2	2	1	2	2	2	3	3	3
Chaaya Lagoon Hakuraa Huraa	3	2	2	1	2	2	2	3	1	3
Chaaya Reef Ellaidhoo	3	1	2	1	2	2	2	3	3	3
Cinnamon Island Resort & Spa	2	2	2	2	3	1	2	3	2	2
Club Faru	3	1	3	2	3	2	1	3	2	3
Club Med Kani	3	1	3	1	3	2	2	3	3	3
Cocoa Island	3	3	1	3	1	3	3	3	3	3
Coco Palm Boduhithi	2	3	2	3	2	3	3	3	3	3
Coco Palm Dhuni Kolhu	3	2	2	2	2	2	2	3	3	3
Conrad Maldives Rangali Island	3	3	1	3	3	3	3	3	3	3
Dhiggiri	2	2	2	2	3	2	2	3	3	2
Dhoni Island	3	3	1	3	0	3	3	3	3	2
Diva Resort & Spa	3	3	2	3	2	3	3	3	3	3
Embudu Village	3	1	2	1	2	2	1	3	3	3
Equator Village	1	1	3	1	2	1	1	3	3	2
Eriyadu	3	2	2	1	1	2	1	3	3	2
Fihalhohi Resort	3	2	2	1	2	2	1	3	2	2
Filitheyo	2	1	2	1	2	2	2	3	1	1
Four Seasons Kuda Huraa	2	2	1	3	3	3	2	3	3	3
Four Seasons Landaa Giraavaru	2	3	2	3	3	3	3	3	3	3
Gangehi Island Resort	2	2	2	3	1	2	2	3	3	2

rice and maybe risotto. There's a trend for 'live cooking stations' at one or more places along the buffet tables, where food is fried or barbecued to taste while you watch – great for fresh fish, prawns, pasta, steak and shish kebab. Whole fish and roast meats are carved and served as you like.

Resort	A	B	C	D	E	F	G	H	I	J
Giravaru	1	1	2	1	1	1	1	3	3	2
Helengeli	3	2	2	1	1	1	2	3	3	0
Holiday Island	3	1	2	1	2	1	1	3	1	2
Huvafen Fushi	3	3	1	3	1	3	3	3	3	3
Irufushi Beach & Spa Resort	3	3	1	3	3	2	2	2	2	3
Island Hideaway	3	3	1	3	3	3	3	3	3	2
J Resort Handhufushi	1	2	2	2	2	1	2	3	3	3
J Resort Kudarah	1	2	2	2	2	2	2	3	3	2
Kandooma	1	2	3	2	3	2	3	3	2	3
Kanuhura	3	3	2	3	3	3	3	3	3	3
Kihaad	3	3	2	2	3	2	2	3	3	2
Komandoo Island Resort	2	3	1	2	0	2	3	3	3	3
Kuramathi Blue Lagoon	3	2	1	2	1	2	3	3	3	3
Kuramathi Cottage & Spa	3	2	1	3	1	2	2	3	3	3
Kuramathi Village	3	1	3	1	1	2	1	3	3	3
Kuredu Island Resort	3	2	3	2	2	2	1	3	3	3
Kurumba Maldives	3	2	2	3	3	3	2	3	3	3
Maayafushi	2	1	1	1	1	2	1	3	3	1
Madoogali	3	3	1	2	1	2	2	3	3	2
Makunudu Island	3	3	1	2	1	2	2	3	3	1
Medhufushi	3	2	2	2	1	2	2	3	3	3
Meeru Island Resort	3	2	2	2	2	2	2	3	3	3
Mirihi	3	2	1	3	2	2	2	3	2	2
Naladhu	2	3	1	3	1	3	2	3	3	2
Nika Island	3	3	1	3	1	3	2	3	3	2
Olhuveli Beach & Spa	3	2	1	3	1	2	2	3	3	3
One & Only Reethi Rah	3	3	2	3	3	3	3	3	1	3
Palm Beach Resort	3	3	2	2	2	2	2	3	1	2
Paradise Island	3	2	3	2	2	1	1	3	3	3
Rania Experience	3	3	0	3	1	3	3	3	3	2
Ranveli Beach Resort	3	2	2	2	2	3	2	3	3	2
Reethi Beach Resort	3	2	2	1	1	2	2	3	3	3
Rihiveli Beach Resort	2	2	3	2	2	2	1	3	1	3
Royal Island Resort & Spa	3	2	1	2	1	2	2	3	3	3
Sheraton Maldives Full Moon Resort & Spa	3	3	1	3	3	3	3	2	2	2
Soneva Fushi	3	3	2	3	3	3	3	3	3	3
Soneva Gili	3	3	1	3	1	3	3	3	3	3
Summer Island Village	3	1	2	1	2	1	1	3	3	3
Sun Island	2	1	3	1	3	3	1	3	3	3
Taj Exotica	3	3	1	3	1	3	3	3	3	2
Thudufushi	3	2	3	1	1	2	2	3	3	2
Thulhagiri	3	2	2	1	1	2	1	3	3	2
Velidhu Island Resort	3	2	2	1	1	1	1	3	3	3
Veligandu	3	2	2	2	1	2	1	3	3	2
Vilamendhoo	2	2	2	1	2	2	2	3	3	2
Vilu Reef	3	3	2	3	1	2	2	3	3	3
W Retreat & Spa	3	3	3	3	1	3	3	3	3	3
Zitahli Kuda-Fanafaru Maldives	3	3	1	3	1	2	3	2	3	3

Fancier resorts feature more and fresher seafood and it's less likely to be overcooked – the best places serve sashimi. Salad is another class marker – a budget resort will serve iceberg lettuce, coleslaw and cucumber with a basic bottled mayo, French or Thousand Island dressing. A better resort will have cos lettuce, rocket, radicchio, spinach leaves and three kinds of cabbage, with freshly made mayonnaise and your choice of vinegars and olive oils. Only the very best resorts have ripe, red, tasty tomatoes.

Desserts can be delicious, with pastries, fruit pies, tarts, tiramisu, mousse, blancmange, custard and cheesecake all on offer at the far end of the buffet. The best resorts might have crêpes prepared at a live cooking station, and a choice of cheeses too.

Budget resorts might offer a set menu only for some meals – perhaps for lunch, or on alternate days for dinner. These are OK, and will give your waistline some respite. At the other end of the market, the best resorts serve some meals à la carte – the chef has a chance to do something special and creative, and the waiters enjoy giving full table service.

As well as the main buffet restaurant, big resorts usually have 'speciality restaurants' serving regional cuisine (Thai, Japanese, Italian, Indian etc) or grills and seafood. These can be expensive (main courses US$15 to US$50) but in better resorts are excellent.

Most resorts have a 'coffee shop' serving light meals, coffee and drinks, often 24 hours a day. They're good for people on half board who want a snack in the middle of the day.

Another alternative to the usual buffet is a 'speciality meal'. This might be a barbecue or a curry night, served on the beach, and open to anyone who pays the extra charge, perhaps US$25 (unlike a theme night in the main restaurant, which is not charged as an extra). Or it can be a much pricier private dinner for two in romantic surroundings – on an inhabited island, on the beach, or on a sandbar a short ride from the resort island. Most resorts will do special meals on request.

> Always ask for desalinated water to drink; any good resort will provide this (preferably free) and not just a US$7 bottle of imported Evian, which is exorbitant in both cash and carbon.

MEAL PLANS

Many guests are on full-board packages that include accommodation and all meals. Others take a half-board package, which includes breakfast and dinner, and pay extra for lunch. Some resorts offer a bed and breakfast plan, and guests pay separately for lunch and dinner. The advantage of not paying for all your meals in advance is that you permit yourself the freedom to vary where you eat (assuming your resort has more than one restaurant). However, at good resorts your full-board plan is usually transferable, meaning you can eat a certain amount at other restaurants, or at least get a big discount on the à la carte prices.

A TASTE OF THE MALDIVES

It used to be rare to find Maldivian food in tourist resorts – the opinion was that Western stomachs couldn't cope with the spices. Now many resorts do a Maldivian barbecue once a week, which is very enjoyable if not totally authentic. These barbecues can be on the beach, by the pool or in the restaurant. The main dishes are fresh reef fish, baked tuna, fish curries, rice and *roshi* (unleavened bread). The regular dinner buffet might also feature Maldivian fish curry. Less common is the Maldivian breakfast favourite *mas huni,* a healthy mixture of tuna, onion, coconut and chilli, eaten with *roshi*. If there's nothing Maldivian on the menu, you could ask the kitchen staff to make a fish curry or a tray of 'short eats' – they may be making some for the staff anyway. Small resorts are usually amenable to special requests. Otherwise, do a trip to Male' or an island-hopping excursion to a fishing village, and try out a local teashop.

RESORT TIPS

It's always worth checking a resort website yourself and even contacting the resort for specific, up-to-date information, as things change regularly. Is there construction work happening on the island? Is the spa finished yet? Do they still offer kite-boarding? Also, be aware that many resort websites have never been updated since they were created. While there are exceptions, it's never a good idea to take the information there as fact – check when the page was last updated.

Check the dive centre website. It might provide a discount if you book your dives before your arrival. Email them for any specific dive information.

If the trip is a honeymoon, or second honeymoon, or if you will be celebrating an anniversary or birthday, let your travel agent or resort know – there's usually something laid on in such circumstances. Some resorts might require a wedding certificate before they do anything – the Maldives is notorious for couples claiming to be on their honeymoon just to get some freebies!

Room-only deals are also sometimes available, but they're rarely a great idea. Never underestimate the sheer expense of eating à la carte in the Maldives at any level, although at the top end it's positively outrageous – think US$75 per head without alcohol for a decent lunch. Self-catering is of course not possible and there's nothing worse than being unable to eat properly due to financial constraints. Unless you're very comfortable financially and want to eat in a variety of different places, we strongly encourage you to book full- or half-board meal plans.

All-inclusive plans are some of the best value of all, although in general they're associated with the core package-tourist market and tend to be available only in budget resorts. These typically include all drinks (non-brand-name alcohol, soft drinks and water) and some activities and water sports/diving thrown in for good measure. Always investigate carefully exactly what's on offer meal-wise before you make a decision – the meal plan can make an expensive package worthwhile or a cheap one a rip-off. One resort that has sought to be the first up-market all-inclusive resort is Lily Beach in Ari Atoll, where you'll get good wines and brand name spirits for your (not inconsiderable!) daily rate.

> Be prepared to get on the weighing scales yourself if you are flying on Maldivian, the domestic airline. The planes are small and everyone's weight needs to be taken into account.

ENTERTAINMENT

Beware the animator! These lively people are forever trying to encourage group work-outs or karaoke competitions in Italian-dominated resorts even though their appeal seems limited to Italian and Russian holiday-makers. Their days in the Maldives are numbered as the country's tourist industry increasingly tries to define the Maldives as a stylish and fashionable destination, but they're still determinedly hanging on in some places for the time being.

The truth is that the Maldives is not a premium destination for entertainment. What little of it there is can be fairly naff and uninspiring, and the resorts that insist on a nightly disco often find them empty. Simply put, honeymooners, divers and families, the core demographic of Maldivian tourism, don't really come here for any kind of entertainment, preferring quiet romance and daily activities to night-time ones.

The biggest party and entertainment resort is Club Med Kani, with its tireless round of animator high jinks and nightly disco, and to a lesser extent Bandos, where visiting air crews can often be the life and soul of the party. One classy exception is the ice-cool stylings of the subterranean nightclub at W Retreat & Spa, where the in-house DJ spins Kraftwerk to the fabulous crowd and there's no chance of hearing ABBA!

> Look out for the barefoot pilots on Maldivian Air Taxi and Trans Maldivian. Not only do they go to work in shorts, many of them spend the nights in luxury resorts before flying back to Male' the next morning – not the world's worst job.

Most resorts have some low-key entertainment a couple of evenings a week. Usually it's a fairly cringe-inducing covers band, although other more interesting performers such as traditional Maldivian *bodu beru* (big drum) players, Sri Lankan fire dancers or a jazz band are also common.

LUXURIES

You've come to the right place if this is your main interest – the Maldives' top-end resorts (and to a good extent even its midrange options) offer an eye-watering range of 'treatments', pampering, and a general level of luxury that you can find in few other places.

The current *sine qua non* of the luxury industry is the personal *thakuru*, or butler, otherwise known as a 'man Friday' or 'villa host'. The *thakuru* is assigned to you throughout your stay. He's your point of contact for all small things (restocking the minibar, reconfirming your flight), but given that one *thakuru* will often be looking after up to ten rooms at a

---

SAFARI CRUISES

Safaris are a superb option for anyone wanting the best possible combination of diving sites, the chance to travel outside the standard tourist zone and a sociable arena where both couples and non-couples will feel totally comfortable.

The massive expansion in the market for safari cruises has meant an increasingly sleek approach from the tour companies that run them; a typical, modern boat is air-conditioned, spacious, and serves varied and appetising meals. It should have hot water, a sun deck, fishing and diving gear, mobile phone, full bar, DVD player and cosy, comfortable cabins.

Costs start at around US$100 per person per day, including the US$8 per day bed tax and all meals, plus roughly US$60 per day for diving trips. There's usually a minimum daily (or weekly) charge for the whole boat, and the cost per person is lower if there are enough passengers to fill the boat. You'll be charged extra for soft drinks and alcohol, which are priced as you'd expect to find in most resorts. You might splurge for the occasional meal at a resort, but generally there are few extras to spend money on.

The most basic boats are large dhonis with a small galley and communal dining area, two or three cramped cabins with two berths each, and a shared shower and toilet. Passengers often drag their mattresses out on deck for fresh air, and sleep under the stars. Food is prepared on board and varies from very ordinary to very good – it usually features lots of freshly caught fish. The bigger, better boats have air-conditioning, more spacious accommodation, and a toilet and shower for each cabin. The best boats, like the best resorts, spare no effort in making their guests comfortable.

Most safari trips are for diving (see p69) or so-called 'surfaris' for surfing (see p91). A minority of safari trips are primarily for sightseeing, and usually offer a fair amount of fishing and snorkelling, stops at fishing villages and resorts, and picnics or a camp-out on an uninhabited island. Obviously it's important to make sure you're joining a trip that will cover what you want to do.

On a scheduled trip, a single passenger may have to share a cabin with another, or pay a premium rate. Compatibility isn't usually a problem on diving or surf trips, where everyone has a common interest, but it can be an issue on longer sightseeing cruises. If you arrange your own group of six or so people, you can charter a whole boat and tailor a trip to suit your interests.

Choosing a Safari Boat

More than 80 safari boats are operating in the Maldives. Some specific suggestions are given here, but you'll need to do some research yourself. When you're considering a safari-boat trip, ask the operator about the following.

■ Boat size – Generally speaking, bigger boats will be more comfortable, and therefore more expensive, than small boats. Boats with more than 20 or so passengers may not have

time, the term 'personal' is pushing it a bit, especially when even in the best hotels in the country there are often language problems and some service issues.

The main centre of luxury at most resorts is the spa – until recently they were considered optional for resorts, whereas now they are usually at the very centre of the luxury experience. Expect to pay from about US$40 for a simple massage at a budget or midrange place to US$300 for a long session of pampering.

Resort spas in good resorts are often run by specialist companies such as ESPA, Serena, COMO Shambhala, Per Aquum and Six Senses. At this very highest level they offer a vast range of treatments from the sublime to the truly ridiculous. Some of our favourite names include Fit For Life Aromatic Moor Mud Wrap, Tamarind Fancy Wipe, Potato Purifier and Happy Man Relaxer (no jokes please). Perhaps it's because we can't afford to spend US$250 on a foot massage, but it all seems rather funny to us;

---

the camaraderie you'd get with a small group. Most boats have about 12 berths or less; few boats have more than 20.

- Cabin arrangements – Can you get a two-berth cabin (if that's what you want)? How many cabins/people are sharing a bathroom?

- Comforts – Does the boat have air-con, hot water and desalinated water available 24 hours?

- Companions – Who else will be on the trip, what language do they speak, have they done a safari trip before? What are their interests – diving, sightseeing, fishing, surfing?

- Food and drink – Can you be catered for as a vegetarian or vegan? Is there a bar serving alcohol and, if so, how much is a beer and wine etc?

- Recreation – Does the boat have a DVD player, iPod dock, fishing tackle or sun deck? Does the boat have sails or is it propelled by motor only?

Safari Boat Operators

Safari boats often change ownership, or get refitted or acquire a new name. The skipper, cook and divemaster can change too, so it's hard to make firm recommendations. The following boats have a good reputation, but there are many others offering decent facilities and services. The boats listed here all have a bar on board, oxygen for emergencies, and some diving equipment for rent. Universal's Atoll Explorer is like a mini-cruise ship with a swimming pool on deck, while the Four Seasons Island Explorer is the most luxurious and the most expensive of all. The websites are those of the boat operators. Many of these operators have other boats as well, which may also be very good. If the website does not give booking information (or it's not in your language), most of these boats can be booked through the bigger tour operators in Male' (see p96), or by overseas travel agents. The official **tourism website** (www.visitmaldives.com) has reasonably up-to-date details on almost every safari and cruise boat (click on Where to Stay then Cruise Boats).

Adventurer 2 (☎ 3326734; www.maldivesdiving.com; 🕿) Boat 31m, eight cabins, 20 berths, hot water.
Atoll Explorer (☎ 3314873; www.atollexplorer.com; 🕿) Boat 48m, 20 cabins, 40 berths, hot water.
Eagle Ray (☎ 3314811; www.maldivesboatclub.com) Boat 26m, seven cabins, 14 berths, hot water.
Four Seasons Explorer (☎ 6644888; www.fourseasons.com; 🕿) Boat 39m, 11 cabins, 22 berths, hot water.
Gulfaam (☎ 3323617, www.voyagesmaldives.com; 🕿) Boat 20m, six cabins, 12 berths.
MV Carina (☎ 3316172; www.seamaldives.com.mv; 🕿) Boat 33m, 11 cabins, 33 berths, hot water.
Sharifa (☎ 3320555; www.guraabu.com.mv; 🕿) Boat 30m, 8 cabins, 19 berths, hot water.
Soleil (☎ 3320555; www.guraabu.com.mv; 🕿) Boat 28m, nine cabins, 17 berths, hot water.
Sting Ray (☎ 3314811; www.maldivesboatclub.com.mv; 🕿) Boat 31m, nine cabins, 22 berths, hot water.
Sultan of Maldives (☎ 3310550; www.sultansoftheseas.com; 🕿) Boat 30m, eight cabins, 16 berths, hot water.

there's a lot to be said for gorgeous relaxing treatments, but you'll meet your fair share of Bubbles DeVere types here who go from treatment to treatment all day long.

BEACHES

There's almost no resort in the Maldives that does not have an amazing beach. Throughout the course of researching this book, the only really mediocre beach we saw was at the Equator Village. It's still swimmable but narrow and strewn with seaweed, making swimming unpleasant. Beaches suffer a great deal from erosion and the tsunami did not help this at all, but resorts work very hard to redress erosion with sandbags in certain places. These can of course be unsightly, but they are necessary to hold the islands' beaches in place. Of course, the more expensive the resort, the more effort is made to ensure that sandbags are never visible. Elsewhere, islands around Male' can suffer from litter washing up on their beaches – Giravaru, near Thilafushi (Rubbish Island) suffers particularly badly – but other than that the quality of beach is almost universally brilliant.

For the record here are a few of our favourites: Kanuhura, One & Only Reethi Rah, Kuredu, Palm Beach, Soneva Fushi, Reethi Beach, Royal Island, Coco Palm, Eriyadu, Angsana Ihuru, Bandos, Baros, Banyan Tree Vabbinfaru, Soneva Gili, Club Med Kani, Rihiveli, Adaaran Club Rannalhi, Paradise Island, Island Hideaway, W Retreat & Spa, Coco Palm Dhuni Kolhu, Sun Island, Veligandu, Vilu Reef, Huvafen Fushi, Filitheyo, Fun Island and Conrad Maldives Rangali Island. This does not mean that resorts not on this list don't make the grade – these are just a few of our top choices.

'If your offspring are happy to spend the day on the beach, then almost every resort will be suitable.'

CHILDREN

If you're bringing children to the Maldives, it's very important to get your choice of resort right, as only a few resorts have kids clubs or babysitters available, and activities for older children can be limited at resorts more used to welcoming honeymooning couples. If you aren't looking for kids clubs and your offspring are happy to spend the day on the beach, then almost every resort will be suitable. Note that Komandoo Island Resort does not accept children aged under six and W Retreat & Spa and Dhoni Island don't accept children under 12.

In general kids will love the Maldives, although for more than a week it might be pushing it unless you're staying in a big and friendly family resort where there are plenty of other children for them to play with and an endless parade of activities.

Some highly recommended resorts for children include: Kuredu, One & Only Reethi Rah, Kanuhura, Bandos, Kurumba Maldives, Filitheyo, Club Med Kani, Paradise Island, the three Kuramathi resorts, Meeru, both Four Seasons resorts, Lily Beach and Sun Island.

Snorkelling, Diving & Surfing

Unless you take some time to explore the magical world underneath the water in the Maldives, you're seeing just one tiny part of this incredibly diverse country. Yes, the flora and fauna on the tiny scraps of land poking their heads above the water are not the most spectacular or varied, but glance into the deep blue all around and you'll see marine life so incredible that you'll quickly understand why the Maldives is a favourite destination for divers from around the world.

The visibility is incredible, the water so warm that many divers don't even wear a wetsuit and the sheer variety of life underwater is fantastic. Because of the thoroughly professional and safety-conscious approach from all resorts and excellent facilities, it's common to learn to dive in the Maldives as well. Even if you don't do a full PADI or equivalent course, a brief scuba introduction is very cheap and lots of fun, while snorkelling can be done by anyone who can swim.

A further boon about the Maldives' submarine life is that as well as being plentiful, beautiful and accessible, it's also extremely unaggressive. Despite its being rich in sharks, there's not one type likely to attack a human, and the only possible reason it would attack in any case would be self-defence.

Diving in particular requires some planning; decide your level, what you want to see and how much diving you want to do before choosing a resort. Snorkelling is similar – some resorts have no good house reef and thus you have to go on a boat trip to see anything worthwhile. Surfing is the most seasonal activity of all - but it's increasingly popular in the east of the country, with some great breaks coming off the Indian Ocean.

SNORKELLING

Snorkelling is the first step into seeing a different world. Anyone who can swim can do it, it's very cheap to rent the equipment (and often free at smarter resorts) and the rewards make themselves known immediately. The colours of the fish and coral are far better at shallow depths, as water absorbs light, and so below 5m colours start to become less sharp (hence why so many divers carry torches to compensate). This means a visual feast awaits any snorkeller on any decent reef.

WHERE TO SNORKEL

Usually an island is surrounded firstly by a sand-bottomed lagoon, and then by the reef flat (*faru*), a belt of dead and living coral covered by shallow water. At the edge of the reef flat is a steep, coral-covered slope that drops away into deeper water. These reef slopes are the best areas for snorkelling – around a resort island this is called the 'house reef'. The slope itself can have interesting features such as cliffs, terraces and caves, and there are clearly visible changes in the coral and marine flora as the water gets deeper. You can see both the smaller fish, which frequent the reef flats, and sometimes much larger animals that live in the deep water between the islands but come close to the reefs to feed.

'The colours of the fish and coral are far better at shallow depths, as water absorbs light.'

You can also take a boat from your resort to other snorkelling sites around the atoll. A giri (coral pinnacle) that rises to within 5m of the surface is ideal for snorkelling, which is not difficult if it's in sheltered waters inside an atoll. A kandu (sea channel) will usually have excellent soft corals, schools of reef fish and large pelagic species.

The best resorts for snorkelling have an accessible house reef, where the deep water is not far offshore, at least around part of the island. There are usually channels you can swim through to the outer-reef slope. To avoid grazing yourself or damaging the coral, always use these channels rather than trying to find your own way across the reef flat. Another option is to walk out on a jetty to the reef edge – all resorts have at least one jetty, though sometimes they don't extend right to the edge of the reef.

Resorts with excellent house reefs tend to be popular with divers too. Some of the best are Chaaya Reef Ellaidhoo, Adaaran Club Bathala, Adaaran Prestige Vadoo, Mirihi, Biyadhoo, Eriyadu, Vilamendhoo, Filitheyo, Reethi Beach Resort, Embudu Village, W Retreat & Spa, Soneva Gili, Olhuveli Beach & Spa and Kuredu Island Resort.

Resorts that don't have an accessible house reef will usually provide a couple of boat trips per day to a good snorkelling site nearby, but this is a lot less convenient as you're limited in time and not usually alone. Many resorts offer island-hopping trips or snorkelling excursions that stop at really superb snorkelling sites, and these are a far better option. Full-day excursions usually cost from US$30 to US$60 or so, but are definitely worth it. Kuredu Island Resort has the most comprehensive snorkelling programme, with guided snorkelling trips to many interesting sites, including a shipwreck. Sometimes snorkellers can go out with a dive boat, if the dive site is suitable and there's space on the boat.

The whale shark (p80) is the largest fish in the world – they regularly reach up to 12m in length and are one of the biggest diving attractions when they cruise the kandus in May.

TOP SNORKELLING SITES

If you stay in a resort with an interesting and accessible house reef, that will probably be your main snorkelling site. You can visit the same reef again and again, and get to know its nooks and crannies, its resident fish and its regular visitors.

A resort excursion can take you to the best snorkelling sites in your atoll, and if you're on a live-aboard safari boat you'll have an unlimited choice. The best snorkelling sites are also dive sites, with a lot of interest in the shallower water. Fit and experienced snorkellers can free-dive to 5m or more without too much trouble, and if the visibility is good they can appreciate any features down to about 10m. Many of the dive sites described in this book are also excellent for snorkelling.

PREPARATION

If you've never tried snorkelling before, you'll soon pick it up. Every resort will have snorkelling equipment that you can rent, but this will cost US$5 to US$10 per day (although less by the week), and it's often free at smarter resorts. It's definitely better to have your own. It's also cheaper in the long run and you can be sure that it fits properly. You can buy good-quality equipment at reasonable prices at the airport shop and in Male'. Most resort shops sell them too, but the range is smaller and the prices are higher. Ideally, you should bring your own set from home.

Mask

Human eyes won't normally focus in water, but a mask keeps an air space in front of your eyes allowing them to focus. Any mask, no matter how cheap, should have a shatterproof lens. Ensure that it fits you comfortably

– press it gently onto your face, breathe in through your nose a little, and the suction should hold the mask on your face.

If you're short-sighted you can get the mask lens ground to your optical prescription, but this is expensive. Alternatively, get a stick-on optical lens to attach to the inside of the mask lens, or simply fold up an old pair of spectacles and wedge them inside the mask. There's no problem with contact lenses under the mask, although theoretically they can be lost if the mask is flooded.

Snorkel

The tube has to be long enough to reach above the surface of the water, but should not be either too long or too wide. If it is too big then you have more water to expel when you come to the surface. Also, each breath out leaves a snorkel full of used air, and if the snorkel is too big, you will rebreathe a larger proportion of carbon dioxide.

Fins

These are not absolutely necessary, but they make swimming easier and let you dive deeper, and they give a margin of safety in currents. Fins either fit completely over your foot or have an open back with an adjustable strap around your heel, designed for use with wetsuit boots.

Shirt

A Lycra swim shirt or thin wetsuit top will protect against sunburn (a real hazard) and minor scratches from the coral or rocks. Even a T-shirt will give sun protection – but don't use a favourite as the sea water won't do the fabric any favours.

SNORKELLING SAFELY

Don't snorkel alone, and always let someone else know where and when you'll be snorkelling. Colourful equipment or clothing will make you more visible. Beware of strong currents or rough conditions – wind chop and large swells can make snorkelling uncomfortable or even dangerous. In open waters, carry a safety balloon and whistle to alert boats to your presence.

'Don't snorkel alone, and always let someone else know where and when you'll be snorkelling.'

DIVING

Taking the proper plunge into the deep blue is one of the most exciting things imaginable and the rewards are massive, especially in the Maldives, which is rightly known as a world-class scuba diving destination. The enormous variety of fish life is amazing, and there's a good chance you'll see some of the biggest marine creatures – a close encounter with a giant manta or a 2m Napoleon wrasse is unforgettable, and the friendly sharks of the Maldives are legendary.

Combine this with warm water, visibility reliably over 25m and professional dive centres, and you'll know why divers come back again and again.

DIVING SAFARIS

On a diving safari, a dozen or so divers cruise the atolls in a live-aboard boat fitted out for the purpose. You can stop at your pick of the dive sites, visit uninhabited islands and local villages, find secluded anchorages and sleep in a compact cabin. If you've had enough diving, you can fish, snorkel or swim off the boat.

Generally, bigger boats are more comfortable, more fully equipped and more expensive. For keen divers, a safari trip is a great way to get in a lot of dives at a variety of sites, and it will probably work out cheaper than a resort-based dive trip. See p64 for general information about cruises and choosing a safari boat.

Everyone on a diving safari should be a qualified diver. If you need to do a diving course, contact the boat operator in advance (you may need a minimum of two to four people for a course). Dive clubs can often get together enough members to fill a safari boat and design a programme and itinerary that suits their needs. Ideally, everyone on board should be of a similar diving standard.

A diving safari should have a separate dhoni that has the compressor and most of the equipment on board. This means that compressor noise doesn't disturb passengers at night, and the smaller boat can be used for excursions near shallow reefs. All dive safari boats will have tanks and weights, and they'll be included in the cost of dives. Regulators, buoyancy control devices (BCDs), depth gauges, tank pressure gauges and dive computers are available on most boats for an additional charge. It's best to bring your own mask, snorkel, fins and wetsuit. Ask about the availability of specialised equipment such as cameras, lights and nitrox. Check www.visitmaldives.com for reasonably up-to-date details on what each boat provides (click on Where to Stay then Cruise Boats).

For safety, every dive-safari boat should have oxygen equipment, a first-aid kit and good radio and telephone communications with Male'. The divemasters should give thorough predive briefings and emergency plans, have a checklist of every diver and do a roll-call after each dive. It's good to have descent lines and drift lines available for use in strong currents, and to be able to hang a safety tank at 5m for deeper dives. Night diving requires powerful lights, including a strobe light.

WHERE TO DIVE

There are hundreds of recognised and named dive sites, and dozens accessible from nearly every resort. Many of the best dives are described in detail in Lonely Planet's *Diving & Snorkeling Maldives*. In general there are four types of dive sites in the Maldives.

> 'Hard corals on inner-reef slopes were badly damaged by bleaching, but are growing back at various rates.'

Reef Dives

The edges of a reef, where it slopes into deep water, are the most interesting part of a reef to dive. Inner-reef slopes, in the sheltered waters inside an atoll, are generally easier dives and feature numerous smaller reef fish. Hard corals on inner-reef slopes were badly damaged by bleaching, but are growing back at various rates. The reef around a resort island is known as its 'house reef', and only the guests of that resort are allowed to dive or snorkel on it.

At some resorts qualified divers can do unguided dives on the house reef. This is cheaper and more convenient than a boat dive, and gives divers a chance to get really well acquainted with the reef. House reefs can be terrific for night dives too. See p68 for more on the resorts with the best house reefs.

Reef	Atoll	Reef type	Page
Banana Reef	North Male'	reef & kandu	113
Devana Kandu	Vaavu	kandu & thila	156
Embudhoo Express	South Male'	kandu	125

Reef	Atoll	Reef type	Page
Fotteyo	Vaavu	kandu	156
Fushifaru Thila	Lhaviyani	thila kandu	153
Kuda Giri	South Male'	giri & wreck	125
Kuda Kandu	Addu	kandu	165
Kuredhoo Express	Lhaviyani	kandu	152
Maa Kandu	Addu	kandu & reef	165
Macro Spot	Dhaalu	giri	160
Manta Reef	Ari	reef & kandu	134
Milaidhoo Reef	Baa	kandu	150
Orimas Thila	Ari	thila	134
Panetone	Ari	kandu	134
Rakeedhoo Kandu	Vaavu	kandu	157
Rasdhoo Madivaru	Ari	outer-reef slope	133
Two Brothers	Faafu	giri	159
Vaadhoo Caves	South Male'	kandu	125

Outer-reef slopes, where the atoll meets the open sea, often have interesting terraces, overhangs and caves, and are visited by pelagics. Visibility is usually good, but surf and currents can make for a demanding dive.

Kandus

These are channels between islands, reefs or atolls. Obviously, kandus are subject to currents and this provides an environment in which attractive soft corals thrive. Water inside an atoll is a breeding ground for plankton, and where this water flows out through a kandu into the open sea, the rich supply of plankton attracts large animals such as manta rays and whale sharks. During the southwest monsoon (May to November), currents will generally flow out of an atoll through kandus on the eastern side, while in the northeast monsoon (December to March), the outward flow is on the western side.

Thilas & Giris

A thila is a coral formation that rises steeply from the atoll floor and reaches to between 5m and 15m of the water surface – often it's a spectacular underwater mountain that divers fly around like birds. The top of a thila can be rich in reef fish and coral, while the steep sides have crannies, caves and overhangs, which provide shelter for many small fish, and larger fish come, in turn, to feed on the smaller fish.

A giri is a coral formation that rises to just below the water surface. It has many of the same features as a thila, but the top surface may be too shallow to dive.

Thilas and giris are found inside kandus, where the nutrient-rich currents promote soft-coral growth. They also stand in the sheltered waters inside an atoll, where the sea is warmer and slower moving. Hard-coral structures on sheltered thilas and giris suffered most from the 1998 coral bleaching, and have been the slowest to recover.

Wrecks

While many ships have foundered on Maldivian reefs over the centuries, there are few accessible wrecks with any historical interest. Most were on outer-reef slopes and broke up in the surf long ago, leaving remnants to be dispersed and covered in coral. Any wreck sites of historical significance will require special permission to dive. The wrecks you can dive at are mostly inside the atolls and not very old. They are interesting for

The whale shark is an evolutionary oddity, skipping almost the whole food chain to ensure its survival: despite being the biggest fish in the water, it feeds solely on plankton.

the coral and other marine life that colonises the hulk within just a few years. Quite a few of the wrecks have been sunk deliberately, to provide an attraction for divers.

TOP DIVING SITES

Some of the better-known dive sites are described in the chapters covering each atoll and marked on the maps. For examples of the different types of dive sites, look up the following.

Dive	Atoll	Dive type	Page
British Loyalty	Addu	wreck	165
Dhidhdhoo Beyru	Ari	outer reef	135
Embudhoo Express	South Male'	kandu	125
Fish Head	Ari	thila & giri	134
Guraidhoo Kandu	South Male'	kandu	125
Halaveli Wreck	Ari	wreck	134
Helengeli Thila	North Male'	thila & giri	113
HP Reef	North Male'	thila & giri	113
Kakani Thila	Baa	thila	150
Maa Kandu & Kuda Kandu	Addu	kandu	165
Maaya Thila	Ari	thila & giri	134
Bodu Hithi Thila	North Male'	thila	113
Shark Point	Addu	outer reef	165

'Diving is not difficult, but it requires knowledge and care, and a lot of experience before you can safely dive independently.'

DIVING SEASONS

January to April are generally considered the best months for diving, and should have fine weather and good visibility. May and June can have unstable weather – storms and cloudy days are common until September. October and November tend to have calmer, clearer weather, but visibility can be slightly reduced because of abundant plankton in the water. Some divers like this period because many large fish, such as whale sharks and mantas, come into the channels to feed on the plankton. December can have rough, windy weather and rain.

LEARNING TO DIVE

Diving is not difficult, but it requires knowledge and care, and a lot of experience before you can safely dive independently. It doesn't require great strength or fitness although if you can do things with minimum expenditure of energy, your tank of air will last longer. An experienced diver will use much less air than a beginner. Women often have an advantage because they don't breathe as much air as men.

There's a range of courses, from an introductory dive in a pool or lagoon, to an open-water course that gives an internationally recognised qualification (usually PADI). Beyond that, there are advanced and speciality courses, and courses that lead to divemaster and instructor qualifications. Courses in the Maldives are not a bargain, but they're no more expensive than learning at home and this way you are assured of high standards, good equipment and extremely pleasant conditions. On the other hand, if you do a course at home you'll have more time for diving when you get to the Maldives.

We recommend all learner divers do an open-water referral course in their home country (ie all the theory and basics in the pool), allowing you to complete the course in the Maldives in just two days rather than

(Continued on page 81)

WATERWORLD MALDIVES

To ignore the brilliant turquoise waters of the Maldives would be to ignore 99% of the country, so make sure you get in and get wet! The diving and snorkelling here is second to none and you'll see everything from schools of bannerfish to turtles and sharks if you're lucky. Out of the deep blue, the powder white beaches that ring every island in the country are some of the best on earth.

1

2

Diving & Snorkelling

The sheer range of diving sites in the Maldives means that even as tourism develops, you're still more than likely to be diving entirely alone. Nearly every resort has a house reef to snorkel on, or failing that, runs daily boat trips to a nearby reef with plenty of fish and coral life to be seen. Here are some of our favourite sites in the Maldives.

3

① Maaya Thila, Ari Atoll

One of the best dives in the country is this thila (a coral formation that rises from the atoll floor almost to the water surface). It's a favourite feeding ground for white-tip reef sharks that can very often be seen here.

② Shipyard, Lhaviyani Atoll

Unique for having two wrecks in easy swimming distance from each other, this site is great for seeing hard corals, nurse sharks and moray eels (who live inside the wrecked boats themselves).

③ Embudhoo Express, South Male' Atoll

This long drift dive in Embudhoo Kandu is very impressive as it teams with life. Huge Napoleon wrasse, sharks and big schools of fish congregate here. The reef top is good for snorkelling as well.

④ Kuda Kandu, Addu Atoll

This spectacular dive site is one of the best places in the country to see bright coral formations – the polyps remained unaffected by the El Niño bleaching in the late '90s and as such are stunning. One day hopefully all coral in the Maldives will look like this again!

⑤ Rasdhoo Madivaru, Rasdhoo Atoll

Also known as Hammerhead Point, this great dive is perennially popular for the large number of pelagics that frequent it. As well as the hammerhead population, it's common to see mantas here too. It's also a great snorkelling site in calm seas.

⑥ Fesdhoo island's house reef, Ari Atoll

Is this the best house reef in the country? We haven't been able to snorkel them all of course, but this one is awesome (Fesdhoo island is home to ultra-stylish W Retreat & Spa). Here we saw manta rays, sharks and several turtles all in the space of 20 minutes.

Beaches

We're often asked where the best beach in the Maldives is and we're always absolutely stumped on how to answer. The simple truth is that in their simplicity nearly all Maldivian beaches are utter stunners: soft white sand lapped by clear blue water and fringed by tall palms – what more do you need? For the record, though, here are some of our absolute favourites.

'... one of the widest and longest beaches in the country, facing onto a dazzling blue lagoon.'

❶ Coco Palm Dhuni Kolhu, Baa Atoll
This long time honeymooner favourite has another classic, long, wide beach backed by the thick foliage of this charming island.

❷ Kanuhura, Lhaviyani Atoll
This mesmerising place has one of the widest and longest beaches in the country, facing onto a dazzling blue lagoon. If you really want solitude, you can take the boat to the next-door desert island of Jehunuhura and enjoy its breathtaking beach too.

❸ Palm Beach Resort, Lhaviyani Atoll
It doesn't really get much better than this. Unusually for an island of this size, there's an almost perfect beach the entire way around Palm Beach Resort, as well as a seasonal sandbar and gorgeous overhanging palms.

❹ Meeru Island Resort, North Male' Atoll
The long beach on Meeru's lagoon side is its best, where its sheer size means you'll never feel crowded despite the large size of the resort. There are plenty of other beaches to discover elsewhere on the island too.

❺ Cocoa Island, South Male' Atoll
The blazing strip of sand and the long sandbank at the end of Cocoa Island are just two of this island's most delightful features. Best of all, it's so uncrowded here that you're likely to have them both to yourself.

❻ Paradise Island, North Male' Atoll
This mass-market resort certainly lives up to its name – the beach on the lagoon side is a faultless strip of gleaming sand lapped by an almost luminous turquoise lagoon.

❼ One & Only Reethi Rah, North Male' Atoll
Unique in the Maldives due to being mostly manmade, the dazzling white sands are arranged into perfect white crescent shapes. You can holiday here for a week and spend each day on a different beach.

❽ Angsana Ihuru, North Male' Atoll
Ihuru island has long been famous in the Maldives as one of the picture-perfect islands so loved by photographers. Perfectly circular, with a gorgeous white sand beach the entire way around it, this is unsurprisingly core honeymooner territory.

Fish-spotters' guide

1. Clown Triggerfish
2. Napoleonfish
3. Moray Eel
4. Stingray
5. Bignose Unicornfish
6. Oriental Sweetlips
7. Emperor Angelfish
8. Powder-blue Surgeonfish
9. Black-footed Anemonefish
10. Blue-striped Snapper
11. Blue-faced Angelfish
12. Lionfish
13. Moorish Idol
14. Batfish

Marine Life

So you've seen lots of brightly coloured schools of fish drifting by on the reef? Good, now get ready for the real highlight – the big marine life you'll see down here too. You'll usually have a much better chance at seeing these creatures on a dive, but you can see many of them while snorkelling on a good reef if you're lucky!

❶ Whale sharks
The largest fish in the ocean (12m long whale sharks are quite normal) is this gentle giant that cruises the atolls filtering plankton. It's the holy grail of Maldivian diving – you'll be lucky to see one, but it's certainly not unheard of.

❷ Rays
These bizarre-looking creatures suddenly become terribly beautiful when you see them 'taking flight' under water, like sub-aquatic birds of prey. The most highly prized is of course the majestic manta ray, the largest of the species, which can easily have a three-metre wingspan.

❸ Turtles
These much-loved creatures are very common in Maldivian waters. There are four types here: loggerhead, green, hawksbill and olive ridley, and can be found in the shallows and anywhere around the reef. They're usually very placid and will allow humans to get quite close.

❹ Sharks
The Maldivians joke that even their sharks are friendly, and they're right – the Maldive waters are home to grey, white and black tip reef sharks, tiger sharks, blue sharks and the hammerhead, to name but a few. Seeing and swimming with one is unforgettable.

(Continued from page 72)

the four or five needed for the full course. After all, you didn't fly half way around the world to sit in a room watching a PADI CD-ROM, did you? If you do this, ensure you have all your certification from the referral course with you, otherwise you'll have to start from scratch.

If you're at all serious about diving, you should do an open-water course. This requires nine dives, usually five in sheltered water and four in open water, as well as classroom training and completion of a multiple choice test. The cost in the Maldives is from US$400 to US$750. Sometimes the price is all-inclusive, but there are often a few extra charges. You can do the course in as little as five days, or take your time and spread it over a week or two. Don't try it on a one-week package – transfers and jet lag will take a day or so, and you shouldn't dive less than 24 hours before a flight. Besides, you'll want to do some recreational dives to try out your new skills.

The next stage is an advanced open-water course, which will involve five dives (including one night dive), and will cost from US$280 to US$400, depending on the dive school. Then there are the speciality courses in night diving, rescue diving, wreck diving, nitrox diving and so on.

Dive Schools & Operators

Every resort has a professional diving operation and can run courses for beginners, as well as dive trips and courses that will challenge even the most experienced diver. The government requires that all dive operations maintain high standards, and all of them are affiliated with one or more of the international diving accreditation organisations – most are with diving behemoth PADI.

Certificates

When you complete an open-water course, you receive a certificate that is recognised by diving operators all over the world. Certificates in the Maldives are generally issued by the Professional Association of Diving Instructors (PADI), the largest and the best-known organisation, but certificates from Confédération Mondiale des Activités Subaquatiques (CMAS; World Underwater Federation), Scuba Schools International (SSI) and a number of other organisations are quite acceptable.

EQUIPMENT

Dive schools in the Maldives can rent out all diving gear, but most divers prefer to have at least some of their own equipment. It's best to have your own mask, snorkel and fins, which you can also use for snorkelling. The tank and weight belt are always included in the cost of a dive, so you don't need to bring them – sealed tanks are prohibited on aircraft anyway, and you'd be crazy to carry lead weights. The main pieces of diving equipment to bring with you are described in the following sections.

Wetsuit

The water may be warm (27°C to 30°C) but a wetsuit is often preferable for comfortable diving. A 3mm suit should be adequate, but 5mm is preferable if you want to go deep or dive more than once per day. Some resorts don't have a good selection of wetsuits for rental, so this is a good item to bring if you can. When dive centres say 'full equipment rental', that doesn't usually include a wetsuit. Renting a suit will cost about US$5 per day. It's possible to dive in a T-shirt if you don't feel the cold too much.

The sea snake is an air-breathing reptile with venom 20 times stronger than any snake on land. Basically, don't touch them if you're lucky enough to see any!

Regulator
Many divers have their own regulator, with which they are familiar and therefore confident about using, and a 'reg' is not cumbersome to carry. Rental will cost from US$3 to US$7 per dive.

Buoyancy Control Device
BCDs are readily available for hire, costing US$3 to US$10 per dive, but bring your own if possible.

Depth Gauge, Tank Pressure Gauge & Timer
These are usually available too, but if you have them, bring them.

Dive Computer
Universally used over dive tables, these are now compulsory in the Maldives. They're available for rent, for US$5 to US$10 per dive.

Logbook
You'll need this to indicate to divemasters your level of experience, and to record your latest dives. You can usually buy them for around US$10 at dive schools.

Other items you might need are an underwater torch (especially for cave and night dives), waterproof camera, compass, and safety buoy or balloon, most of which are available for rental. Some things you won't need are a spear gun, which is prohibited, and diving gloves, which are discouraged since you're not supposed to touch anything anyway.

DIVING COSTS
The cost of diving varies between resorts, and depends on whether you need to rent equipment. A single dive, with only tank and weights supplied, runs from US$40 to US$100, but is generally around US$45 or US$50 (night dives cost more). If you need to rent a regulator and a BCD as well, a dive will cost from US$50 to US$110. Sometimes the full equipment price includes mask, snorkel, fins, dive computer and pressure gauge, but they can cost extra. A package of 10 dives will cost roughly from US$275 to US$500, or US$350 to US$600 with equipment rental. Other possibilities are five-, 12- and 15-dive packages, and packages that allow you as many dives as you want within a certain number of consecutive days. In addition to the dive cost, there is a charge for using a boat – about US$12 for half a day, US$20 for a full day. There may also be a service charge of 10% if diving is billed to your room.

If you plan to do 10 dives in a week, budget around US$700, perhaps US$100 or US$150 less if you bring all your own equipment.

DIVING HEALTH & SAFETY
Health Requirements
Officially, a doctor should check you over before you do a course, and fill out a form full of diving health questions (see p183). In practice, most dive schools will let you dive or do a course if you're under 50 years old and complete a medical questionnaire, but the check-up is still a good idea. This is especially so if you have any problem at all with your breathing, ears or sinuses. If you are an asthmatic, have any other chronic breathing difficulties or any inner-ear problems you shouldn't do any scuba diving.

Young male anemone-fish living within the anemone are under the control of a single dominant female. When she dies the largest male fish changes sex and replaces her as the dominant female.

Diving Safely

In the Maldives the dive base will ensure you are aware of the following points to ensure a safe and enjoyable experience, whether scuba diving, skin diving or snorkelling:

- If you are scuba diving, you must possess a current diving certification card from a recognised scuba diving instructional agency. The resort dive base will check your card and provide training if you need it. A check dive is nearly always required.
- Be sure you are healthy and feel comfortable diving.
- Obtain reliable information about physical and environmental conditions at the dive site. The dive base will always provide this.
- Be aware of local laws, regulations and etiquette about marine life and the environment.
- Dive only at sites within your experience level.

Note that underwater conditions vary significantly from one site to another. Seasonal changes can significantly alter any site and dive conditions. These differences influence the way divers dress for a dive and what diving techniques they use.

The following laws apply to recreational diving in the Maldives, and divemasters should enforce them:

- Maximum depth is 30m – this is the law in the Maldives.
- Maximum time is 60 minutes.
- No decompression dives.
- Each diver must carry a dive computer.
- Obligatory three-minute safety stop at 5m.
- Last dive no later than 12 hours before a flight.

Decompression Sickness

This is a very serious condition – usually, though not always, associated with diver error. The most common symptoms are unusual fatigue or weakness; skin itch; pain in the arms, legs (joints or mid-limb) or torso; dizziness and vertigo; local numbness, tingling or paralysis; and shortness of breath. Signs may also include a blotchy skin rash, a tendency to favour an arm or a leg, staggering, coughing spasms, collapse or unconsciousness. These symptoms and signs can occur individually, or a number of them can appear at one time.

The most common causes of decompression sickness (or 'the bends' as it is commonly known) are diving too deep, staying at depth for too long, or ascending too quickly. This results in nitrogen coming out of solution in the blood and forming bubbles, most commonly in the bones and particularly in the joints or in weak spots such as healed fracture sites.

Other factors contributing to decompression sickness include excess body fat; heavy exertion prior to, during and after diving; injuries and illness; dehydration; alcohol; diving in cold water; hot showers or baths after diving; carbon dioxide increase (eg through smoking); and age.

Avoid flying after diving, as it causes nitrogen to come out of the blood even faster than it would at sea level. No resort in the Maldives will allow you to dive less than 24 hours before a flight. Low-altitude flights, like a seaplane transfer to the airport, may be just as dangerous because the aircraft are not pressurised. There are various opinions about the risks and the time required to minimise them – a lot depends on the frequency, depth and duration of dives over several days before the flight. Seek the advice of an instructor when planning the dives during the final few days of your stay, and try to finish up with shallow dives.

Anemonefish are so called as they cover themselves in a special mucous from the anemone, which protects them from its sting.

The only treatment for decompression sickness is to put the patient into a recompression chamber. That puts a person back under pressure similar to that of the depth at which they were diving so nitrogen bubbles can be reabsorbed. The time required in the chamber is usually three to eight hours. The treatment is usually effective, with the main problem being caused by delay in getting the patient to the chamber. If you think that you or anyone else you are diving with is suffering from the bends, get to a recompression chamber as soon as possible; there are two in the Maldives, at Bandos and the Kuramathi resorts.

Ear Problems

Many divers experience pain in the ears after diving, which is commonly caused by failure of the ears to compensate properly for changes in pressure. The problem will usually fix itself, but injuries are often caused when people try to treat themselves by poking cotton buds or other objects into the ear.

Emergencies

The **Divers Alert Network** (DAN; in USA ☎ 919-684-4326; www.diversalertnetwork.org) operates a 24-hour diving emergency hotline in the USA. **DAN Maldives** (p118; ☎ 6640088) is based at Bandos Island Resort, on North Male' Atoll, where there's a recompression chamber and a complete divers health service. There's also a recompression facility and fully staffed diving clinic at **Kuramathi** (p133; ☎ 6660527), in Rasdhoo Atoll at the far north of Ari Atoll. They are both commercial facilities.

Insurance

All divers must purchase compulsory Maldivian diving insurance before their first dive in the Maldives. This will automatically be done at the dive school where you do your first dive, and is not expensive. This remains valid for 30 days, no matter where in the country you dive.

In addition to normal travel insurance, it's a very good idea to take out specific diving cover, which will pay for evacuation to a recompression facility and the cost of hyperbaric treatment in a chamber. Evacuation would normally be by chartered speedboat or seaplane (both very expensive). **DAN** can be contacted through most dive shops and clubs, and it offers a DAN TravelAssist policy that provides evacuation and recompression coverage.

> Male sharks show their interest in females by biting them on the sides, often causing wounds, even though the female shark skin has evolved to be thicker than the male equivalent!

MARINE ENVIRONMENT PROTECTION

The waters of the Maldives may seem pristine but, like everywhere, development and commercial activities can have adverse effects on the marine environment. The Maldivian government recognises that the underwater world is a major attraction, and has imposed many restrictions and controls on fishing, coral mining and tourism operations. Twenty-five Protected Marine Areas have been established, and these are subject to special controls.

Visitors must do their best to ensure that their activities don't spoil the experience of those who will come in the future. The following rules are generally accepted as necessary for conservation, and most of them apply equally to snorkellers and divers.

- Do not use anchors on the reef, and take care not to ground boats on coral. Encourage dive operators and regulatory bodies to establish permanent moorings at popular dive sites.

- Avoid touching living marine organisms with your body or dragging equipment across the reef. Polyps can be damaged by even the gentlest contact.
- Never stand on corals, even if they look solid and robust. If you must hold on, to prevent being swept away in a current, hold on to dead coral.
- Be conscious of your fins. Even without contact the surge from heavy fin strokes near the reef can damage delicate organisms. When treading water in shallow reef areas, take care not to kick up clouds of sand. Settling sand can easily smother the delicate organisms of the reef.
- Collecting lobster or shellfish is prohibited, as is spearfishing. Removing any coral or shells, living or dead, is against the law. All shipwreck sites are protected by law.
- Take home all your rubbish and any litter you may find as well. Plastics in particular are a serious threat to marine life. Turtles can mistake plastic for jellyfish and eat it. Don't throw cigarette butts overboard.
- Resist the temptation to feed fish. You may disturb their normal eating habits, encourage aggressive behaviour or feed them food that is detrimental to their health.
- Practise and maintain proper buoyancy control. Major damage can be done by divers descending too fast and colliding with the reef.
- Take great care in underwater caves. Spend as little time within them as possible as your air bubbles may be caught within the roof and thereby leave previously submerged organisms high and dry. Taking turns to inspect the interior of a small cave will lessen the chances of damaging contact.

Male and female shark populations live in same-sex groups and rarely meet, save for mating.

BACK FROM THE BLEACHING

It's true that coral bleaching killed nearly all of the hard coral in the Maldives, but that's not the end of the story. In a few places old coral has unaccountably survived, and you can occasionally be surprised by a big-table coral or a long-branching staghorn. Soft corals and sea fans were less affected by coral bleaching and have regrown more quickly. Magnificent soft-coral gardens thrive at many dive sites, especially around channels that are rich with water-borne nutrients, and a few fine specimens can be seen at snorkelling depths on many house reefs.

The underlying hard-coral structure is still there of course – new coral grows on the skeletons of its predecessors. The healthiest living coral has many metres, perhaps kilometres, of dead coral underneath. New coral is growing on reefs all over the Maldives, though the large and elaborately shaped formations will take many years to build. It's fascinating to observe the new coral growth – the distinctly coloured patches with the finely textured surface of a living, growing organism. The first regrowth often occurs in crevices on old coral blocks, where it's protected from munching parrotfish. The massive Porites-type corals seem to come first, but they grow slowly – look for blobs of yellow, blue or purple that will eventually cover the whole block in a crust or a cushion or a brainlike dome. The branching corals (Acropora) appear as little purplish trees on a coral block, like a pale piece of broccoli. Growing a few centimetres per year (15cm in ideal conditions), they will eventually become big, extended staghorn corals or wide, flat-topped tables.

The recovery for coral is not uniform. Some parts of a reef can be doing very well, with 80% or 90% of the old surfaces covered with new and growing coral, while 100m along the same reef, new coral growth cover is less than 20%. Reef formation is a very complex natural process, but surprisingly the marine ecosystem as a whole seems to be undamaged by the coral bleaching. Fish life is as abundant and diverse as ever.

FISH-SPOTTER'S GUIDE

You don't have to be a hardcore diver to enjoy the rich marine life of the Maldives. You'll see an amazing variety just snorkelling, walking in the shallows, or peering off the end of a jetty. This guide will help you identify a few of the most colourful and conspicuous varieties; see the colour pictures on pp78–79. A point to remember is that even within the same species, colour and patterning can vary greatly over a fish's life cycle, as well as according to gender.

For a comprehensive online guide to the fish of the Maldives, visit www.popweb.com/maldive. For more information, try *Photo Guide to Fishes of the Maldives* by Rudie H Kuiter (Atoll Editions), the classic guide to the fish of the Maldives.

'Remember that even within the same species, colour and patterning can vary greatly over a fish's life cycle, as well as according to gender.'

Anemonefish

Maldives anemoncfish (also known as black-footed anemonefish; p78) are indigenous to the Maldives. They are around 11cm long, orange, dusky orange or yellow, with differences in face colour and the shape and thickness of the head bar marking. Their mucous coating protects them from the venomous tips of sea anemone tentacles, allowing them to hide from predators among the anemones' tentacles. In return for this protection, they warn the anemones of the approach of fish such as butterflyfish, which feed on the tentacle tips. Juveniles are lighter in colour than adults, and have greyish or blackish pelvic fins.

Angelfish

Of the many species, there are 14 in the Maldives, mostly found in shallow water, though some inhabit reef slopes down to 20m. They can be seen individually or in small groups. Small species are around 10cm, the largest around 35cm. They feed on sponges and algae. Regal (or empress) angelfish have bright yellow bodies with vertical dark blue and white stripes. The emperor, or imperial, angelfish (p78) are larger (to 35cm) and live in deeper water, with almost horizontal blue-and-yellow lines and a dark blue mask and gill markings; juveniles are quite different in shape and markings. The shy blue-faced angelfish (p79) also change colour dramatically as they age.

Butterflyfish

There are over 30 species in the Maldives; they are common in shallow waters and reef slopes, singly, in pairs or small schools. Species vary in size from 12cm to 30cm, when mature, with a flattened body shape and elaborate markings. Various species of this carnivorous fish have specialised food sources, including anemones, coral polyps, algae and assorted invertebrate prey. Bennett's butterflyfish, bright yellow and 18cm long, is one of several species with a 'false eye' near the tail to make predators think it's a larger fish facing the other way. Spotted butterflyfish, which grow to 10cm long, are camouflaged with dark polka dots and a dark band across its real eye.

Flutemouth

One species of flutemouth (or cornetfish) is very common in shallow waters in the Maldives, often occurring in small schools. They are very slender, elongated fish, usually around 60cm in length, but deep-sea specimens grow up to 1.5m. Flutemouths eat small fish, often stalking prey by swimming behind a harmless herbivore. The silver colouring seems almost transparent in the water, and it can be hard to spot flutemouths even in shallow sandy lagoons.

Moorish Idol

One species of moorish idol (p79) is commonly seen on reef flats and reef slopes in the Maldives, often in pairs. Usually 15cm to 20cm long, the moorish idol is herbivorous, feeding primarily on algae. They are attractive, with broad vertical yellow-and-black bands, pointed snouts, and long, streamer-like extensions to the upper dorsal fin.

Parrotfish

More than 20 of the many parrotfish species are found in the Maldives they include some of the most conspicuous and commonly seen reef fish. The largest species grow to more than a metre, but those around 50cm long are more typical. Most parrotfish feed on algae and other organisms growing on and around a hard-coral structure. With strong, beaklike mouths they scrape and bite the coral surface, then grind up the coral chunks, swallowing and filtering to extract nutrients. Snorkellers often hear the scraping, grinding sound of parrotfish eating coral, and notice the clouds of coral-sand faeces that parrotfish regularly discharge. Colour, pattern and even sex can change as parrotfish mature – juveniles and females are often drab, while mature males can have brilliant blue-green designs. Bicolour parrotfish start life white with a broad orange stripe, but the mature males (up to 90cm) are a beautiful blue with hot-pink highlights on the scale edges, head, fins and tail. Green-face parrotfish grow to 60cm, with the adult male identified by its blue-green body, bright green 'face' and white marks on fins and tail. Heavybeak (or steephead) parrotfish can be 70cm long, and have a distinctive rounded head.

Reef shark

Several smaller shark species frequent reef flats and reef edges inside Maldivian atolls, often in schools, while larger pelagic species congregate around channels in the atoll rim at certain times of the year. Most reef species are small, typically 1m to 2m. Reef sharks hunt small fish (attacks on swimmers and divers are totally unknown). White-tips grow from 1m to 2m long and have white tips on dorsal fins. They are often seen in schools of 10 or more in the sandy shallows of a lagoon. Black-tips, distinguished by black tips on dorsal fins and tail, grow to 2m. Grey reef sharks are thicker in the midsection and have a white trailing edge on the dorsal fin.

Guided seaplane surfaris around the Maldives are offered year round by Tropicsurf (www.tropic surf.net) in Australia. Spot the best surf from the sky, land and you're surfing in minutes.

Rock Cod

Hundreds of species are currently classified as Serranidae, including rock cod and groper, which are common around reefs. Smaller species reach 20cm; many larger species grow to 50cm and some to over a metre. Rock cod are carnivorous, feeding on smaller fish and invertebrates. Vermillion rock cod (or coral groper) are often seen in shallow waters and near the coral formations in which they hide; they are a brilliant crimson colour covered with blue spots, up to 40cm long.

Snapper

There are 28 species of snapper that have been documented in the Maldives, mostly in deep water. Small species are around 20cm and the largest grow to 1m (snapper, themselves carnivorous, are popular with anglers as a fighting fish, and are excellent to eat). Blue-striped snapper (p79), commonly seen in schools near inshore reefs, are an attractive yellow with blue-white horizontal stripes. Red snapper (or red bass) are often seen in lagoons.

Stingray

Several species of stingray (p78), such as the black-spotted stingray, are often seen in very shallow water on the sandy bed of a lagoon, where they are often well camouflaged. Most rays seen inshore are juveniles, up to about 50cm across; mature rays can be over a metre across, and maybe 2m long including the whiplike tail. A barbed and venomous spine on top of the tail can swing up and forward, and will deliver a painful injury to anyone who stands on it.

Sea urchins are rare in the sandy shallows of the lagoons, but numerous deeper on the reefs – wearing fins or other protective footwear is always a good idea to avoid their nasty needles.

Surgeonfish

The surgeonfish are so named for the tiny scalpel-sharp blades that are found on the sides of their bodies, near their tails. When they are threatened they will swim beside the intruder swinging their tails to inflict cuts, and can cause nasty injuries. Over 20 species of surgeon, including the powder-blue surgeonfish (p78), are found in the Maldives, often in large schools. The adults range from 20cm to 60cm. All species graze for algae on the sea bottom or on coral surfaces.

Sweetlips

Only a few of the many species are found in the Maldives, where they inhabit outer-reef slopes. Some species grow up to 1m, but most are between 50cm and 75cm; juveniles are largely herbivorous, feeding on algae, plankton and other small organisms; older fish hunt and eat smaller fish. Oriental sweetlips (p78), which grow to 50cm, are superb-looking with horizontal dark and light stripes, dark spots on fins and tail, and large, lugubrious lips. Brown sweetlips are generally bigger, duller and more active at night.

Triggerfish

There are over a dozen species in the Maldives, on outer-reef slopes and also in shallower reef environments. Small species grow to around 25cm and the largest species to over 75cm. Triggerfish are carnivorous. Orange-striped triggerfish (30cm) are common in shallow reef waters. Titan triggerfish have yellow and dark-brown crisscross patterning, grow up to 75cm and can be aggressive, especially when defending eggs, and will charge at divers. The clown triggerfish (up to 40cm; p78) is easily recognised by its conspicuous colour pattern with large, round, white blotches on the lower half of the body.

Hammerhead sharks are some of the most spectacular underwater creatures in the Maldives. Your best chance of seeing them is early in the morning in Northern Ari and Rasdhoo Atolls.

Unicornfish

From the same family as the surgeonfish, unicornfish grow from 40cm to 75cm long (only males of some species have the horn for which the species is named), and are herbivores. Spotted unicornfish are very common blue-grey or olive-brown fish with narrow dotted vertical markings (males can change their colours for display, and exhibit a broad white vertical band); their prominent horns get longer with age. Bignose unicornfish (or Vlaming's unicorn; p78) have only a nose bump for a horn.

Wrasse

Some 60 species of this large and very diverse family can be found, some on reefs, others on sandy lagoon floors, others in open water. The smallest wrasse species are only 10cm; the largest over 2m. Most wrasse are carnivores; larger wrasse will hunt and eat small fish. Napoleonfish (also called Napoleon wrasse and humphead wrasse; p78) are the largest wrasse species, often seen around wrecks and outer-reef slopes; they are generally green with fine vertical patterning. Large males have a humped head.

Moon wrasse, about 25cm, live in shallow waters and reef slopes, where adult males are beautifully coloured in green with pink patterning and a yellow marking on the tail. Cleaner wrasse have a symbiotic relationship with larger fish, which allows the wrasse to eat the small parasites and food scraps from their mouths, gills and skin surface. At certain times, large numbers of pelagic species congregate at 'cleaning stations' where cleaner wrasse abound – a great sight for divers.

SURFING

Surfing has been slow to take off in the Maldives, but its popularity is on the increase. There's some great surf throughout the country although only a few breaks are easily accessible from resorts, and they are only surfable from March to November. Surfers have a choice of basing themselves at a resort and taking a boat to nearby breaks, or arranging a live-aboard safari cruise. In either case, make arrangements in advance with a reputable surf travel operator who knows the area well. The Maldives is definitely not the sort of place where a surfer can just turn up and head for the waves.

The period of the southwest monsoon (May to November) generates the best waves, but March and April are also good and have the best weather. June can have bad weather and storms, and is not great for boat trips, but it is also a time for big swells. The best breaks occur on the outer reefs on the southeast sides of the atolls, but only where a gap in the reef allows the waves to wrap around.

Surfing in the Maldives was pioneered by Tony Hussein (also known as Tony Hinde), a Sydney surfer who was shipwrecked in the Maldives in the early 1970s. Before the first tourist resorts were opened, he discovered, surfed and named all the main breaks, and had them all to himself for many years.

'May to November generate the best waves, but March and April are also good and have the best weather.'

NORTH MALE' ATOLL

This is where the best-known breaks are, and they can get a bit crowded, especially if there are several safari boats in the vicinity. The following breaks are listed from north to south.

Chickens A left-hander that sections when small, but on a bigger swell and a higher tide it all comes together to make a long and satisfying wave. It's named for the old poultry farm onshore, not because of any reaction to the conditions here.

Cola's A heavy, hollow, shallow right-hander; when it's big, it's one of the best breaks in the area. This is a very thick wave breaking hard over a shallow reef, so it's definitely for experienced, gutsy surfers only. Named for the Coca-Cola factory nearby on the island of Thulusdhoo, it's also called Cokes.

Honky's During its season, this is the best wave in the Maldives. It's a super long, wally left-hander that wraps nearly 90 degrees and can nearly double in size by the end section.

Jailbreaks A right-hander that works best with a big swell, when the three sections combine to make a single, long, perfect wave. There used to be a prison on the island and the surrounding waters were off-limits, but now it's open to surfers.

Lohi's A solid left-hander that usually breaks in two sections, but with a big enough swell and a high enough tide the sections link up. You can paddle out there from the resort island of Lohifushi, and guests of that resort have exclusive access to the break.

Pasta Point A perfect left that works like clockwork on all tides. There's a long outside wall at the take-off point, jacking into a bowling section called the 'macaroni bowl'. On big days the

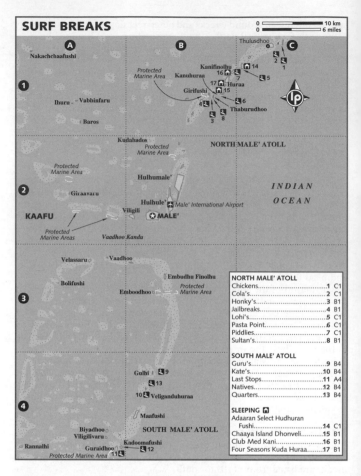

SURF BREAKS

NORTH MALE' ATOLL		
Chickens	.1	C1
Cola's	.2	C1
Honky's	.3	B1
Jailbreaks	.4	B1
Lohi's	.5	C1
Pasta Point	.6	C1
Piddlies	.7	C1
Sultan's	.8	B1

SOUTH MALE' ATOLL		
Guru's	.9	B4
Kate's	.10	B4
Last Stops	.11	A4
Natives	.12	B4
Quarters	.13	B4

SLEEPING 🏠		
Adaaran Select Hudhuran Fushi	.14	C1
Chaaya Island Dhonveli	.15	B1
Club Med Kani	.16	B1
Four Seasons Kuda Huraa	.17	B1

break continues to another section called 'lock jaws', which grinds into very shallow water over the reef. It's easily reached from the shore at the Chaaya Island Dhonveli resort, whose guests have exclusive use of this break.

Piddlies A slow, mellow, mushy right-hander, a good Malibu wave. It's also called Ninja's because of its appeal to Japanese surfers. It's off the island of Kanifinolhu, home of the Club Med Kani resort, but it's very difficult to reach from the shore, and the wave is available to any boat-based surfer, not just Club Med guests.

Sultan's This is a classic right-hand break, and the bigger the swell, the better it works. A steep outside peak leads to a super-fast wall and then an inside section that throws right out, and tubes on every wave.

SOUTH MALE' ATOLL

The breaks in South Male' Atoll are smaller than those in North Male' Atoll and generally more fickle. It will be harder here to find a boatman who really knows the surf scene.

Guru's A nice little left off the island of Gulhi; it can get good sometimes.

Kate's A small left-hander, rarely more than a metre.

Last Stops This is a bowly right-hander breaking over a channel reef. It's a Protected Marine Area, and can get very strong currents when the tides are running.
Natives A small right-hander, rarely more than a metre.
Quarters Another small right-hander, rarely more than a metre.

OUTER ATOLLS

Only a few areas have the right combination of reef topography and orientation to swell and wind direction. Laamu and Addu both have surfable waves on occasions, but they're not reliable enough to be worth a special trip.

Gaaf Dhaal has a series of reliable breaks that are accessed by safari boats in the season. From west to east, the named breaks are Beacons, Castaways, Blue Bowls, Five Islands, Two Ways (also called Twin Peaks; left and right), Love Charms, Antiques and Tiger. They can currently only be visited with permits from Atolls Administration.

RESORT-BASED SURFING

The most accessible surf breaks are in the southeastern part of North Male' Atoll. Half a dozen resorts are within a short boat ride, but only a couple of them cater for surfers by providing regular boat service to the waves.

Chaaya Island Dhonveli (p117) is the resort that's best set up for surfers – the reliable waves of the 'house break', Pasta Point, are just out the back door, while Sultan's and Honky's are close by. A surfside bar provides a great view of the action. Surfing packages at Chaaya Island Dhonveli include unlimited boat trips to the other local breaks with surf guides who know the conditions well, leaving and returning on demand.

Adaaran Select Hudhuran Fushi (p119), a few kilometres northeast of Dhonveli, is a bigger, more expensive resort with more facilities and it also has its own, exclusive surf break at the southern tip of the island. A bar and a viewing terrace overlook the wave, which has hosted international surfing competitions.

Club Med Kani (p119) is the other resort island with an adjacent surf break, but you need a boat to reach it from the resort. There's no surfing programme, no surf guides and no boats available for surfers. The nearby Four Seasons Kuda Huraa can also arrange boat trips to the surf for guests.

SURFING SAFARIS

Most of the safari boats in the Maldives claim to do surfing trips, but very few of them have a specialised knowledge of surfing or any experience cruising to the outer atolls. Ideally, a surfing safari boat should have an experienced surf guide and a second, smaller boat to accompany it, for accessing breaks in shallower water and getting in close to the waves. A surfing safari ('surfari') boat should also be equipped with fishing and snorkelling gear, for when the surf isn't working or you need a rest.

An inner-atolls surfari will just cruise around North Male' Atoll, visiting breaks that are also accessible from resorts in the area. If the swell is big and the surf guide is knowledgeable, the boat may venture down to South Male' Atoll to take advantage of the conditions. A one-week inner-atoll surf trip will start at around US$900 per person. This might be cheaper than resort-based surfing, but it won't be as comfortable, and it won't give access to a handy and uncrowded house break.

An outer-atolls surfari is the only feasible way to surf the remote waves of Gaaf Dhaal – an experienced outer-atoll guide is essential. Ideally, the

'Ideally, a surfing safari boat should have an experienced surf guide and a second, smaller boat to accompany it.'

safari boat should be based in Gaaf Dhaal, and the surfers take a Maldivian flight to the domestic airport on the island of Kaadedhoo where the boat crew meets them. They should also have a good relationship with Atolls Administration, so that they can get the necessary permits before you arrive.

You need at least six people to make a safari boat affordable; the surfing specialists should be able to put together the necessary numbers. Don't book into a safari trip that is primarily for diving or cruising. Allow at least two weeks for the trip or you'll spend too much of your time getting to the waves and back. A 10-night surfari will cost from about US$2000 per person, including domestic airfares.

Did You Know? The hump on the head of a napoleon wrasse becomes larger and more pronounced as the fish ages.

SURF TRAVEL OPERATORS

The following agents specialise in surf travel and book tours and safaris to the Maldives.

Atoll Travel (☎ 03-5682 1088; www.atolltravel.com; PO Box 205, 4 Bridge St, Foster, Vic 3960, Australia) Australian and international agent for Atoll Adventures. It offers surfing packages to the Chaaya Island Dhonveli resort, premium surfing safari tours in Male' Atoll and to the outer atolls.

Maldives Scuba Tours (☎ 01284-748010; www.scubascuba.com; Innovation House, Boldero Rd, Bury St Edmonds, Suffolk, IP32 7BS, UK) Maldives dive travel agency and UK agent for Atoll Adventures. Also offers Chaaya Island Dhonveli packages.

Surf Travel Company (☎ 02-9222 8870; www.surftravel.com.au; Level 11, Chifly Sq, Sydney, NSW 2000, Australia) Venerable surf travel operator; it books surfers into Hudhuran Fushi, Four Seasons Kuda Huraa and Paradise Isand. It also does boat-based tours throughout the country.

Turquoise Surf Travel (☎ 04 91 13 94 82; www.turquoise-voyages.fr; 8 rue Neuve St Martin, 13001 Marseille, France) This agent offers surfing safaris in Gaaf Dhaal atoll as well as resort-based surfing at Hudhuran Fushi.

World Surfaris (☎ 1800-611163, 07-5444 4011; www.worldsurfaris.com; PO Box 180, 2/147 Brisbane Rd, Mooloolaba, Qld 4557, Australia) Offering tours to various surfing destinations, it books surfers into Dhonveli and also does boat-based trips in the inner atolls.

Male'

The pint-sized Maldivian capital is the throbbing, mercantile heart of the nation, a densely crowded and extraordinary place, notable mainly for its stark contrast to the laid-back pace of island life elsewhere in the country.

Male' (*mar-lay*) is well worth giving up half a day on a beach for, if for no other reason than it offers by far the best chance to see the 'real' Maldives away from the resort buffet. Overlooked by brightly coloured tall buildings and surrounded by incongruously turquoise water, Male' is a hive of activity, the engine driving the Maldives' economy and the forum for the country's now-vibrant political debate.

Far smaller than the neighbouring airport island of Hulhule', Male' nevertheless feels like an important place, where the leaders of the republic congregate, where the country's exports arrive and where travellers find themselves from time to time. That said, Male' is interesting to visit mainly for a taste of Maldivian life more than for its inherent wealth of things to see and do. Independent travellers will find that this is a place they see a lot of – it's also one of the few places where palm trees and sandy beaches aren't on the menu.

Male' is pleasant and pleasingly quirky – its alcohol-free bars and restaurants jostle with its shops and lively markets and the general hubbub of a capital is very much present. This city island offers a chance to get a real feel for the Maldives, what makes its people tick and to meet Maldivians on an equal footing.

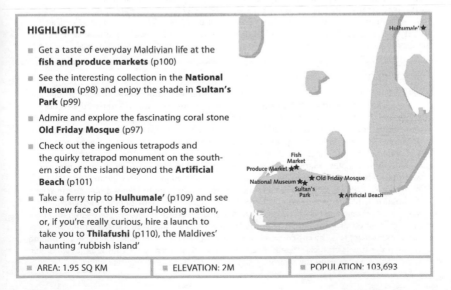

HIGHLIGHTS

- Get a taste of everyday Maldivian life at the **fish and produce markets** (p100)

- See the interesting collection in the **National Museum** (p98) and enjoy the shade in **Sultan's Park** (p99)

- Admire and explore the fascinating coral stone **Old Friday Mosque** (p97)

- Check out the ingenious tetrapods and the quirky tetrapod monument on the southern side of the island beyond the **Artificial Beach** (p101)

- Take a ferry trip to **Hulhumale'** (p109) and see the new face of this forward-looking nation, or, if you're really curious, hire a launch to take you to **Thilafushi** (p110), the Maldives' haunting 'rubbish island'

- ▪ AREA: 1.95 SQ KM ▪ ELEVATION: 2M ▪ POPULATION: 103,693

MALE'

HISTORY

Male' has been the seat of the Maldives' ruling dynasties since before the 12th century, though none left any grand palaces. Some trading houses appeared in the 17th century, along with a ring of defensive bastions, but Male' didn't acquire the trappings of a city and had a very limited range of economic and cultural activities. Visitors in the 1920s estimated the population at only 5000.

Growth began with the 1930s modernisation, and the first banks, hospitals, high schools and government offices appeared in the following decades. Only since the 1970s, with wealth from tourism and an expanding economy, has the city really burgeoned and growth emerged as a problem.

But a problem it has very definitely become; despite extending the area of the city through land reclamation over the island's reef, Male' is unable to extend any further and so the government is looking to projects such as nearby Hulhumale' to accommodate the future overspill of the city.

ORIENTATION

Male' is a roughly rectangular shape, its centre being spread out along the north side of the island – where all the main jetties and harbours are. The main street is the waterfront Boduthakurufaanu Magu, which goes all the way around the island. Many central government institutions are on this street and it opens up half-way down to include the city's main square, Jumhooree Maidan.

Male' is divided into four administrative districts, from west to east: Maafannu, covering most of the western end of the island; Machangolhi, running north-south across the middle; Galolhu, a crowded residential maze in south-central Male'; and Henveiru, covering the east and northeast. These districts are indiscernible to visitors, but taxi drivers understand the addresses. Street numbers are rarely used – the building name will do.

Maps

Given Male's size, the two maps in this book should be sufficient. The Maldives Tourism Promotion Board's *Resort/ Hotel Guide* brochure has an adequate map of Male'; it's given out free at the airport and at the MTPB office (p96). There are town plans pointing out the major sights of the island along Boduthakurufaanu Magu.

INFORMATION
Bookshops

Asrafee Bookshop (Map p98; ☎ 3323424; Chandanee Magu) Sells a good selection of English paperbacks upstairs.

Asters Bookshop (Map p98; ☎ 3335505; www.asters .com.mv; Majeedee Magu) Has one of the best choices of English books in town, a good history section and more highbrow fiction than most.

Novelty Bookshop (Map p95; ☎ 3318899; Fareedhee Magu) Although it has almost no novels worth reading, here you'll find the best range of books about the Maldives, as well as some imported titles.

MALE' IN ONE DAY

Take a stroll down Boduthakurufaanu Magu, the main street running along the waterfront, and enjoy a relaxed breakfast at **Shell Beans** (p105). Carry on down the waterfront past the President's Office and the main square, turning left to visit the **Grand Friday Mosque** (p99), if you're dressed respectfully enough. Next door, drop in to see the small but interesting collection at the **National Museum** (p98) and enjoy the gardens of **Sultan's Park** (p99) before some shopping around Fareedhee Magu. For lunch, try local 'short eats' at **Dawn Café** (p106), after which you can explore the fascinating **market** (p100), where you'll see the morning catch being brought in and gutted (you'll be glad you ate beforehand) and everything else imaginable on sale. Carry on to the President's Jetty; if you're a non-diver, you might want to take the boat to the **Whale Submarine** (p100) for a fascinating trip to the reef nearby (book by phone in advance), and if you still have some energy left, head over to the artificial beach on the east of the island, where you can cool off or just chill out with the locals after work and watch the impromptu soccer matches. As night falls, the city comes alive with promenading couples and young people zipping through the streets on their mopeds. Round the day off with a meal at **Thai Wok** (p105) or join the crowds walking along the seafront – the closest Male' has to a nightlife scene.

Emergency

Ambulance ☎ 102
Fire ☎ 118
Police ☎ 119
Police station (Boduthakurufaanu Magu) On the corner of Jumhooree Maidan (Map p98)

Internet Access

There is a real shortage of internet cafes in Male' – your best bet if you're without a laptop is the **Luckyhiya Hotel** (p103), where there's a small cybercafe in the lobby.

Those with laptops or other wi-fi-enabled devices can connect in many places, including **Bistro Jade** (Map p98; Boduthakurufaanu Magu; ☺ 8am-11pm Sat-Thu, 3-11pm Fri), a hub for expats that offers free wi-fi to its patrons,

although the food is thoroughly lacklustre. Free wi-fi also operates in the lobby of the Hulhule' Island Hotel (p104).

Paid wi-fi can be found all over town – look for the Dhiraagu hotspot signs.

Laundry

Any hotel will take care of your laundry for a few dollars per item. Guesthouses will do it more cheaply. Allow a couple of days if the weather is rainy. There are no laundromats.

Left Luggage

There are no dedicated left-luggage facilities in Male' itself. The only option is taking a day room at a hotel, or asking nicely at

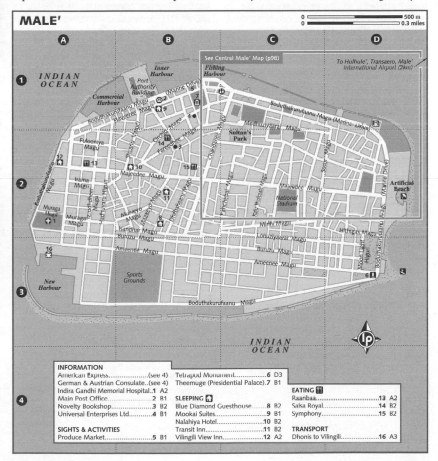

INFORMATION
American Express...................(see 4)
German & Austrian Consulate..(see 4)
Indira Gandhi Memorial Hospital..**1** A2
Main Post Office.......................**2** B1
Novelty Bookshop.......................**3** B2
Universal Enterprises Ltd............**4** B1

SIGHTS & ACTIVITIES
Produce Market.......................**5** B1

Tetrapod Monument.................**6** D3
Theemuge (Presidential Palace).**7** B1

SLEEPING
Blue Diamond Guesthouse.......**8** B2
Mookai Suites..........................**9** B1
Nalahiya Hotel.......................**10** B2
Transit Inn............................**11** B2
Vilingili View Inn...................**12** A2

EATING
Raanbaa..............................**13** A2
Salsa Royal..........................**14** B2
Symphony............................**15** B2

TRANSPORT
Dhonis to Vilingili...............**16** A3

MALE'

reception if you can leave your bags. There is a left-luggage service at the airport that costs US$3 per item, per 24 hours.

Libraries

National Library (Map p98; Majeedee Magu; ☾ closed Fri) Has quite a few English titles. Nonresidents can't borrow books, but are welcome to sit and read in the library.

Medical Services

Both the following will make arrangements with travel insurance companies, and both have doctors trained to do a diving medical check. There are a large number of well-stocked chemists outside both establishments.

ADK Private Hospital (Map p98; ☎ 3313553; Sosun Magu) Private facility with Western-trained doctors and dentists, excellent standards of care and quite high prices.

Indira Gandhi Memorial Hospital (Map p95; ☎ 3316647; Buruzu Magu) Modern public facility, well-equipped and staffed with English-speaking doctors.

Money

For reliable service, try the State Bank of India, Bank of Maldives, Bank of Ceylon or HSBC, all near each other on Boduthaku-rufaanu Magu (Map p98). All have ATMs that accept international cards.

More local banks are clustered near the harbour end of Chandanee Magu and east along Boduthakurufaanu Magu. They all change travellers cheques, usually for a small transaction fee. Bank of Maldives doesn't charge a fee if you change travellers cheques for Maldivian rufiya, but does charge if you want US dollars.

Universal Enterprises Ltd (Map p95; ☎ 3323080; www.unisurf.com; 39 Orchid Magu) The Amex agent in the Maldives.

Post

Main post office (Map p95; ☎ 3315555; www.maldivespost.com; Boduthakurufaanu Magu; ☾ 8.15am-9pm Sun-Thu, 3-9pm Fri, 9.15am-9pm Sat) The main post office is just opposite the Maldives Port Authority building, though a new building was being constructed by the airport ferry dock at the time of writing. There's a post office at the airport too.

Telephone

Although they seem to go largely unused, there are Dhiraagu telephone booths around the town. Lots of shops offer discounted calls abroad and phone cards. Any-

one in the Maldives for a long time will save a lot of money by getting a local SIM card for their mobile phone (see p176). Go to either **Dhiraagu** (Map p98; ☎ 123; www.dhiraagu.com; Chandhanee Magu) or **Wataniya** (Map p98; ☎ 929; www.wataniya.com.mv; Majeedee Magu).

Toilets

The most conveniently located public toilet (Rf2) is on the back street between Bistro Jade (see p95) and the small mosque on Ameer Ahmed Magu. However, you can also pop in and use the toilets of most cafes or restaurants; the owners are almost universally polite and don't seem to mind.

Tourist Information

Maldives Tourism Promotion Board (MTPB; Map p98; ☎ 3323228; www.visitmaldives.com; 12 Boduthaku-rufaanu Magu ☾ 7.30am-2.30pm Sun-Thu) The MTPB has an information counter on the 3rd floor of an office building on the seafront. It gives away free booklets and maps and can answer specific inquiries. The information desk at the airport is supposedly open when international flights arrive, but sometimes this isn't the case. Even when it's not staffed, look on the shelf out the front for some useful booklets.

Travel Agencies

You're unlikely to use a travel agency in the Maldives as most people book their holidays from home and have little need to arrange anything in the country. However, anyone travelling independently can try the following agencies, which vary enormously in terms of services offered. Consistently the best agency for FITs (fully independent travellers) is Inner Maldives, which can tailor-make itineraries. If you're an independent traveller looking for a resort or a safari tour, be prepared to do some shopping around – ask in town, or call one or more of those listed below. A full list of Male' travel agents can be found at www.visitmaldives.com.

Crown Tours (Map p98; ☎ 3329889; www.crowntoursmaldives.com; Fasmeeru Bldg, 5th fl, Boduthakurufaanu Magu)

Inner Maldives (Map p98; ☎ 3315499; www.innermaldives.com.mv; Ameer Ahmed Magu)

Sultans of the Sea (Map p98; ☎ 3320330; www.sultansoftheseas.com; Fasmeeru Bldg, ground fl, Boduthakurufaanu Magu)

Sunland Travel (Map p98; ☎ 3324658; www.sunland.com.mv; STO Trade Centre, Orchid Magu)

Voyages Maldives (Map p98; ☎ 3323617; www.voyagesmaldives.com; Chandhanee Magu)

DANGERS & ANNOYANCES

The main danger in Male' is posed by the mopeds that seem to appear from nowhere at great speeds. Keep your wits about you and look around before crossing the road. Crime against travellers is not unknown, but it is rare. Pickpocketing is probably the biggest threat, particularly in crowded shopping areas and around the markets; but again, it is not common. The main annoyance in Male' is the lack of alcohol. If you really want a drink, take the approximately hourly ferry from Jetty No 1 to the Hulhule' Island Hotel (p104) near the airport, or take the airport ferry and walk the ten minutes to the hotel for a cold beer by the pool.

SIGHTS & ACTIVITIES

Male' is more of an experience than a succession of astonishing must-sees. The best thing to do is enjoy a stroll and absorb the atmosphere of this oddest of capitals. That said, there are a few genuine sights to keep you occupied for a day.

Old Friday Mosque

Hukuru Miskiiy (Map p98; Medhuziyaarai Magu) is the oldest mosque in the country, dating from 1656. It's a beautiful structure made from coral stone into which intricate decora-

tion and Quranic script have been carved. Even though an ugly protective corrugated-iron sheet covers the roof and some of the walls, this is still a fascinating place. The interior is superb and famed for its fine lacquer work and elaborate woodcarvings. One long panel, carved in the 13th century, commemorates the introduction of Islam to the Maldives. Visitors wishing to see inside are supposed to get permission from an official of the **Ministry of Islamic Affairs** (☎ 3322266). However, most of the staff are officials of the ministry and, if you are respectful and well dressed, they will usually give you permission to enter the mosque on the spot – just hang around outside and try to get the attention of someone, although don't bother if you're underdressed.

The mosque was built on the foundations of an old temple that faced west to the setting sun, not northwest towards Mecca. Consequently, the worshippers have to face the corner of the mosque when they pray – the striped carpet, laid at an angle, shows the correct direction.

Overlooking the mosque is the solid, round, blue-and-white tower of the *munnaaru* – the squat minaret. Though it doesn't look that old, it dates from 1675. West of the mosque is a graveyard with many elaborately carved tombstones. Stones with rounded tops are for females, those with pointy tops are for males and those featuring gold-plated lettering are the

---

THE MAGNIFICENT TETRAPOD

The installation of tetrapod walls around much of Male' saved it from huge potential devastation by the Indian Ocean tsunami in 2004. Tetrapods are concrete blocks with four fat legs, each approximately 1m long, sticking out like the four corners of a tetrahedron. These blocks can be stacked together in rows and layers so they interlock together to form a wall several metres high, looking like a giant version of a child's construction toy. A tetrapod breakwater has gaps that allow sea water to pass through, but collectively the structure is so massive and its surface so irregular that it absorbs and dissipates the force of the waves and protects the shoreline from the physical impact of a storm. As Male' has expanded through land reclamation to cover its entire natural coral reef, its natural buffer from the force of strong waves has disappeared.

A severe storm in 1988 was the prompt that lead to the scheme being built. Huge waves broke up tons of landfill that was part of a land-reclamation scheme, and much of this land was re-reclaimed by the sea. The solution was to protect the whole island with a rim of tetrapod breakwaters, constructed as part of a Japanese foreign-aid project. In some places the tetrapod walls are used to retain landfill, and have a path on top forming an attractive seaside promenade. In other places, tetrapod walls enclose an artificial harbour that provides a sheltered anchorage for small boats, and a safe spot for kids to swim. So beloved are these curious structures to locals, there's even a tetrapod monument (p101) in the southwestern corner of town.

MALE'

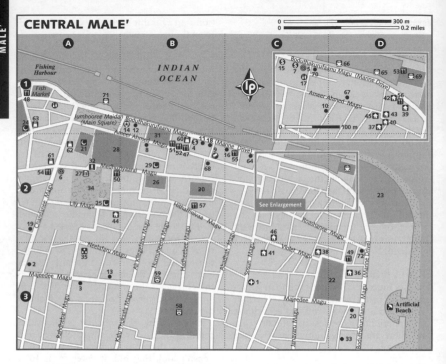

graves of former sultans. The small buildings are family mausoleums and their stone walls are intricately carved. Respectably dressed non-Muslims are welcome to walk around the graveyard; you don't require permission for this.

National Museum & Sultan's Park

The small **National Museum** (Map p98; ☎ 3322254; Medhuziyaarai Magu; adult/child under 12 US$3/1; ⏰ 8am-6pm Sun-Thu, closed holidays) is well worth a visit. Housed in a small, three-storey building in one corner of the Sultan's Park, it is the only remaining part of the original sultan's palace – the rest was demolished in 1968 at the beginning of the second republic. At the time of writing, a rather gaudy new Chinese-gifted building was being built next door, which the museum will eventually move in to, making way for the old building to house a reconstruction of how the Sultan's Palace's interiors would have looked.

For the time being, the museum has a small collection that is displayed over three floors and well labelled in English. You'll

be accompanied throughout by one of the staff. A useful, illustrated guide to the museum, sold at the entrance for Rf50, has colour pictures and more detailed descriptions of the exhibits. Many are items once owned by the sultans – clothing, utensils, weapons and a throne. Some of the fabrics are beautiful, especially the rich brocades. Excellent, traditional lacquer work is displayed on large bowls and trays used to bring gifts to the sultan. Weapons include *bonthi* sticks, which were used in martial arts, and a *silvan bonthi*, used by a husband to punish an unfaithful wife.

Especially interesting are the museum's pre-Islamic stone carvings collected by Thor Heyerdahl, and other examples from sites all over the country. They include a fine Buddha's head and various phallic images. Most of them are labelled, but little is known about the significance or historical context of these fascinating finds. Quirky additions to the historic collection include a tiny Maldivian flag taken on one of the Apollo missions and some moon rock, both gifts from Richard Nixon.

Surrounding the museum, **Sultan's Park** (8am-6pm Sun-Thu, 4-6pm Fri) was once part of the grounds of the sultan's palace. It's an attractive place full of flowers and trees and is the nicest public space in Male'.

Grand Friday Mosque & Islamic Centre

The golden dome of this impressive but rather sterile **mosque** (Map p98) dominates the skyline of Male' and has become something of a symbol for the city. Set back off the main square, Jumhooree Maidan, and opposite the National Security Service Headquarters, this is the biggest mosque in the country.

Opened in 1984, and built with help from the Gulf States, Pakistan, Brunei and Malaysia, the Grand Friday Mosque is striking in its plainness, built in white marble and virtually free from decoration. From a boat coming into Male's harbour, you can still see the gold dome glinting in the sun, although the gold is actually anodised aluminium. The *munnaaru*, with its space-age shape and distinctive zigzag decoration, was supposed to be the tallest structure in Male', but that title now goes to the telecommunications towers.

Visits to see the Grand Friday Mosque must be between 9am and 5pm, and outside prayer times. It closes to all non-Muslims 15 minutes before prayers and for the following hour. Before noon and between 2pm and 3pm are the best times to visit. Invading bands of casual sightseers are not encouraged, but if you are genuinely interested and suitably dressed, you'll be welcomed by one of the staff members who hang out by the entrance. Men must wear long trousers and women a long skirt or dress.

The main prayer hall inside the mosque can accommodate up to 5000 worshippers and has beautifully carved wooden side panels and doors, a specially woven carpet and impressive chandeliers. The **Islamic Centre** also includes a conference hall, library and classrooms.

Muleeaage & Medhu Ziyaarath

Across the road from the Old Friday Mosque is a blue-and-white building with colourful gateposts. This is the **Muleeaage** (Map p98), built as a palace in the early 20th century. The sultan was deposed before he could move in and the building was used for government offices for about 40 years. It became the president's residence in 1953 when the first republic was proclaimed, but lost the honour in 1994 to **Theemuge** (Map p95), a newer residence on Orchid Magu. At the eastern end of the building's compound, behind an elaborate blue-and-white gatehouse, the **Medhu Ziyaarath** (Map p98) is the tomb of Abul Barakat Yoosuf Al Barbary, who brought Islam to Male' in 1153.

Tomb of Mohammed Thakurufaanu

In the back streets in the middle of town, in the grounds of a small mosque, is the **tomb of Mohammed Thakurufaanu** (Map p98), the Maldives' national hero who liberated the country from Portuguese rule and was then the sultan from 1573 to 1585. Thakurufaanu is also commemorated in the name of the road that rings Male', Boduthakurufaanu Magu (*bodu* means 'big' or 'great').

National Art Gallery

This small **exhibition space** (Map p98; ☎ 3337724; www.artgallery.gov.mv; 131 Majeedhee Magu; admission free; ☷ 9am-6pm Sun-Thu) is the only one of its kind in the Maldives and is therefore the important centre of the nation's fledgling art scene. Solo exhibits from painters rotate, while the biennial Maldives Contemporary exhibition is a great chance to see the varied art produced in the country, from photography to painting and conceptual works.

Mosques

There are over 20 *miskiiys* (mosques) in Male'; some are simple coral buildings with an iron roof and others are quite stylish with elegant minarets. Outside there is always a well or an outdoor bathroom, because Muslims must always wash before they pray. Visitors usually can't go inside, but there's no need – the doors are always wide open, and you can clearly see that the interior is nearly always devoid of furniture or decoration.

Markets

The busy **produce market** (Map p95) gives a real flavour of the Maldives – people from all over the country gather here to sell homegrown and imported vegetables. Coconuts and bananas are the most plentiful produce, but look inside for the stacks of betel leaf, for wrapping up a 'chew'. Just wandering around, watching the hawkers and the shoppers and seeing the vast array of products on display is fascinating and as real a Maldivian experience as possible.

Nearby is the **fish market** (Map p98), which is not to be missed, although the squeamish may well object to the buckets of entrails or the very public gutting of fish going on all around. This is the soul of Male' – and it's great fun watching the day's catch being brought in to the market from the adjacent fishing harbour. Look out for some truly vast tuna, octopus and grouper. Fishing and marketing are men's work here, and Maldivian women don't usually venture into these areas, although foreign women walking around won't cause any raised eyebrows.

Whale Submarine

The **Whale Submarine** (☎ 3333939; www.whale submarine.com.mv; adult/child/family US$75/38/170) can hardly be described as a sight of Male', but it's a popular excursion. First things first, this is not a submarine for whale watching – its name is slightly misleading. It is, in fact, a submarine for looking at life on a reef. It's hard to recommend for divers as the trip can't really compare to a real dive, but for kids (under-threes not allowed) and those who don't dive, this is a great, if pricey, little excursion. As the submarine departs from a point off the coast you have to get a boat either from the airport or Jetty No 1 (the jetty in front of Jumhooree Maidan, also known as the President's Jetty; Map p98) – one boat picks up from both about 30 minutes before the scheduled departure of the submarine. You should ring ahead and book a place (there are several departures daily) so the boat can pick you up. At the submarine dock (the 'Whale House') you pay your money, have a cool drink and board the sub.

The sub takes a few minutes to get to its dive spot, and then descends to about 35m while passengers gaze out through large, lenslike windows. A variety of fish come very close to the windows, attracted partly by the food that the sub dispenses. Surgeonfish, blue-striped snapper and unicornfish are among the most commonly seen, but you have an excellent view of smaller creatures too, such as lionfish and anemonefish. The sub goes very close to a reef wall, and its lights illuminate crevices and show up colours that wouldn't be visible in natural light.

Underwater time is about 45 minutes, but allow 1½ hours for the whole trip. Many people manage to fit in a submarine trip if they have a few hours to spare at the airport before their departure flight. The sub maintains normal surface pressure inside, so it's quite safe to fly straight afterwards.

Artificial Beach

The western seafront of Male' is its recreational centre. Here, a sweet little **beach** has been crafted from the breakwater tetrapods and there's a whole range of fast food cafes next to it as well as open fields for ad hoc games of soccer and cricket. Further up towards the airport ferry there are fairground attractions at the **Majeediyya Carnival** (Map p98) including a bowling alley and more eateries. The other way you'll see the charming **tetrapod monument** (Map p95), a local salute to the mini concrete structures that together form a life-saving breakwater for the city (see the box p97).

WALKING TOUR

Male' is best seen on foot – you can circumnavigate the entire island in around an hour; but to get a proper feel for the place, try to get into the crowded, chaotic backstreets in the island's centre.

Start from the waterfront near **Jumhooree Maidan (1)**, the main square, conspicuous for the huge Maldivian flag flying on its eastern side. This was the setting for antigovernment demonstrations in August 2004, and where, four years later, democratically elected President Nasheed was inaugurated. You'll notice that it remains a well-guarded place, with the police station on one side and the white **National Security Service Headquarters (2)** to the south.

To the right of the NSS is the **Grand Friday Mosque (3**; p99). Walk down the sandy street past its main entrance and you'll arrive at the **Republican Monument (4)**, a modern-style centrepiece to a roundabout unveiled in 1999 to commemorate 30 years of Maldivian independence. Avoiding the traffic, cross over to the **Sultan's Park (5**; p99) and walk through its well laid-out flowerbeds and plantings to Lily Magu. Exit the park and turn left, where you'll see a charming coral stone **mosque (6)** in the corner of the park, typical of the intricate 17th-century Maldivian design. Continue south from here through streets that are far more typical of the crowded capital until you reach the **Tomb of Mohammed Thakurufaanu (7)**, a much-loved shrine honouring the man who liberated the Maldives from the Portuguese in the 16th century. Cut down to Majeedee Magu, the city's main thoroughfare, and absorb the shops, noise and bustle of the town's commercial heart as you walk west. Cut up through the good shopping streets of Fareedhee Magu and Orchid Magu, passing the striking **Theemuge** (Presidential Palace; **8**), supposedly the official residence of the President, though the current incumbent apparently prefers living in his flat to the trappings of high office. The charming **mosque (9)** next door is also worth a peek at from the street.

From here head north towards the seafront and turn left for the wonderful **produce market (10**; p100). Continue for a few more blocks along the waterfront, a bustling area with hardware shops and hangouts for sailors and fishermen. Go back along the seafront to the **fish market (11)**, which, along with the adjacent **fishing harbour (12)**,

---

HOUSE NAMES

Street numbers are rarely used in Male', so most houses and buildings have a distinctive name, typically written in picturesque English as well as in the local Thaana script. Some Maldivians prefer rustic titles like Crabtree, Forest, Oasis View and Banana Cabin. Others are specifically floral, like Sweet Rose and Luxury Garden, or even vegetable, like Carrot, or the perplexing Leaf Mess. There are also exotic names like Paris Villa and River Nile, while some sound like toilet disinfectants – Ozone, Green Zest, Dawn Fresh.

Some of our quirkier favourite house names include Hot Lips, Subtle Laughter, Remind House, Pardon Villa, Frenzy, Mary Lightning and Aston Villa.

Shop names and businesses, on the other hand, often have an overt advertising message – People's Choice Supermarket, Bless Trade, Fair Price and Neat Store. Premier Chambers is not a pretentious house name – it's where you'll find Male's first barrister.

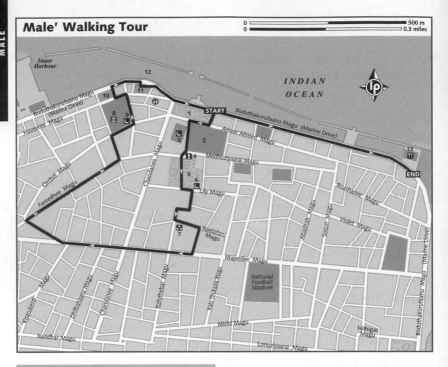

Male' Walking Tour

0 ————————————— 500 m
0 ————————————— 0.3 miles

Inner Harbour

INDIAN OCEAN

START

Boduthakurufaanu Magu (Marine Drive)

END

WALK FACTS

Start Jumhooree Maidan
Finish Sea House
Distance 3km
Duration One hour

is a must-see for anyone in Male'. Wander along the seafront, which is always fascinating as people crowd on and off boats, and you can see more and more obscure cargo being brought ashore. Finish up at **Sea House (13**; p105) for a drink with a view of the harbour.

DIVING SITES

There is some excellent diving within a short boat ride of Male' even though the rubbish and pollution of the capital can be seen underwater. The **Sea Explorers Dive School** (Map p98; ☎ 3316172; www.seamaldives.com.mv; Bodufungadhu Magu) is a very well-regarded operation that does dive courses and trips for locals and the expat community. It costs US$50 per dive including all equipment and boat

trip, or US$40 for just tanks and weights. If you do nine dives, the 10th dive is free.

Some of the best dives are along the edges of Vaadhoo Kandu (the channel between North and South Male' Atolls), which has two Protected Marine Areas. There is also a well-known wreck.

Hans Hass Place (also called Kikki Reef) is a demanding wall dive beside Vaadhoo Kandu in a Protected Marine Area. There is a lot to see at 4m or 5m, so it's good for snorkellers and less-experienced divers when the current is not too strong. There's a wide variety of marine life, including many tiny reef fish and larger species in the channel. Further down are caves and overhangs with sea fans and other soft corals.

Lion's Head is a Protected Marine Area that was once a popular place for shark feeding, and although this practice is now strongly discouraged, grey reef sharks and the occasional turtle are still common here. The reef edge is thick with fish, sponges and soft corals; although it drops steeply, with numerous overhangs, to over 40m, there is still much to see at snorkelling depth.

The wreck of the **Maldive Victory** is an impressive and challenging dive because of the potential for strong currents. This cargo ship hit a reef and sank on Friday 13 February 1981 and now sits with the wheelhouse at around 15m and the propeller at 35m. The ship has been stripped of anything movable, but the structure is almost intact and provides a home for a rich growth of new coral, sponges, tubastrea and large schools of fish.

MALE' FOR CHILDREN

The **Whale Submarine** (p100) will appeal to kids of all ages (although those under three aren't allowed), while the **Artificial Beach** (p101) and the recreational areas nearby is also a great place for them to swim, and older kids can join in football or cricket match with local children. The nearby Majeediyya Carnival also has some fun activities for children, including the Slam Bowling Alley.

SLEEPING

Male' makes Hong Kong look spacious, and as you'd expect on this densely crowded island, space is at a premium. Even top-end rooms are not large. Compared to the rest of Asia, prices are very high here, though a night in Male' costs peanuts compared to one in a resort. Nearly all Male' hotels offer 'day rooms' to passengers in transit to a resort, at between half and two thirds the price of a night.

Budget

Extra Haven Guesthouse (Map p98; ☎ 3327453; s/d with fan US$33/40, with air-con US$45/50; ✖) In the back streets at the east end of town, Extra Haven attracts a mixed clientele of visiting workers and budget travellers. The rooms with air-con are small and nothing fancy, and the fan-cooled rooms are even smaller and plainer, but they're all clean and have bathrooms.

Blue Diamond Guesthouse (Map p95; ☎ 3326125; fax 3316404; Badifasgandu Magu; s/d with fan US$37/42) On a little street south of Majeedee Magu, the Blue Diamond has small, simple ensuite rooms. It's in a residential part of town, interesting for its authentic local ambience, but not very convenient for shops, restaurants or transport.

Fariva Inn (Map p98; ☎ 3337611; amsha@dhivehi net.net.mv; Boduthakurufaanu Magu; s/d US$45/50; ✖)

Male' on a tight budget is not much fun – if you want centrality too then this is your only real option; but don't expect much charm – of the 18 rooms, eight have air-con. All have TV, a fridge and a need to be painted!

Transit Inn (Map p95; ☎ 3320420; transit@dhive hinet.net.mv; Maaveyo Magu; s/d US$45/50; ✖ 🛜) The Transit Inn is above the busy Junways Café in a residential neighbourhood of the capital. It's a slightly chaotic place with just four rooms that all include a fridge, TV and free wi-fi.

Skai Lodge (Map p98; ☎ 3337098; skailodge@ dhivehinet.net.mv; Violet Magu; s/d/tr US$49/63/78; ✖) This attractive town house boasts 13 clean but rather poky rooms with bathroom, hot water, phone, TV and air-con; some have a balcony. Meals are available, but must be requested in advance.

Fuana Inn (Map p109; ☎ 3350610; www.fuana.net /inn; Hulhumale' island; s/d incl breakfast US$50/65; ✖) Staying on Hulhumale' gives you the great combination of surreal, budget and beach. Surreal because this manmade island is a centrally planned vision for 21st-century Maldives (see p109), but it's also on the beach and a snip at these prices. The rooms are modern and clean, and all doubles come with balconies over the sea.

Midrange

Maagiri Lodge (Map p98; ☎ 3328787; www.maagiri lodge.com.mv; Boduthakurufaanu Magu; s/d US$60/70; ✖) This centrally located place is a tad overpriced for its level of accommodation, but its functional rooms are comfortable enough, albeit totally lacking in charm. Avoid the two dark downstairs rooms, where the drone of the lobby television is audible at all times. English can sometimes be a problem at reception.

Vilingili View Inn (Map p95; ☎ 3318696; www.tropicalisland.com.mv; Majeedee Magu; s/d/ste US$65/80/105; ✖ 🖥 🛜) At the far west end of Majeedee Magu, this place is not very convenient for the rest of town and, despite the name, views to the sea are hard to come by. But there's charm here, regardless of the flaking paint and damp in some rooms. There's also free guest wi-fi and a great restaurant that's perfect for a non-alcoholic sundowner.

Luckyhiya Hotel (Map p98; ☎ 3315856; info@ luckyhiyahotel.mv; off Violet Magu; s/d/ste incl breakfast US$68/76/78; ✖ 🖥) This highrise hotel in the centre of Male' has small, clean rooms and some great views. It's located off Violet Magu at the end of a thin and apparently nameless side street. There's a cybercafe in reception, where you can pay to use the internet.

Baani Hotel (Map p98; ☎ 3303530; www.baani hotels.com.mv; Filigas Hingun; s/d/ste incl breakfast US$79/94/159; ☒ ▯) Newly opened in 2008, this great hotel overlooks one of Male's two football fields and offers spacious, bright rooms (avoid the dark ones at the back of the building), free in-room internet and a complimentary driver to pick you up from the airport ferry. The downside is that the breakfast sucks – eat out.

Park House (Map p98; ☎ 3306600; info@theparkhouse .com.mv; off Lily Magu; s/d incl breakfast US$82/95; ☒ ☎) Another brand-new hotel, the brightly painted Park House offers 20 large yellow-and-green rooms, dark wood furniture and all mod cons. It's a good find, with free wi-fi and a pizza restaurant downstairs.

our pick Candies (Map p98; ☎ 3310220; www.candies .mv; Dheefuram Gholhi; s/d/tr US$85/97/120; ☒ ☎) This is overall the best deal in the city for our money – the 16 rooms are comfortable, not too cramped and overlook a charming pool and popular garden cafe frequented by locals in the evening. Guests have access to free wi-fi and overall the whole place feels more like a large house than a hotel. A good breakfast comes in at an extra US$8. Booking is advised.

Top End

Relax Inn (Map p98; ☎ 3314531; www.hotelrelaxinn .com; Ameer Ahmed Magu; s/d/ste from US$91/103/157; ☒ ☎) The Relax has been gradually doing up its rooms, with the result that they now look more modern and the furniture is less garish. Those on the higher floors have wonderful views. Suites are very large and have balconies, while doubles and singles are far smaller.

Mookai Hotel (Map p98; ☎ 3338811; www.mookai .com.mv; Meheli Golhi; s/d US$97/115; ☒ ▣ ☎) With a good location just seconds from the waterfront, rooms with great views on the higher floors and a tiny but effective swimming pool to cool down in, the Mookai is a solid choice. Rooms are small but clean and well furnished. Wi-fi, only available in the lobby, costs a ridiculous US$15 per day. Opposite, the **Kam Hotel**

(Map p98; ☎ 3320611; rohana@kam.com.mv; Meheli Golhi; s/d from US$90/102; ☒ ☎) is run by the same company and offers similar standard rooms and service.

Mookai Suites (Map p95; ☎ 3309911; www.mookai suites.com.mv; Haveeree Higun; s/d/tr US$97/115/150; ☒ ▣ ☎) These new business-oriented suites are a welcome addition to Male' accommodation, though ADSL is charged at US$5 per 24 hours, which seems cheeky at these prices. Each of the sleek though rather sterile rooms shares a sitting room and kitchen area with one other room. Rooms at the front have balconies – some with great harbour views.

Nalahiya Hotel (Map p95; ☎ 3346633; www.bee hivehotels.com; Majeedee Magu; s/d/ste US$99/117/193; ☒ ☎) This impressive new hotel has by far the smartest lobby in town, a chic air-conditioned oasis from the busy crossroads outside. The rooms are tastefully furnished and feature local artwork, though they fall short of charming and can be quite small. Don't miss the fantastic rooftop restaurant for great Male' views. There's free wi-fi throughout.

Hulhule' Island Hotel (Map p109; ☎ 3330888; www.hih.com.mv; Hulhule' island; s/d/ste incl breakfast US$263/289/464; ☒ ▣ ☎) The poshest hotel in Male' is not actually in the capital, but across the lagoon on the airport island, a 10-minute dhoni ride from the bustle of the city. This is a well-run business hotel with clean and spacious rooms and the only hotel in Male' serving alcohol, for which expats frequently make the pilgrimage across the lagoon. The pool is another great attraction – it's by far the nicest in Male'. Many transit passengers take a room on a 'day use' basis (until 10.30pm) for US$189.

EATING

Rather like the accommodation scene, eating in Male' is perfectly decent without being excellent, but it's blessedly less expensive than eating à la carte at any resort.

Restaurants

Typically restaurants in Male' have several different cuisines on offer – most popular are Thai, Indonesian, Indian, Italian and American-style grills. Nearly everything is imported, including the prawns and the lobsters, which are the most expensive items.

None of the Male' restaurants serves alcohol, but some serve nonalcoholic beer for about Rf10 to Rf20 per can. Nearly every restaurant has now acquired an espresso machine, and you can get a good cup of coffee, cappuccino or latte almost anywhere.

Raanbaa (Map p95; ☎ 3336010; Shaheed Ali Hingun; mains Rf40-70; ⏱ 8am-1am Sun-Thu, 3.30pm-1am Fri) Is this the largest restaurant in Male'? It's certainly a contender, with its tree-house-like extensions into the sky. The huge menus encompass everything from tasty red cuttlefish curry to chicken chimichangas.

Symphony (Map p95; ☎ 3326277; Athamaa Goalhi; mains Rf50-100; ⏱ 11am-midnight Sat-Thu, 6pm-midnight Fri; ☒) This long-time favourite for Male' residents, located off Majeedee Magu, has an exceptionally dark interior, chilly air-con and a smart look. The menu is comprehensive and the Indian cuisine is especially good. This has one of the best vegetarian selections in town.

Thai Wok (Map p98; ☎ 3310007; Hithaffivinivaa Magu; mains Rf60-110; ⏱ noon-3.30pm Sun-Thu, 7pm-midnight daily; ☒) This Male' institution has now moved to rather better premises, though there's still something weirdly sterile about it. But the Thai food is excellent and authentic, and this is the reason to come – especially if you can get a table on the balcony.

Aïoli (Map p98; ☎ 3304984; Lotus Goalhi; mains Rf75-250; ⏱ 11.30am-3pm Sun-Thu, 7-11.30pm daily; ☒) Definitely the sleekest eating option in the capital, this large restaurant has the feel of a boutique hotel, decked out all in dark wood and cream furnishings. The menu is just as fabulous – chose from Wagyu ribeye steak, spicy aïoli crab and chilli prawn linguini, for example – all served up on a great outdoor balcony or in one of two dining rooms.

Sala Thai (Map p98; ☎ 3345959; Ameer Ahmed Magu; mains Rf75-160; ⏱ noon-1am Sat-Thu, 6pm-1am Fri; ☒) With the most impressive interior on the capital's eating scene, a mint-infused atmosphere and friendly staff, Sala Thai is an inviting venue for a meal. The menu is equally enticing, with a huge choice of soups, noodles and curries. Booking is a good idea for evening meals.

Salsa Royal (Map p95; ☎ 3335008; Orchid Magu; mains Rf95-180; ⏱ 11.30am-3.30pm Sat-Thu, 6.30-11.30pm; ☒) This airy, high-ceilinged hall serves up Italian and Thai food from two separate menus. The restaurant is non-smoking throughout, extremely clean and with good service.

Cafes

Shell Beans (Map p98; ☎ 3333686; Boduthakurufaanu Magu; snacks Rf30-60; ⏱ 8.30am-11.30pm Sun-Thu, 3pm-1am Fri) This lifeline by the seafront serves up tasty sandwiches, burgers, takeaway coffee and pastries. It's a great spot for lunch on the run, although there's seating both upstairs and downstairs for a less hurried meal.

Royal Garden Café (Map p98; ☎ 3320288; Medhuziyaaraai Magu; mains Rf40-80; ⏱ 8am-1am Sun-Thu, 3pm-1am Fri) This great little place, with a charming garden and an air-conditioned, stylish dark-wood interior, is housed in a rare surviving example of a *ganduvaru*, a noble's house. The menu is a combination of Italian, Indonesian, American and Indian cuisines.

Sea House (Map p98; ☎ 3332957; Boduthakurufaanu Magu; mains Rf40-80; ⏱ 24hrs, closed 10am-1pm Fri) This breezy (and sometimes downright windy) place above the Hulhumale' ferry terminal has expansive harbour views and a great menu that runs from pizza and sandwiches to full meals. It's very popular and a great place to meet friends.

Seagull Café (Map p98; ☎ 3323792; cnr Chandanee Magu & Fareedhee Magu; mains Rf50; ⏱ 9am-11pm Sun-Thu, 3-11pm Fri) One of the most pleasant and popular places, the Seagull boasts a delightfully shaded outdoor eating area and a delicious American-style menu with a kicking club sandwich. There's also a rightly popular gelataria attached, serving up the city's best ice cream.

Saffron Café & Kitchen (Map p98; Ameer Ahmed Magu; mains Rf50-100; ⏱ 8am-1am, 2pm-1am Fri) This great courtyard affair offers a tempting array of both local 'short eats' and international food such as beef fajitas, nasi goreng and fish curry. It's good for a quick lunch, and the set breakfast (Rf30-40) is also recommended.

Teashops

Local teashops are frequented by Maldivian men; it's not the done thing for local women to visit one, although there is no law against it. Foreign women use them sometimes, generally with a male companion, and there's no problem. Some traditional teashops have broadened the menus, installed air-conditioning and improved service – you should feel quite comfortable in

MALE'

these places and they're a great way to meet locals. A bigger and slightly better teashop might be called a cafe or 'hotel'.

Teashops have their goodies displayed on a counter behind a glass screen, and customers line up and choose, cafeteria style – if you don't know what to ask for, just point. Tea costs around Rf2 and the *hedhikaa* ('short eats'; finger-food snacks) from Rf1 to Rf3. You can fill yourself for under Rf10. At meal times they also serve 'long eats', such as soups, curried fish and *roshi* (unleavened bread). A good meal costs from Rf12 to Rf25.

Teashops open as early as 5am and close as late as 1am, particularly around the port area where they cater to fishermen. During Ramazan they're open till 2am or even later, but closed during the day.

Irudhashu Hotaa (Map p98; Filigas Hingun) Our favourite 'short eats' place in town is this perennially busy meeting place by the Henveiru football field. After prayers at the next door mosque, it's always rammed, and the spicy fish curries and selection of *hedhikaa* are delicious.

Dawn Café (Map p98; Haveeree Higun) This is one of the bigger teashops in the area, and it's near the fish market. You can get a brilliant meal here. Try it on Friday afternoon when people come in after going to the mosque.

South Beach (Map p98; Boduthakurufaanu Magu) Another popular place convenient for the airport ferry, this friendly hangout serves up delicious 'short eats' from dawn until well into the night.

Self-Catering

The city's biggest supermarket is the **STO Trade Centre** (Map p98; Orchid Magu), which includes fresh fruit and veg. It's handy for self-catering, which is a sensible option during Ramazan.

ENTERTAINMENT

Nobody comes to a dry town for nightlife, let's face it, but despite the worrying sobriety of the Male' populace, there's a surprising amount going on after dark. The evening is popular with strolling couples and groups of friends who promenade along the seafront and Majeedee Magu until late in the night. Thursday and Friday nights are the busiest, after prayers at sundown. There are even sporadic club nights put on,

although there's nothing regular. Keep your eye out for notices along the seafront, as such events are usually advertised.

Most expats in town make the pilgrimage across the lagoon to the **Hulhule' Island Hotel** (p104) bar for alcohol.

The **Olympus** (Map p98; Majeedee Magu), opposite the stadium, shows Maldivian and Indian films as well as the occasional Hollywood blockbuster.

The **National Stadium** (Map p98; Majeedee Magu) hosts the biggest football matches (tickets cost Rf15 to Rf40) and the occasional cricket match. More casual games can be seen any evening in the sports grounds at the east end of the island and near New Harbour.

SHOPPING

Most of the shops selling imported and locally made souvenirs are on and around Chandanee Magu, Fareedhee Magu and Orchid Magu. Many of the tourist shops have a very similar range of stock, but it's worth browsing in several if you're looking for something special.

The most popular purchases are T-shirts, sarongs, cotton clothing, picture books and small handicraft items (carved fish, lacquer boxes and coconut-shell spoons). Prices are negotiable: they're generally lower in Male' than in resorts, but higher than on village islands.

Male' is definitely the best place to shop for more unusual antiques and Maldivian craft items – come here for old, wooden measuring cups, coconut graters, ceremonial knives and finely woven grass mats. **Gloria Maris** (Map p98) on the east side of Chandanee Magu is worth visiting for such souvenirs. For less conventional items, such as giant fish-hooks, boat balers, hookahs (water pipes) and medicinal herbs, try the local hardware, chandlery and general stores along the waterfront west of the fish market and down Fareedhee Magu.

The best range of surfboards, accessories and surf wear is available at **Atoll Surf** (Map p98; ☎ 3334555; Boduthakurufaanu Magu). Two of the best diving shops are next door to each other: **Dive Shop** (Map p98; Chandanee Magu) and **Water World** (Map p98; Chandanee Magu). Both supply a full range of equipment and are authorised dealers for big-name brands.

For bookshops, see p94.

LOCAL VOICE: ABDULLA ('ALLO') SAEED

Allo, a PADI Dive Instructor at Sea Explorers Dive School (p102), talks about living and diving in the Maldives.

So, diving around Male' – is it any good, or is it too polluted so close to the capital? Diving around Male' is excellent. Some of the best dive sites in the country are located in North & South Male' Atolls, all of which are a short boat ride from Male'. As well as plentiful fish life and coral growth, I've seen whale sharks, manta rays, sharks, and Napoleon wrasse in my diving here. The unusual geography of the islands actually means that any pollution from humans living on islands remains concentrated on the house reef of that island and doesn't get dispersed to the surrounding areas. Local divers are also generally very vigilant in taking care of the dive sites and we encourage experienced divers to remove any rubbish they see entangled on the reefs.

Is the Maldives a good place to learn to dive? Yes, the Maldives is a great place to learn to dive as, unlike elsewhere, you are exposed to real diving conditions and sights from the very first training dive. Confined-water sessions are done in shallow lagoons with plenty to see and experience. There's nothing quite like that instant exposure to a coral reef to make you realise how extraordinary the underwater world can be.

What's the best advice you can give to a tourist coming to dive in the Maldives? The Maldives has good diving throughout the year, although visibility varies with monsoon periods. When deciding to come here for diving, think about what you're most interested in seeing and find out when and where those things are most commonly sighted. Mantas and whale sharks are frequently seen in Ari Atoll from December to May and, after May, also in South Male' Atoll. Anyone after physically challenging dives will enjoy South Male' Atoll and Vaavu Atoll, both of which have great channels to cross in order to watch large pelagics such as sharks, barracuda and tuna. North Male' Atoll and Ari Atoll offer fantastic drift dives at colourful thilas (underwater pinnacles) for those more interested in soft corals and smaller marine creatures. Also, the very first resorts are being built in Gaaf Alif Atoll at the moment, opening up a brand new atoll to divers. I've not yet dived there myself, but from what I hear, it's pretty terrific, so I'm looking forward to getting there soon. The diving in the south is great as the atolls from Gaaf Alif to Addu were not badly affected by the coral bleaching. The coral growth on the reefs is fantastic and the atoll topography offers some exhilarating channel dives with plenty of shark sightings. If you're having difficulty deciding which resort to choose for your dive holiday, I'd suggest contacting the dive base at the resort and asking about the dive packages available, and also getting more information on their regular dive sites. Anyone thinking about doing a speciality dive course while on holiday should make sure that the relevant instructor will be available during their stay.

What is the most impressive dive you've done in Maldives? One of the most impressive dives I have done in the Maldives is with manta rays; being totally surrounded by these magnificent creatures is a completely unforgettable experience. However, overall my favourite dive site in the country is Maaya Thila in North Ari Atoll. It's a wonderful dive site with beautiful coral growth and a marine population that is most active at night. It's great for a night dive throughout the year.

GETTING THERE & AWAY
Air

Nearly all international flights to the Maldives use **Male' International Airport** (www.airports.com.mv), which is on a separate island, Hulhule', about 2km east of Male' island. Domestic flights and seaplane transfers to resorts also use Hulhule', although the seaplane terminal is on the far side of the island, involving a free five-minute bus ride around the runway. Male' is linked by daily flights to Colombo, Qatar, Dubai and Trivandrum and less frequently with Bangalore, Kuala Lumpur, London, Milan, Moscow, Paris, Singapore, Tokyo, Vienna and Zurich.

Boat

The airport functions as the biggest transport hub in the country, so if you want to travel to a resort from Male', take the airport ferry and get a transfer. You'll need to book the transfer in advance and pay for it at the resort. Dhonis to and from the airport dock at the east end of Boduthaku-rufaanu Magu. This is also the best place to charter a dhoni for a day trip. Boats to Hulhumale', which is the overspill island for the capital and is located on the other side of the airport island, depart from the smart ferry terminal east of the airport ferry dock.

Dhonis to nearby Viligili use the New Harbour on the southwest corner of Male'.

Safari boats and private yachts usually moor between Male' island and Viligili, or in the lagoon west of Hulhumale'. Safari-boat operators will normally pick up new passengers from the airport or Male' and ferry them directly to the boat.

GETTING AROUND
To/From the Airport
Dhonis shuttle between the airport and Male' all day and most of the night, departing promptly every 10 minutes. At the airport, dhonis leave from the jetties just north of the arrivals hall. In Male' they arrive and depart from the landing at the east end of Boduthakurufaanu Magu. The crossing costs Rf10 per person or US$1 if you don't have any local cash.

Bicycle
A bicycle is a good way to get around, but there's no place to rent one. Your guesthouse might be able to arrange something, although nearly all the locals get around on motorised scooters, so you can expect to be overtaken a lot.

Taxi
The numerous taxis in the city offer a few minutes of cool, air-conditioned comfort and a driver who can usually find any address in Male'. Many streets are one way and others may be blocked by construction work or stationary vehicles, so taxis will often take roundabout routes.

Fares are the same (Rf20) for any distance, though this rises to Rf25 after midnight. Taxis may charge Rf10 extra for luggage. You don't have to tip. There are various taxi companies, but don't worry about the names – just call one of the following numbers: ☎ 3323132, ☎ 3325757 or ☎ 3322454.

AROUND MALE'

VILIGILI
Probably the most obvious day trip from Male' is the short ferry ride to Viligili, the closest thing Male' has to a suburb, just 1km from the western shore of the capital. The short boat ride takes you into a different world. Far more relaxed than Male', Viligili has something of a Caribbean feel to it, with its brightly painted houses and laid-back pace. Here Male' residents come to enjoy some space, play football and go swimming (usually fully clothed after the conservative fashion typically found on inhabited islands here – this is no place to be seen in a bikini). While it's still a great deal more cosmopolitan than most inhabited islands in the Maldives, if you only visit Male' and resorts, this is perhaps the best chance you'll have of seeing everyday life. The Symphony Garden, a pretty outdoor cafe by the harbour, is the most convenient place for refreshments. Viligili is easy to get to. Just catch one of the frequent dhoni ferries from New Harbour on the southwest corner of Male' (Rf3, 10 mins, every 5 mins).

HULHULE'
Better known as the airport island, Hulhule' was once densely wooded with very few inhabitants – just a graveyard and a reputation for being haunted. The first airstrip was built here in 1960, and in the early 1980s it had a major upgrade to accommodate long-distance passenger jets. Airport facilities have expanded to keep pace with the burgeoning tourist industry and now include a sizable terminal, workshops, administrative buildings, staff housing and the **Hulhule' Island Hotel** (p104). Seaplanes land in the lagoon on the east side of the island. Everyone passes through on their way in and out of the country, but it's also a serious leisure option from Male' due to both the excellent swimming pool and the availability of booze at the hotel, which is popular with expats. The hotel runs a free transfer boat 14 times a day, from beside the President's Jetty (Jetty No 1) in Male'. Day membership that allows use of the swimming pool costs US$15; annual membership is available.

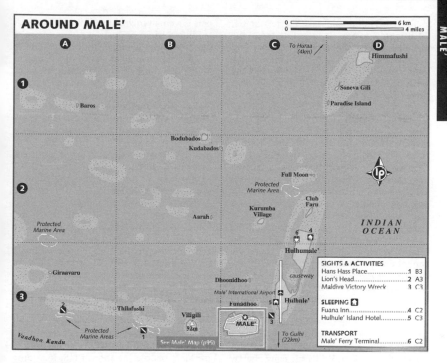

AROUND MALE'

SIGHTS & ACTIVITIES
Hans Hass Place......................1 B3
Lion's Head..............................2 A3
Maldive Victory Wreck 3 C3

SLEEPING
Fuana Inn..............................4 C2
Hulhule' Island Hotel..........5 C3

TRANSPORT
Male' Ferry Terminal..............6 C2

HULHUMALE'

A fascinating half-day trip from Male' is to easily accessible Hulhumale' – or, as many people see it – the future of the Maldives. Here, on the other side of the airport, 1.8 sq km of reef has been built up to create a brand-new and entirely manmade island – the first phase of an ambitious project to relieve the pressure of growth on Male'. Sand and coral were dug up from the lagoon and pumped into big heaps on the reef top. Then bulldozers pushed the rubble around to form a quadrilateral of dry land about 2km long and 1km wide, joined by a causeway to the airport island. It's built up to about 2m above sea level to provide a margin of protection against the possibility of sea-level rises.

This utopian project began in 1997 and now the northern section (about an eighth of the island's total area) is a fully functioning town, complete with rather Soviet-looking apartment blocks, a school, pharmacy, an array of shops and a huge mosque – the golden glass dome of which is visible from all over the southern part of North Male'

Atoll. There's even a surprisingly attractive artificial beach down the eastern side of the island. Coming here makes a fascinating contrast to the chaotic capital – the planning is so precise and mathematical you could be on the set of *Brave New World*. Walking across the hectares of as-yet-empty plots of land towards the tiny conurbation on the far side is an eerie experience and a bewildering glimpse into the future of the Maldivian nation if sea levels continue to rise.

When the first-phase land is fully developed by 2020 it will accommodate 50,000 people and have waterfront esplanades, light industrial areas, government offices, shopping centres, boulevards of palm trees, a marina and a national stadium. The basic layout has been carefully planned, but the details are still flexible, allowing for some natural, organic growth through multiple private developments. The second phase, a long-term proposal, involves reclaiming a further 2.4 sq km of land (engulfing all of Farukolhufushi, currently the Club Faru resort) and bringing the total population of Hulhumale' to around 100,000 people.

MALE'

To visit Hulhumale' take the ferry (Rf5, 20 minutes, every 30 minutes) from the terminal next to the airport ferry jetty and opposite the Maagiri Lodge. On the island a bus service connects the ferry terminal to the settlement, but it's an easy 10-minute walk if there's not one waiting when you arrive.

OTHER ISLANDS

With so many small islands in the Maldives, it's not uncommon for individual islands to be allocated to specific activities or uses. One example is **Funadhoo**, between the airport and Male', which is used for fuel storage – it's a safe distance from inhabited areas, and convenient for both seagoing tankers and smaller boats serving the atolls.

One of the fastest-growing islands in the country, west of Viligli, is **Thilafushi**, also known as 'Rubbish Island'. It's where the capital dumps its garbage. The land is earmarked for industrial development, and its three conspicuous, round towers are part of a cement factory. It's perfectly possible to visit Thilafushi, though you'll need to hire a launch or get a lift there – a cruise around its post-apocalyptic rubbish mountains is a sobering flipside to more conventional images of the country. While the truly ghastly part is the south part of the island, the north part is a small township of migrant workers tending various industrial plants – you're free to wander about if you can get here.

The island of **Dhoonidhoo**, just north of Male', was the British governor's residence until 1964. The house was used during the Gayoom era for detaining political prisoners, all of whom have now been set free.

Slightly further north, **Aarah** is a small island that was used as the president's holiday retreat during the Gayoom era. President Nasheed has insisted that he will not use it as such, and various ideas have been put forward for Aarah's future, including its use as a writers' retreat.

Another 3km further north, the island of **Kudabandos** was saved from resort development and became the Kuda Bandos Reserve, to be preserved in its natural state for the people's enjoyment. It has a few facilities for day-trippers, but is otherwise undeveloped – a small island encircled by a white beach. Tourists come to Kudabandos on 'island-hopping' trips from nearby resorts. Maldivian families and groups come on weekends and holidays. The **Bandos Island Resort's Male' office** (☎ 3325529) arranges a boat most Fridays for local people for about Rf45, including the Rf10 entry fee.

North & South Male' Atolls

At the centre of the country, the two atolls either side of Vaadhoo Kandu are the focal point of Maldivian tourism, where the first resorts cautiously developed in the 1970s. Today they're home to the Maldives' main international airport as well as many of the country's most famous and best-established island resorts.

The lively national capital, Male', the economic and political centre of the country, lies between North and South Male' Atolls, and yet it's hard to imagine anywhere much more pristine than the islands that surround its bustle. The nature of Maldivian geography means that, once you leave the area around the capital and the airport, you're immediately in a desert island paradise, even in the most developed part of the country.

Some excellent dive sites are found on these atolls, despite the coral bleaching caused by El Niño back in the 1990s. Some of the most interesting sites are on either side of Vaadhoo Kandu, the channel that runs between North and South Male' Atolls. At the outer edge of the atolls, the dive sites are accessible from only a few resorts or by safari boat, and you'll probably have them all to yourself. Gaafaru Falhu Atoll, north of North Male' Atoll, has at least three diveable shipwrecks. Some of the Maldives' best surf breaks are also in North Male' Atoll, and this is home to a small, seasonal surfer scene.

North and South Male' Atolls will be where most people experience the Maldives and both atolls are stunning visions of cobalt-blue water, white sand and island idyll – both worthy introductions to this extraordinary paradise.

NORTH MALE' ATOLL

North and South Male' Atolls together are officially known as Kaafu Administrative District. The capital island is **Thulusdhoo**, on the eastern edge of North Male' Atoll, with a population of about 1150. Male' itself is not the capital as it is considered to be its own administrative district.

Thulusdhoo is an industrious island, known for *bodu beru* (big drums), traditional dancing and a government warehouse for salted fish. It is also unique for its Coca-Cola factory, the only one in the world where the drink is made from desalinated water.

The island of **Huraa** (population 850) is visited by tourists on island-hopping trips, but it's not yet as touristy as other North Male' islands. Huraa's dynasty of sultans, founded in 1759 by Sultan Al-Ghaazi Hassan Izzaddeen, built a mosque on the island.

Many tourists visit **Himmafushi** (population 1000) on excursions arranged from nearby resorts. The main street has two long rows of shops, where you can pick up some of the least expensive souvenirs in the country. Carved rosewood manta rays, sharks and dolphins are made locally. If you wander into the back streets, you quickly get away from the tourist strip to find an attractive, well-kept village with many modern amenities, including an attractive cemetery with coral headstones.

A sand spit has joined Himmafushi to the once separate island of **Gaamaadhoo**, where there used to be a prison. The surf break here, aptly called **Jailbreaks**, is a great right-hander, accessible by boat from nearby resorts.

Further north, **Dhiffushi** is one of the most appealing local islands, with approximately 760 people, three mosques and two schools.

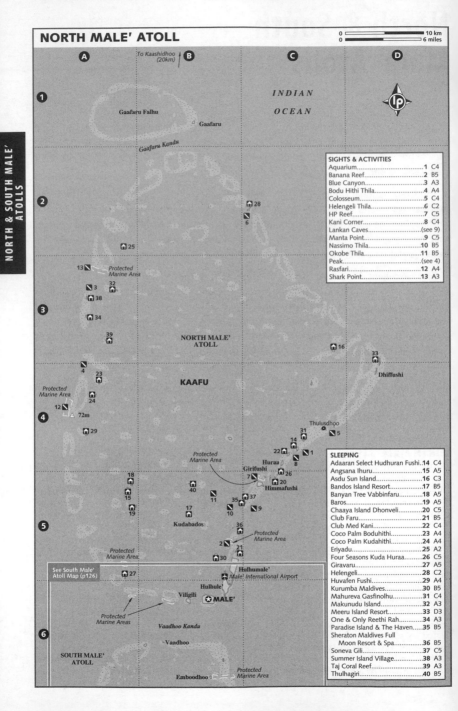

NORTH MALE' ATOLL

| 0 | 10 km |
| 0 | 6 miles |

INDIAN OCEAN

To Kaashidhoo (20km)

Gaafaru Falhu

Gaafaru

Gaafaru Kandu

SIGHTS & ACTIVITIES

Aquarium	1	C4
Banana Reef	2	B5
Blue Canyon	3	A3
Bodu Hithi Thila	4	A4
Colosseum	5	C4
Helengeli Thila	6	C2
HP Reef	7	C5
Kani Corner	8	C4
Lankan Caves	(see 9)	
Manta Point	9	C5
Nassimo Thila	10	B5
Okobe Thila	11	B5
Peak	(see 4)	
Rasfari	12	A4
Shark Point	13	A3

Protected Marine Area

NORTH MALE' ATOLL

KAAFU

Dhiffushi

Protected Marine Area

Thulusdhoo

Protected Marine Area

Huraa

Girifushi

Himmafushi

Kudabados

Protected Marine Area

Protected Marine Area

See South Male' Atoll Map (p126)

Hulhumale'
Male' International Airport

Hulhule'

Viligili

★MALE'

Protected Marine Areas

Vaadhoo Kandu

Vaadhoo

SOUTH MALE' ATOLL

Emboodhoo

Protected Marine Area

SLEEPING

Adaaran Select Hudhuran Fushi	14	C4
Angsana Ihuru	15	A5
Asdu Sun Island	16	C3
Bandos Island Resort	17	B5
Banyan Tree Vabbinfaru	18	A5
Baros	19	A5
Chaaya Island Dhonveli	20	C5
Club Faru	21	B5
Club Med Kani	22	C4
Coco Palm Boduhithi	23	A4
Coco Palm Kudahithi	24	A4
Eriyadu	25	A3
Four Seasons Kuda Huraa	26	C5
Giravaru	27	A5
Helengeli	28	C2
Huvafen Fushi	29	A4
Kurumba Maldives	30	B5
Mahureva Gasfinolhu	31	C4
Makunudu Island	32	A3
Meeru Island Resort	33	D3
One & Only Reethi Rah	34	A3
Paradise Island & The Haven	35	B5
Sheraton Maldives Full Moon Resort & Spa	36	B5
Soneva Gili	37	C5
Summer Island Village	38	A3
Taj Coral Reef	39	A3
Thulhagiri	40	B5

Mainly a fishing island, it has lots of greenery and grows several types of tropical fruit. Tourists from Meeru Island Resort are regular visitors.

Sights & Activities
DIVING

North Male' Atoll has been well explored by divers and has some superb dives. Some are heavily dived, especially in peak seasons. The following is just a sample of the best-known sites, listed from north to south.

Helengeli Thila, also called Bodu Thila, is a long narrow thila on the eastern edge of the atoll famous for its prolific marine life. Reef fish include surgeonfish, bannerfish, butterflyfish and dense schools of snapper and fusilier. Larger fish and pelagics are also common – sharks, tuna, rays and jacks. Soft corals are spectacular in the cliffs and caves on the west side of the thila at about 25m. The large hard coral formations here are recovering from coral bleaching quite quickly, possibly because of the strong, nutrient-rich currents.

Also called Saddle, or Kuda Faru, **Shark Point** is in a Protected Marine Area and is subject to strong currents. Lots of white-tip and grey reef sharks can be seen in the channel between a thila and the reef, along with fusiliers, jackfish, stingrays and some impressive caves.

The alternative, less-picturesque name of **Blue Canyon** is Kuda Thila, which means 'small thila'. A canyon, 25m to 30m deep and lined with soft, blue corals, runs beside the thila. The numerous overhangs make for an exciting dive: this is one for experienced divers.

Bodu Hithi Thila is a prime manta-spotting site from December to March, with a good number of sharks and many reef fish. The soft corals on the sides of the thila are in excellent condition. If currents are moderate, this site is suitable for intermediate divers, and the shallow waters atop the thila offer superb snorkelling. Nearby, the **Peak** is another great place to see mantas in season; it is also home to some large Napoleon wrasse.

The outer-reef slope of **Rasfari** drops down to a depth of more than 40m, but a couple of thilas rise up with their tops at about 25m. Grey reef sharks love it here – you might see 20 or 30 of them, as well as white-tip sharks, barracuda, eagle rays and trevally. It's a Protected Marine Area.

A curving cliff near a channel entrance forms the **Colosseum**, where pelagics do the performing. Sharks and barracuda are often seen here. Experienced divers do this as a drift dive, going right into the channel past ledges and caves, with soft corals and the occasional turtle. Even beginners can do this one in good conditions.

As the name suggests, **Aquarium** (a coral rock formation about 15m down) features a large variety of reef fish. A sandy bottom at 25m can have small sharks and rays, and you might also see giant wrasse and schools of snapper. It's an easy dive and suitable for snorkelling.

Across the kandu from the Aquarium, **Kani Corner** is the start of a long drift dive through a narrow channel with steep sides, past caves and overhangs decorated with soft corals. Lots of large marine life can be seen, including sharks, barracuda, Napoleon wrasse and tuna. Beware of fast currents.

HP Reef, also called Rainbow Reef or Girifushi Thila, sits beside a narrow channel where currents provide much nourishment for incredibly rich growths of soft, blue corals, and support a large variety of reef fish and pelagics. The formations include large blocks, spectacular caves and a 25m vertical, swim-through chimney. It is a Protected Marine Area.

Also called Barracuda Giri, the attraction of **Okobe Thila** is the variety of spectacular reef fish that inhabit the shallow caves and crannies, including lionfish, scorpionfish, batfish, sweetlips, moray eels, sharks and big Napoleon wrasse.

The demanding dive at **Nassimo Thila** follows the north side of a fine thila, also known as Paradise Rock, which has superb gorgonians and sea fans on coral blocks, cliffs and overhangs. Numerous large fish frequent this site.

The best time to see the mantas for which **Manta Point** is famous is from May to November. Coral outcrops at about 8m are a 'cleaning station', where cleaner wrasse feed on parasites from the mantas' wings. Cliffs, coral tables, turtles, sharks and numerous reef fish are other attractions, as are the nearby **Lankan Caves**.

The Protected Marine Area of **Banana Reef** has a bit of everything: dramatic cliffs, caves and overhangs; brilliant coral growths; big predators such as sharks, barracuda and groper; and prolific reef fish including jackfish, morays, Napoleon wrasse and blue-striped snapper. It was one of the first dive sites in the country to become internationally known. The reef top is excellent for snorkelling.

Resorts

Most of the resorts in North Male' Atoll are reached by speedboat from the airport, though some of the more distant and smarter ones also offer transfers by seaplane. Unless otherwise noted, airport transfers to the following resorts are by speedboat.

BUDGET

Giravaru (Giraavaru island; ☎ 6640440; www.giravaru. com; s/d US$145/175; airport transfer 15min, US$50; 65 rooms; ✖ ▢ ▣) is a cheap and cheerful diving resort that has been threatening to close and renovate itself for some years now, but it still showed no sign of doing so at last visit. And to be honest, that's something of a relief, as cheap and cheerful resorts seem to be going the way of the dodo in the Maldives.

Giravaru has an unusual history – the Giravaru people are believed to descend from the earliest inhabitants of the Maldives, and as such they are ethnically distinct from the rest of the population. About 30 years ago the number of people on the island had declined to the point where they no longer included the 40 adult males required to support a mosque, so the islanders all moved

to Male' and Giravaru became available for resort development. Sadly, there's nothing left of the aboriginal Giravaran culture on the island.

The diving school here is excellent and extremely friendly, with plenty of good diving sites nearby. Yet the whole place remains pretty average otherwise – particularly suffering from its proximity to Thilafushi (or Rubbish Island as it's known to one and all), meaning that your desert island idyll can be slightly spoiled by the odd plastic bag washing up on the beach. The tiny swimming pool is also in a state of bad repair. Lunch and breakfast are somewhat lacklustre, although there's often a good choice at the big dinner buffet. The majority Italian guests seem entirely happy with the experience, however, perhaps preferring to concentrate on the fantastic diving and cheap evening drinks in the bar. Rooms are simple but comfortable units spread around the island in small clusters, all with private bathroom and air-conditioning.

Small, intimate and low-key, **Thulhagiri** (Thalhaagiri island; ☎ 6645930; www.thulhagiri.com.mv; s/d/wb US$175/200/350; airport transfer 30min, US$90; 69 rooms; ✖ ▢ ▣) is as laid back as it is pretty. Its wide, sloping white beaches and a thick vegetation of palms greet you as you arrive at its small jetty, beyond which a new row of water villas was nearing completion on our most recent visit (the second set on the island, and testament to their great popularity). The resort itself is very rustic, with a charming open-air reception area and other nice touches including a lily pond

---

HOW TO SPOT A FASHIONABLE RESORT

In case you have any doubts about where you're staying, this checklist should help you confirm you're in the very smartest of Maldivian resorts:

■ You will not be given a fruit cocktail on arrival, but an iced ginger tea, home-made ice cream or fresh melon juice, served in dainty earthenware cups.

■ Infinity pools all the way, and preferably your own lap pool so you don't have to mix with the hoi polloi in the main one.

■ No glass floors in water villas – you should have your own sea garden or at least a staircase into the sea from your veranda.

■ You have more towels than you know what to do with in your room, and more brand-name bath products than you can actually be bothered to steal.

■ Staff members you have never even seen magically address you by your first name.

■ Every time you leave your room a fleet of staff will swarm in to clean it.

among the dense foliage. Thulhagiri represents a great choice for its price range, because although it's less expensive, its small size gives it a more exclusive feel than some of the bigger budget places.

The diving school offers a full programme of courses, and individual dives at US$46 each, plus equipment. The problem here is that each piece of equipment you borrow is charged separately and therefore quickly adds up – so if you want to do a lot of diving here, bring as many of the basics as possible. There's a good water sports centre with catamarans and waterskiing available although the small, rather murky swimming pool is the only real evidence that this is a budget resort. Rooms are in a rustic style, featuring thatched roofs and wooden interiors. The older 17 water villas have four-poster beds, colourful fabrics and coffee-making facilities – they're decent, but not especially great value at their high-season price. All meals are buffets, and they're very good for a resort in this range.

Primarily favoured by Italian divers, delightfully laid-back **Asdu Sun Island** (Asdhoo island; ☎ 6645051, 7779480; www.asdu.com; s/d full board US$180/240; airport transfer 1½hr, US$150; 30 rooms; 🖳) is about as far away from the luxury super resorts as can be imagined. All the staff on the island are members of owner Ahmed's family, whose quarters are not hidden but enjoy equal status on the island to those of the guests. Chickens run around freely and reception's own computer is yours to use for checking your email.

The tiny island itself is thickly forested and with a stunning white beach around much of it, though erosion is a problem on one side. Accommodation is in two- and three-unit white-painted concrete huts, all terribly simple and rather worn, free of air-con, TV and glass windows, but clean. The **Submaldive diving school** (www.submaldive.com) offers comprehensive daily excursions and courses at reasonable rates, with full diving equipment available for US$25 per day.

Helengeli (Helengeli island; ☎ 6644615; www.helengeli.net; s/d/tr US$185/210/280; airport transfer by speedboat 1hr, US$180, by seaplane 15min, US$230; 50 rooms; 🖳🖳 🛜 🖳), one of the most laid-back resorts, is paradise for divers. It's a totally out-of-the-way gem at the top of North Male' Atoll from where around 40 dive sites are accessible, used almost exclusively by

Helengeli guests and the occasional passing safari boat. It's a European diving resort through and through, with 85% of the guests from Switzerland, and the remainder from Germany, Austria and the UK.

Accommodation is in two-room blocks, which are simple, clean and pleasant, all with air-con, minibar, safe and outdoor bathrooms. Despite a 'soft' renovation in 2004, the rooms are far from luxury, but absolutely fine. The public areas have sand floors throughout, so this is a place you can leave your shoes in your luggage. The focus of the resort is on the swimming pool and bar-restaurant area, where all meals are served up as buffets.

The 2km-long house reef is excellent, so you need not venture far for snorkelling either, and qualified divers can do unguided scuba dives from the beach. Nearby Helengeli Thila is considered one of the best dive sites in the country. Dive costs start at US$46 for a boat dive with tanks and weights, or US$315 for a package of five dives with all equipment provided. An open-water course costs US$698. The **Ocean-Pro dive base** (www.oceanpro-diveteam.com) aims for personalised service and tries to keep guests with the same dive guides for their whole stay.

There's no windsurfing, sailing or other water sports, but a few excursions are offered, including dolphin watching and trips to the inhabited island of Gaafaru nearby. There's also a small spa. Evening entertainment is very low-key, consisting mainly of a few drinks at the delightful beachfront bar, and an early night in preparation for the next day's diving activity. Wireless internet is available for US$15 per 24 hours, while 15 minutes of internet access from the library terminal costs US$5.

ourpick Meeru Island Resort (Meerufenfushi island; ☎ 6643157; www.meeru.com; full board s/d/tr/wb US$185/220/230/380; airport transfer 50min, US$60; 286 rooms; 🖳🖳 🛜 🖳) will have you smitten at first sight – it's a beautiful long, verdant stretch of land with a dazzling white beach. The resort is enormous, the third largest in the country, and offers almost every conceivable activity. Indeed, so large is the resort that for convenience there are two receptions and two buffet restaurants, to avoid guests having to walk too far.

Rooms come in a startling number of categories, from prefab timber-clad self-contained units that are very cosy and sweet to the 87 water villas. The latter range from rustic-style older rooms in bright colours with open-air bathrooms and jacuzzis to newer, sleeker but perhaps less-charming water villas, all in dark wood and with extra luxuries such as espresso machines and direct water access.

All nonmotorised water sports are included here, which makes it a great place for enthusiasts. There are two excellent spas, the newest of which is entirely over water, and two swimming pools. Other amenities include a nine-hole golf course, two tennis courts, a gym and a golf driving range. Even more unusual is the extraordinary blue whale skeleton on display in the middle of the island, and a small and rather neglected museum of Maldivian history and traditions above the barn-like main reception.

Meerufenfushi actually means 'Sweet Water Island' in Dhivehi, and the island's wells were used to replenish passing dhonis in the past. The unusual retention of ground water here has created a large amount of natural vegetation and now some of the 28-hectare island is used for growing fruit and vegetables. Most guests are from Britain, Germany, France, Italy and other parts of Europe. There's a massive range of activities and excursions, and the evenings can be lively in the various bars, as many guests are on all-inclusive packages.

The house reef can only be reached by boat and these leave every two hours to take snorkellers and divers off to the outer reef, where the aquatic life is fantastic. All the usual water sports are offered, fishing trips are popular and the vast lagoon is perfect for learning sailing and windsurfing. Meeru has its own safari boats, and two- or three-day cruises can be taken from the resort. Inexpensive excursions go to the fishing village on neighbouring Dhiffushi.

Ocean-Pro (www.oceanpro-diveteam.com) is the large diving centre. Diving quickly adds up here, however; while a single dive is US$46 with tank and weights only, or US$63 including full equipment rental, there's a boat charge of US$17/29/34 for one/two/three boat trips. An open-water course costs US$698. A whole slew of great dive sites are accessible in the channels within 5km.

Overall, Meeru gets great reviews from guests. It caters to a wide variety of interests and budget levels – it's a big resort but it's not crowded and has retained its personal, friendly feel.

Summer Island Village (Ziyaaraifushi island; ☎ 6641949; www.summerislandvillage.com; s/d/tr/wb all-inclusive US$200/280/350/346; airport transfer by dhoni 1½hr, US$120; 118 rooms; ✷ ▣) is a long, thin island that's all about affordable fun. It's popular with repeat visitors from Germany and Britain who enjoy the laid-back approach and profit from the good-value, all-inclusive packages. The management's efforts to increase the vegetation and wildlife on the island have paid off and the vegetation was looking much healthier on our last visit than it did on our previous one.

Accommodation is a little spartan but clean and adequate, all rooms being on the beach and all having an extra bed and a spacious outdoor bathroom. The units are tightly packed together, and some rooms are in two-storey units. The modern-style water bungalows at the island's southern end are a recent addition and they're nothing fancy, with no direct access to the water and just a small hole in the floor looking into the sea, but they're bigger and more comfortable than the standard rooms.

Sand floors in the public areas and friendly staff give the whole place a relaxed feel. Meals are buffets with a modest selection of curry, fish, salads and vegetables. Weekly theme nights feature Asian and international cuisine.

The lagoon is wide and shallow, so the resort is more suited to windsurfing, waterskiing and sailing than to snorkelling or swimming. The island has quite good beaches on both sides, though some stretches are protected by somewhat unattractive breakwaters.

There are some great dive sites within about 5km – the **Diverland dive centre** offers a single dive with equipment for US$55 or an excellent deal on ten dives starting at just US$400 including tanks and weights; an open-water course costs US$495. A daily snorkelling trip is included in the package (excluding equipment), as are table tennis, volleyball and badminton. There's also the Serena Spa.

A decent, economical choice and rightly popular with divers.

Just beyond the Male' overflow island of Hulhumale', **Club Faru** (Farukolufushi island; ☎ 6640553; www.clubfaru.com; all-inclusive s/d

US$205/230; airport transfer 20min, US$35; 152 rooms; (icons) is the latest incarnation of an island that was a Club Med until its lease expired in 2005. The island will eventually become part of the Hulhumale' development (see p109) and will be closed at some point before then to allow for building and redevelopment work that will turn it from a resort into a residential island. Until that day comes though, Club Faru remains an all-inclusive resort and the rooms are basic but modern, all housed in two-storey blocks, not making it ideal for peace and quiet or privacy. There's a large pool, excellent beaches and plenty of activities ranging from a dive school to water sports and animation.

Located right at the top of North Male' Atoll, **Eriyadu** (Eriyadhoo island; ☎ 6644487; www.eriyadumaldives.com; half board s/d/tr US$200/290/455; airport transfer 50min, US$110; 60 rooms; (icons)) is pleasantly remote, which is a major incentive for divers who come here for the uncrowded waters that surround the resort. It's also wonderfully laid back without the fussy over-attentive service that characterises so many Maldivian resorts.

The island is full of repeat visitors – the vast majority of whom are German. Children aren't really encouraged as there are no facilities tailored to them, and this leads to a very quiet and undisturbed atmosphere.

The island is an oval shape, which even more than its counterparts appears to be slowly disappearing into the sea. Erosion is a big problem here, but the beaches are still attractive, with a beautiful sandbank sometimes created by the changing current. There's a good reef, great for snorkelling, with turtles and dolphins regular fixtures just metres from the beach. There's no pool but there is a spa.

The **Euro-Divers** (www.eurodivers.com) dive centre offers a single lagoon dive for US$50, while a six-day no-limit dive package will cost US$414 – making it a great deal. An open-water course is equally great value at US$375.

The rooms are divided into two categories – most are in two-room units on the beach, each with its own sea-facing patio, though views can be blocked by the island's mature foliage. The six cheaper rooms (euphemistically called 'garden villas') are in a two-storey block set back from the beach.

Rooms have polished timber floors, TV and minibar. The island itself is quite heavily developed, but the buildings are interspersed with lots of shady trees and shrubbery. The sand-floor restaurant serves most meals in buffet style, with a varied selection of European dishes, curries and seafood.

The usual water sports and excursions are available, as is some low key evening entertainment, but this resort is mainly for diving, snorkelling and relaxing on the beach.

It's been a dramatic few years for old-timer **Chaaya Island Dhonveli** (Kanuhuraa island; ☎ 6640055; www.chaayahotels.com; half board s/d/tr/wb US$230/250/350/290; airport transfer 30min, US$75; 145 rooms; (icons)). Following full-scale devastation in the tsunami that saw its water bungalows washed away, the resort was rebuilt and then later became part of the Chaaya group. It's now a well-run and unpretentious resort with plenty to recommend it, including a great pool, its own surf break and tennis courts.

There are six categories of room catering for everyone from honeymooners to groups of surfers who come here in big numbers from June to September. The charming-looking new water villas have thatched roofs and Indian-style carved wood frames, although they are more impressive outside than in, where furnishings are rather garish and cheap. The older water villas that survived the tsunami are a bit poky and similarly garish. Better value are the cheaper rooms on the island itself, which are simple but attractive.

While having some attractive beaches, the island is quite sparse in places, and beach erosion is a real problem, with some unsightly sandbags in sight. Elsewhere, the resort is more attractive, with some banyan trees and thicker foliage around the swimming pool. The beach on the north side of the island is great for swimming and sunbathing, as well as being safe for children. All meals are buffet style and feature a fair selection of good-quality food. Dhonveli is not a big diving destination, but there are lots of good dive sites nearby (the Protected Marine Area at HP Reef is very close).

Diving is done through **Albatros Top Diving** (www.albatrostopdiving.com), where dives start at US$55 without equipment and boat fees and an open-water course costs US$592. Surfers, who come here in the summer to enjoy the island's private surf break, a consistent left-hander called Pasta Point, are well catered for too, with board hire for US$100 per four-day period. All in all, there's a lot going for Dhonveli, as it offers a good standard of service and facilities for the price.

Paradise Island (Lankanfinolhu island; ☎ 6640011; www.villahotels.com; half board s/d/tr/wb US$232/240/324/700; airport transfer 20min, US$50; 322 rooms; ⊠ 🖥 🛜 🛋) is one of the Maldives' biggest resorts, and offers some great deals for people seeking a huge range of facilities and services and at a bargain price. The beaches are gorgeous and the whole place is well run and friendly, though the atmosphere is hardly intimate. Extras from diving to drinking add up quickly here, so be careful if your package price sounds too good to be true.

Paradise has recently expanded, building the Haven, a luxury resort within a resort, which aims to satisfy the apparently limitless appetite for water villas, though given its prices are comparable to other more intimate, less mass-market resorts, its appeal is rather limited.

Rooms in Paradise proper are simple, with white tiles, white walls, air-con and satellite TV. They are absolutely fine, but unlikely to be places you'll want to spend much time. By contrast, the 62 brand-new rooms in the Haven come in four categories. They are very sleek, stylish and rather minimalist, the higher categories coming with enormous slate pools and all having large sun terraces with direct access to the water.

Packages with meals at the resort are definitely worth it: you get a decent buffet for every meal and the other three restaurants are nothing to shout about so you won't find yourself wanting to eat elsewhere that much. Guests staying at the Haven have two restaurants for their exclusive use.

The island is well landscaped and has good beaches and a swimming pool. Some rooms are a long way from the restaurant, and some don't have much of a view. Activities include gym, squash, badminton, tennis and billiards, all at extra cost, while darts and table tennis are free. There's a huge spa here too. Snorkelling is excellent in the lagoon and on the house reef, which is full of fascinating marine life. The **Delphis dive**

centre (www.delphisdiving.com) is very friendly but not the cheapest around, charging a US$20 boat fee per trip. However, there are plenty of excellent diving sites nearby and the resort's location is unquestionably one of its highlights.

One of the largest resorts in the country, **Bandos Island Resort** (Bodubados island; ☎ 6640088; www.bandosmaldives.com; s/d/tr/wb US$241/302/383/900; airport transfer 20min, US$70; 225 rooms; ⊠ 🖥 🛜 🛋 🛞) has developed and expanded enormously since it opened as the second resort in the Maldives in 1972. It has an enviable range of facilities – a 500-seat conference centre, coffee shop, several restaurants, a disco, tennis courts, a billiard room, sauna, gym, swimming pool, beauty salon and spa-massage service. The child-care centre is free during the day, and babysitters are only US$8 per hour in the evening, so in general the resort is very child-friendly. With all these facilities, the island is quite intensely developed and resembles a well-manicured town centre rather than a typical tropical island. Many visitors love it just for that reason, though you may be disappointed if you're yearning to get away from it all.

Sailing and windsurfing are available, along with a full range of motorised water sports and an active big-game fishing centre. Fine, narrow beaches surround the island, and the house reef is handy for snorkelling and diving. Lots of fish and a small wreck can be seen here. The state-of-the-art dive centre does trips to about 40 dive sites in the area, and offers a full range of courses, including nitrox and rebreather training. A single boat dive costs US$70, including all equipment and boat charges, or US$55 with your own equipment. The diving health clinic here has a decompression chamber. An open-water course costs US$564.

Bandos caters for evening visitors and day-trippers from Male', but currently does not provide a regular boat – call the resort if you want to arrange something. Airline crews and travel agents often use Bandos for short-term stays, as well as guests from all over Europe and Asia, so there can be a very mixed group here.

Rooms are modern, with red-tiled roofs, white-tiled floors, air-con, hairdryer, minibar and phone. Other categories include the Jacuzzi Beach Villa and the luxurious Water Villas that include services such as a private butler, although they're a lot more expensive.

The main Gallery Restaurant does three international buffet meals daily. Other eateries include a fine-dining restaurant, the 24-hour Seabreeze Café for à la carte pasta and curries, and the Harbour Grill for steak and seafood. The Sand Bar hosts live bands, disco nights, cultural shows or karaoke several nights a week. This is one of the liveliest resorts in the country. Bandos is great for families and those who like big resorts where there's potential to meet lots of new people and to have a huge range of activities available. For a romantic break you might want to look elsewhere, though.

MIDRANGE

Adaaran Select Hudhuran Fushi (Lohifushi island; ☎ 6641930; www.hudhuranfushimaldives.com; s/d/tr US$256/320/432; airport transfer 25min, US$100; 158 rooms; ✶ ▣ ☎ ☒ ⅍) is a good choice for a family holiday where activities are laid on in bucket loads. Remodelled from its previous incarnation as Lohifushi by the Sri Lankan Adaaran group, this large and high-quality resort is centred on a huge hangar-like reception surrounded by restaurants, bars and a great pool. The rooms are bright and tasteful with a rustic feel, despite being full of mod cons and featuring outdoor showers in the higher categories.

The island is one of the best places for an active water sports holiday. As well as the usual sailing, windsurfing and waterskiing, there's a very surfable left-hand wave called Lohi's off the southeast corner of the island, overlooked by a surfers' bar and viewing deck. Other breaks are accessible by boat on paid excursions.

Also on the island, and effectively a resort within a resort, is Ocean Villas, the new water villa category on one side of the island. Villas are very stylishly appointed and designed in a sleek, minimalist Japanese style with private sun decks and espresso makers in each, not to mention an à la carte restaurant exclusively for Ocean Villa guests.

Plenty of good dive sites are accessible, and the resort is quite popular with divers who are catered for by the five-star PADI dive centre. Other draws include the Coconut Spa, a children's playground and a large selection of restaurants.

People who like Club Med tend to love Club Med – and the couples and families at **Club Med Kani** (Kanifinolhu island; ☎ 6643152; www.clubmed.com; all-inclusive s/d US$260/290; airport transfer 30min, US$50; 225 rooms; ✶ ▣ ☎), the only Club Med resort in the Maldives, seem to love every minute of it. You pretty much have to come through a Club Med package to stay here, as FIT (fully independent traveller) reservations aren't even accepted until 24 hours before arrival. French guests make up half of the resort's guests at any time, while Italians are the second biggest group.

The resort is large and well set up for activities, with a big pool, diving school and water sports centre, not to mention the nightly live entertainment and disco, which make it one of the livelier resorts in the country.

There are three room categories – the beachfront rooms cost a little more than garden rooms, and water bungalows are pricier still. They're all comfortably furnished and feature lots of natural timber, air con, a phone and minibar. The meals are very good with accompanying wine, beer or soft drinks included in the package price. Drinks at the bar cost extra.

The island itself is quite large and well vegetated, and the beachside bar and entertainment areas are particularly spacious. The wide lagoon is a good place to learn sailing or windsurfing (both included in the price), but not as good for snorkelling (though snorkelling trips to other reefs are also included). Fitness sessions, one daily scuba dive, volleyball and other games and activities are all included, but you pay extra for excursions and spa treatments.

our pick **Makunudu Island** (Makunudhoo island; ☎ 6646464; www.makunudu.com; half board s/d US$402/473; airport transfer 50min, US$170; 36 rooms; ✶) is wonderful, and one of our very favourite resorts in the country. Just 2.4 hectares in area, the tiny island almost looks like it might sink under the sheer weight of lush vegetation on it – and the surrounding reef is so big that it's hard for unaccustomed speedboats to find their way into the dock through the shallow lagoon.

Things are extremely tasteful here, but almost unbelievably low-key as well, with individual thatched-roof bungalows hidden among the jungle-like foliage. All rooms face the beach and feature natural finishes, varnished timber, textured white walls, open-air bathrooms, and all facilities except the purposefully excluded TV. The service is of a high standard and the food is excellent. Breakfast and lunch are buffets, while most dinners are a choice of thoughtfully prepared set menus, served in the delightful open-sided restaurant. Beach barbecues are a weekly event.

Guests are mainly German, British, French and Italian couples who come to relax, or who are on their honeymoon. Honeymooners from all over the world have planted the island with memorial trees with plaques. This has become too popular, though, and the management has had to stop the practice due to a huge proliferation of trees growing everywhere.

There are excellent dive sites in the area, the house reef is great for snorkelling, and an introductory dive is free with the small diving school. Dive groups tend to be small and friendly. Windsurfing and sailing are free, as are shorter excursions. If you want a small, exclusive, natural-style resort, Makunudu is one of the very best in the Maldives.

Established in 1972, **Kurumba Maldives** (Vihamanaafushi island; ☎ 6642324; www.kurumba.com; s/d/tr US$420/430/550; airport transfer 15min, US$78; 180 rooms; ✱ ▭ ⚲ ⚑ ⚱) was the first resort in the country. It was completely refurbished in 2003 and reopened as a very high-quality place with a relative sense of history. Some may feel its overly manicured gardens and foliage as well as its relentlessly modern architecture combine to make the resort feel a little sterile; others, however, will like its grand country-club style – golf buggies rule the roads here and the resort is big enough for this to be justifiable.

Kurumba is the closest resort to Male', and as such it regularly caters for business conferences and conventions as well as daytrippers from the capital who come for the renowned restaurants. If you're sensitive to aircraft noise, you may find it a little too close to the airport, although Male' International is hardly Heathrow or JFK.

The rooms come in a large range of categories, the pool villas being especially impressive, each with its own pool in a private back garden. For those wanting to splurge there are presidential villas and the Royal Kurumba Residence, which should satisfy even the most demanding international jet-setters.

There's no end to the facilities available, from a huge and well-equipped dive school (US$57 per dive with all equipment) to a water sports centre offering every conceivable discipline, tennis courts, babysitters, a gorgeous spa, two gyms, two pools and an incredible seven restaurants. Kurumba is a place for scale and grandeur rather than a desert island hideaway, but it remains a popular choice for both couples and families.

Magnificently laid out with real style and class, **Sheraton Maldives Full Moon Resort & Spa** (Furanafushi island; ☎ 6642010; www.fullmoonmaldives.com; r/wb US$485/785; airport transfer 20min, US$60; 156 rooms; ✱ ▭ ⚲ ⚑) has the ambience of an upmarket country club rather than a remote tropical island. This is in part due to its proximity to the capital, but everything here is clearly aimed at the urbane sophisticate, from the gorgeously understated public areas to the luxurious spa, housed on its own island linked to the resort by a footbridge.

Recently taken over by the Sheraton group as its first Maldives property, this place continues to offer midrange luxury in its 52 water villas and its standard beachfront deluxe rooms, all of which feature thatched roofs, shuttered windows and private gardens or terraces.

The Thai restaurant, Mediterranean restaurant and the Italian grill/pizza place serve more interesting food than the buffets at the main restaurant, so it might be best to take a bed-and-breakfast package and bring extra cash to spend in the speciality restaurants, although this will be more expensive, of course.

A full range of facilities is squeezed onto this small island, including an inviting swimming pool that has its own waterfall, tennis courts, a gym, a gorgeous spa and a business centre. There are no motorised water sports, and the lagoon is unsuitable for snorkelling. The efficient dive centre charges about US$72 for a boat dive with all equipment, and a very reasonable US$475 for a complete open-water course. Windsurfing and sailing are available, as is big-game fishing. Full Moon is a great choice for an upscale break.

TOP END

Understated, sophisticated class jumps out at you from the moment you arrive at **Baros** (Baros island; ☎ 6642672; www.baros.com; r/wb US$560/775; airport transfer 30min, US$110; 75 rooms; ✖ 🖳 ☏), the jewel in the crown of Universal Resorts, one of the country's largest resort groups. Refitted in 2005, Baros reopened as a magnificently rejuvenated place the same year and is a classic luxury resort at surprisingly decent prices.

The centrepiece of the resort is the impressive Lighthouse Restaurant, a white circus top-style fine-dining and cocktail bar establishment, which has the feel of an exclusive yacht club. Other dining can be had at the far less formal Cayenne Grill overlooking the reef, where you can have your food cooked any way you choose by the fleet of chefs. All guests are on a bed-and-breakfast basis, allowing them to enjoy the variety of eating opportunities throughout their stay (although this does add up quickly).

The atmosphere is intimate and quiet, with children under six not allowed – this is upmarket European honeymoon territory through and through. There's 'gentle' jazz and Maldivian music three times a week, and that's about the scope of the nightlife. During the day most people seem to be enjoying diving, swimming and treatments in the luxurious spa. The three room categories are all beautiful. Even the standard 'luxe villa' is a 95 sq metre work of gorgeous refinement with a sumptuous outdoor bathroom, while the water bungalows are proper holiday-of-a-lifetime stuff.

Baros is one of many upmarket resorts that has made a conscious decision not to have a swimming pool. This is a superb resort that has rightly earned a huge following of loyal visitors and is a great choice for a luxurious romantic getaway.

Angsana Ihuru (Ihuru island; ☎ 6643502; www.angsana.com; full board r US$800; airport transfer 30min, US$120; 45 rooms; ✖ 🖳 ☏) is just across the water from its sister resort Banyan Tree, and characterises itself with an innovative management team who combine luxury with thought.

With its canopy of palm trees and surrounding a gorgeous white beach, Angsana conforms exactly to the tropical-island stereotype and often features in photographs publicising the Maldives. The house reef forms a near-perfect circle around the island, brilliant for snorkelling and shore dives. Look near the jetty for the 'barnacle', the oldest of several metal structures on which a small electric current stimulates coral growth.

All nonmotorised water sports are free, including all snorkelling equipment. The best dive sites are some distance away on the edges of the atoll, but boats take divers out morning and afternoon costing US$65/75 for a dive without/with equipment.

The stylish rooms are decorated in contemporary style, with black furniture, lime-green fabrics and designer bathrooms. There's a modern look in the restaurant too, but most guests prefer to eat dinner on the deck overlooking the sea. The luxurious spa consists of eight treatment rooms, almost all doubles. Angsana offers a very Banyan Tree mix of cuisine, comfort and indulgence, but it's somewhat more relaxed and informal.

The smaller of the two Four Seasons properties in the Maldives, **Four Seasons Kuda Huraa** (Kuda Huraa island; ☎ 6644800; www.fourseasons.com; r/wb from US$850/1200; airport transfer 25min, US$220; 96 rooms; ✖ ⚓ 🖳 ☏ 🖳) is also the more intimate and laid back. The style here is apparently that of a Maldivian village, although you'd be hard pressed to find many Maldivians living in this amount of luxury!

The charming rooms range from the beach bungalows with their quaint brick walls and high thatched roofs to the glamorous water villas on the far side of the resort. The furnishings combine tropical luxury with modern design and are sleek and attractive. All categories of rooms have private plunge pools, save the water villas.

The beaches on the island are lovely and there's an enormous curved infinity pool around which the main restaurant is curled. There's always something going on here, and there's the feel of glamorous country club about the place.

The most unique feature of the gorgeous and well-run spa is its location on a smaller island a short boat ride across the lagoon. The trip is done on a mini-dhoni that goes back and forth whenever guests want to get there. A kids club and a teens club are both free and make this a great option for a family holiday. Wi-fi on the island is charged, but there is a terminal in the library that can be used for free by guests. All nonmotorised water sports are free, and the gym is excellent. The dive school rates start at US$100 for a dive with tanks and weights, while an open-water course comes in at US$895 – all as luxurious as you'd expect at a Four Seasons resort.

The island itself is long and very attractive, and the nearby inhabited island of Bodhu Huraa is a short hop away by boat, and is popular with guests for its large number of craft workshops where souvenirs can be bought.

Four Seasons Kuda Huraa is a glamorous and stylish place with exceptionally friendly staff and a laid-back approach to luxury. It has a very different feel to its grander sister island Landaa Giravaru (see p152), and is often combined with it on a two-centre holiday.

Rejuvenated in a post-tsunami refit, **Coco Palm Boduhithi** (Boduhithi island; ☎ 3345555; www .cococollection.com.mv; s/d/wb US$997/1052/1144; airport transfer 40min, US$180; 100 rooms; ✖ ▢ ☎ ▣ ♨) is now right up there with the big names of the Maldivian luxury market. A large resort, Boduhithi nevertheless makes all its guests feel special, whether it be through the gorgeous rooms, the stylish public areas or the helpful staff.

The rooms come in several different categories. The island villas are sublimely stylish, with a big bathtub central to the room and lots of designer-fabulous touches. The top categories are the Escape villas and residences, a mini resort-within-a-resort found on their own private over-water pier. These are gorgeously sleek, with huge windows onto the sea, private lap pools and enormous bathrooms stuffed with Molton Brown goodies. Escape guests also have their own buggy service anywhere on the island.

The rest of the island pretty much manages to tick every box – there are five superb restaurants, a magnificent wine collection, a water sports centre offering everything from wakeboarding to windsurfing, a top-notch dive school with easy access to a host of excellent sites, a large and beautiful spa, free wi-fi, great beaches and one of the most interesting pools in the Maldives (an infinity pool with glass sides in front of the main restaurant). No wonder this is one of the top resorts in the Maldives today.

Along with its new look comes a very progressive environmental policy – Coco Palm plans to be the first carbon neutral resort in the country and offers excellent educational activities through its marine biology department.

The rightly popular **Banyan Tree Vabbinfaru** (Vabbinfaru island; ☎ 6643147; www.banyantree .com; full board r US$1250; airport transfer 25min, US$120; 48 rooms; ✖ ▢) is a wonderful mix of outright luxury and ecotourism project. Part of the international Banyan Tree chain, it's actually about as un-chainlike as can be imagined. Remote enough from Male' to feel like the true desert island experience, Banyan Tree offers a refreshing take on the top-end experience given that it doesn't have many of the features (such as a swimming pool) that many resorts would take for granted. This is intentional and ties in with the overall guiding policy that tourism must be sustainable and eco-friendly.

This is a romantic resort, extremely quiet and popular with couples. Its most unique feature is the marine laboratory on the island, run by a charming team of marine biologists. Guests are able to help out in various capacities – from planting their own coral in the coral garden, helping with reef cleans and even monitoring the sharks and turtles kept under observation in cages just off the island shore. All of these activities are free and marine biology lessons are given twice a week to any guest whose interest in the sea has suddenly been piqued.

The rooms are similarly unique, with the use of lots of wood imported from Indonesia; they have a gorgeous feel with terrific and unusual outdoor bathrooms.

The house reef is excellent for snorkelling and diving, but the very best dive sites are some distance away on the edges of the atoll. A single boat dive is US$75 with all equipment (packages are much cheaper).

Guests come from all over Europe and Asia, and the superb buffet meals cater to all tastes. The restaurant and bar are both casually elegant, open-sided spaces with sand floors and quality furniture.

This was one of the first resorts to have a spa, and it's one of the best in the country, with Thai-trained therapists offering everything from a turmeric and honey body cleanser to a Hawaiian Lomi Lomi for two. For the more active, night fishing, windsurfing, sailing and snorkelling are included in the price.

Angsana, Banyan Tree's 'little sister' resort, is just across a small channel next door – a boat goes back and forth every half-hour, allowing guests at each resort to enjoy the other's facilities.

ourpick One & Only Reethi Rah (Medhufinolhu island; ☎ 6648800; www.oneandonlyresorts.com; r/wb from US$1250/1800; airport transfer by luxury yacht 50min, $165, by seaplane 10min, price varies; 130 rooms; 🍴 🖥 🏊) is still a king of the Maldivian resorts. There may be plenty of resorts that cost more, but none have surpassed this extraordinary place, which remains the most famous and gossiped about in the country.

Reethi Rah is about glamour and style, and shamelessly so. If you aren't comfortable with almost mind-boggling pampering and fly anything other than first class, this probably isn't the place for you. Rooms have every possible convenience, and are some of the most enormous in the country, with vast high ceilings and beautifully furnished in a modern style that picks and mixes different Asian designs. Some have their own pools.

The most controversial thing about Reethi Rah is also one of its biggest draws – the island is largely manmade, which means there's an unusual number of beaches, all in perfect crescents around the island. From its original 15.8 hectares, the island now stands at an incredible (for the Maldives, at least) 44 hectares. Most impressively of all, it's impossible to tell that this is land reclamation as it has been done so beautifully.

All guests get around by bicycle, although those unable to ride can call club cars from reception to take them around – the island is too large to be covered comfortably on foot. Other unique features include a charming canal that was built for the sea to flow through the island (a unique example of this in the Maldives), a sumptuous lap pool built out over the ocean and a reception like a Balinese palace. Vegetation has improved vastly since our first visit – with 16,000 trees and two million plants planted since One & Only took over the resort from a low-budget, far smaller one.

There are three superb restaurants: the main one, Reethi Restaurant; a chic Japa-

nese restaurant, Tapasake; and perhaps the most magical, the open-air Fanditha, at the northern tip of the island, an informal Middle Eastern-style restaurant where meals are served on the beach.

The huge ESPA-run spa focuses on Asian treatments, including Balinese and Thai massage. Other attractions include two tennis courts and a pro tennis trainer, a superb diving school and a full water sports programme. Guests from Germany, the UK, Russia and Japan predominate, many of whom are honeymooners.

Book as far in advance as you can; it can be impossible to get a room at short notice. Reethi Rah remains the most talked about resort in the Maldives, not least as it's alleged behind-the-scenes shenanigans are subject of a popular holiday paperback called *Beach Babylon* (see p16) – set in a place easily recognisable as Reethi Rah.

Soneva Gili (Lankanfushi island; ☎ 6640304; www.sixsenses.com; wb US$1352; airport transfer 20min, US$150; 45 rooms; 🍴 🖥 🏊) is essentially Swiss Family Robinson meets *Condé Nast Traveller* and we're smitten. Where to begin? All villas (for there are no mere rooms here) are over water, ranging from the standard Villa Suite, which has three rooms as well as a sea garden, a sun deck and bed on the roof for stargazing, to the incredible Private Reserve, a free-standing lagoon complex sleeping nine people in the lap of luxury a short boat ride from the main island.

All the buildings are made from natural materials – wood imported from elsewhere in Asia is the main material used – and all villas are as open to the elements as possible (it's only the bedroom that is air-conditioned; the rest of the villa is open-air). The attention to detail is incredible, with luxurious treats hidden away under natural fibres in what is one of the Maldives' most environmentally conscious resorts.

The island itself is very pretty, crisscrossed with sand pathways through which guests can cycle to the main communal areas – the infinity pool overlooking the beach, the charming bar and beachside restaurant where elaborate buffets and à la carte menus are equally impressive. The diving school allows you to dive from a luxury dhoni complete with waiters. The water sports centre offers all nonmotorised sports for free and the lagoon is great for snorkelling a little further out by 'one palm island' – a desert island belonging to the resort. The most recent addition to the place is the Gourmet Cellar, a sumptuous subterranean space for private degustation dinners and wine tasting around a huge driftwood table.

Staff are positively obsequious – this is not a good place for those who don't like to be fussed over by staff, all of whom appear to know your name – but this is the sum total of any gripe we could have with this intelligent, sumptuous place. Robinson Crusoe never had it so good...

Huvafen Fushi (Nakatchafushi island; ☎ 6644222; www.huvafenfushi.com; r/wb US$1600/2700; airport transfer 30min, US$160; 43 rooms; ⊠ ▣ ⊜ ▣) really set tongues wagging when it opened to massive acclaim in 2004 and it seems to have subsequently inspired countless resorts in the country. Yet while Huvafen Fushi can rightly be cited as the resort that standardised private plunge pools, few imitators come close to this place in terms of the less-tangible signs of luxury – namely style, atmosphere and service.

Understated and more than a little fabulous, Huvafen Fushi is the last word in privacy and modern romance. The rooms are stunning in their simplicity, space and design savvy, all somehow still managing to feature 40-in plasma-screen TVs, Bose surround systems, iPod plug-in points, espresso machines and remote-control everything. The water villas that have been so widely copied remain some of the most impressive in the country – each with its own sizeable plunge pool on an enclosed deck overlooking the sea, with access to the lagoon down a staircase. The bedrooms and bathrooms are massive, with luxuries

such as rain showers and some of the largest king-sized beds we've ever come across. Linen is from Frette and furniture by names such as Frank Gehry – the vibe is architect-designed through and through.

Despite this, the atmosphere within the resort is informal and relaxed. The international clientele is made up mainly of honeymooners and couples, who spend the day by the enormous infinity pool overlooking the sea, lunching in one of the four superb restaurants (Celsius for international, Salt for fish and seafood, Raw for Japanese and Fogliani's for pizza) and being treated at the spa – unique for having an amazing underwater treatment room. There's also a huge wine cellar.

Diving and water sports are catered for amply, and the entire place feels eerily empty even at full capacity, such is the way in which the resort has been laid out. This is a great place for a honeymoon or a romantic break with a funky feel.

KAASHIDHOO

Though in the Kaafu (Male') administrative district, the island of Kaashidhoo is way out by itself, in a channel north of North Male' Atoll. The island has a clinic, a secondary school, and over 1700 people, which makes it one of the most populous in Kaafu. Some of the ruins here are believed to be remains of an old Buddhist temple. Local crops include watermelon, lemon, banana, cucumber and zucchini, but the island is best known for its *raa* – the 'palm toddy' made from the sap of a palm tree, drunk fresh or slightly fermented.

Local boats going to or from the northern atolls sometimes shelter in the lagoon in Kaashidhoo in bad weather. Dive boats on

---

ALSO IN NORTH MALE' ATOLL

Taj Coral Reef (Hembadhoo island; www.tajhotels.com) is one of two Taj resorts in the Maldives and is currently closed for renovation. When it reopens in late 2009 it will be as very smart top-end luxury hotel like the Taj Exotica in South Male' Atoll (see p130).

   Coco Palm Kudahithi (Kudahithi island; www.cococollection.com) The smaller of the two islands run by Coco Collection in North Male' Atoll, Coco Palm Kudahithi, a short distance away from Coco Palm Boduhithi, will be a resort catering for one single couple staying in mind-blowing luxury when it finally opens.

   Mahureva Gasfinolhu (Gasfinolhu island; ☎ 6642078; airport transfer 40min, free; 40 rooms; ⊠) Catering exclusively to the Italian market, Mahureva offers all-inclusive packages on this long, attractive property. All bookings are by the week, through the Italian tour company Valtur.

longer trips might stop to dive Kaashidhoo East Faru, a good place to see large pelagic marine life.

GAAFARU FALHU

This small atoll has just one island, also called Gaafaru, with a population of 850. The channel to the north of the atoll, Kaashidhoo Kuda Kandu, has long been a shipping lane, and several vessels have veered off course and ended up on the hidden reefs of Gaafaru Falhu. There are three diveable wrecks – SS *Seagull* (1879), *Erlangen* (1894) and *Lady Christine* (1974). None is anywhere near intact, but the remains all have good coral growth and plentiful fish. Dive trips are possible from Helengeli and Eriyadu, but most visitors are from liveaboard dive boats.

SOUTH MALE' ATOLL

Crossing the Vaadhoo Kandu, the choppy channel between North and South Male' Atolls, you'll quickly notice that South Male' Atoll has a very different feel from its busy northern neighbour. This is partly due to the lack of population – there are only three inhabited islands here, all of which are on the eastern edge of the atoll and none of which have a big population – and partly to do with the fact that the even the uninhabited islands here are spread out and so you really feel that you're remote from the hustle and bustle of Male' and its surrounding islands.

The biggest island in South Male' Atoll is **Maafushi** (population 2000), which is a notorious prison and a reformatory, providing skill training and rehabilitation for wayward youths. It is not possible to land here.

Guraidhoo island, which with around 1200 people is the atoll's most major town, has a lagoon with a good anchorage, used by both fishing dhonis and passing safari boats. Sultans from Male' sought refuge here during rebellions from as early as the 17th century. Island-hopping visitors come here from the resorts, and a dozen or so shops sell them souvenirs, sarongs and cool drinks.

The island of **Gulhi**, north of Maafushi, is not large but is inhabited by around 660 people. Fishing is the main activity, and there's also a small shipyard.

Sights & Activities
DIVING

Some of the best dive sites are around the Vaadhoo Kandu, which funnels a huge volume of water between the North and South Male' Atolls. Various smaller kandus channel water between the atoll and the surrounding sea, and also provide great diving. Some typical, well-known sites are listed here.

The rugged **Velassaru Caves** and overhangs, on the steep wall of the Vaadhoo Kandu, have very attractive coral growth. You may see sharks, turtles and rays on the bottom at around 30m. This dive is not for beginners, but if the current isn't too strong there's excellent snorkelling on the reef edge.

Vaadhoo Caves consists of a row of small caves, plus a bigger one with a swim-through tunnel, as well as excellent soft corals, gorgonians, jackfish and the odd eagle ray. If the current is strong, this is a demanding dive; if not, it's great for snorkelling.

Embudhoo Express is a 2km drift dive through the Embudhoo Kandu, which is a Protected Marine Area. With the current running in, rays, Napoleon wrasse and sharks often congregate around the entrance. The current carries divers along a wall with overhangs and a big cave. The speed of the current makes for a demanding dive, but also provides the ideal environment for soft corals and a large variety of fish. The reef top is good for snorkelling.

Also called Yacht Thila, the attraction of **Kuda Giri** is the hulk of a small freight ship, deliberately sunk here to create an artificial reef. Sponges and cup corals are growing on the wreck, and it provides a home for morays, gropers and large schools of batfish. A nearby thila has recovering coral growth and lots of reef fish to be seen at snorkelling depths. Sheltered from strong currents, this a good site for beginners and for night dives.

Vaagali Caves is an exciting dive and not especially demanding. It's in a less-exposed location and has many caves on its north side, at around 15m, filled with sponges and soft corals. There is good coral regrowth and lots of fish on the top of the reef, much of it visible to snorkellers.

A central reef splits **Guraidhoo Kandu** into two channels, with many possibilities for divers, even those with less experience.

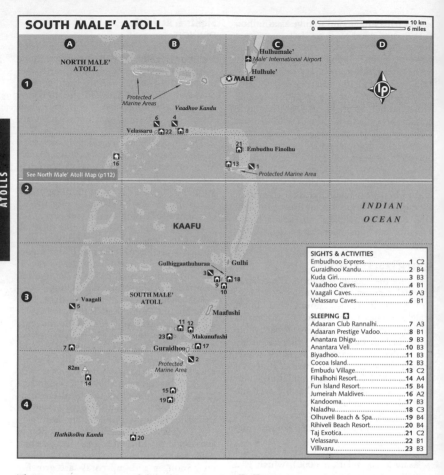

SOUTH MALE' ATOLL

0 _____ 10 km
0 _____ 6 miles

SIGHTS & ACTIVITIES

Embudhoo Express	1 C2
Guraidhoo Kandu	2 B4
Kuda Giri	3 B3
Vaadhoo Caves	4 B1
Vaagali Caves	5 A3
Velassaru Caves	6 B1

SLEEPING

Adaaran Club Rannalhi	7 A3
Adaaran Prestige Vadoo	8 B1
Anantara Dhigu	9 B3
Anantara Veli	10 B3
Biyadhoo	11 B3
Cocoa Island	12 B3
Embudu Village	13 C2
Fihalhohi Resort	14 A4
Fun Island Resort	15 B4
Jumeirah Maldives	16 A2
Kandooma	17 B3
Naladhu	18 C3
Olhuveli Beach & Spa	19 B4
Rihiveli Beach Resort	20 B4
Taj Exotica	21 C2
Velassaru	22 B1
Villivaru	23 B3

There are numerous reef fish, larger pelagics near the entrance and mantas when the current is running out. The kandu is a Protected Marine Area.

Resorts

Most resorts in the South Male' Atoll are reached by speedboat from the airport, but some of the closer, cheaper resorts may offer a slower, less-expensive transfer by dhoni. Unless otherwise specified, all transfer prices are by speedboat.

BUDGET

our pick **Embudu Village** (Emboodhoo island; ☎ 6644776; www.embudu.com; full board s/d/tr/wb US$116/200/270/300; airport transfer by dhoni 45min, US$52; 124 rooms;

⌘ ▢) is a very popular and enduring budget resort with a heavy focus on divers and couples. It's as relaxed as its sand-floor reception suggests, and has lots of thoroughly unpretentious charm. This is a resort where people make friends and socialise without it really being a party island – it's just a friendly and straightforward place. The island has lots of shady trees, some gorgeous beaches and a very accessible house reef.

All accommodation is on a full-board basis, with buffet meals. The standard rooms are fan-cooled, and don't have heated water but are still very acceptable. Superior rooms, with air-con, hot water, fridge and phone, cost about US$20 more. There are also 16 deluxe over-water bungalows, although budget water bungalows are always something of a letdown – these are bare and functional and you may be disappointed if you're after romance. An 'all-inclusive' option, for US$26 per person per day, includes most drinks and afternoon snacks.

The food is decent enough for an inexpensive resort, with a varied selection and fresh fruit and vegetables daily. Entertainment is organised one night per week, but the main attraction is watching the sunset from the casual beach bar.

Diving is popular here, thanks to the very professional **Diverland** (www.diverland.com) and the great dive sites in the area (over 90 different sites are reached on a regular basis). A single dive is US$42 with all equipment (and there are discounts for multi-dive packages). A full open-water course costs US$409 – extremely good value. Windsurfing is also popular, and there's a good range of excursions to Male' and various other islands. Massage is available at the small but well-run Serena Spa. Internet access is charged from a PC in the lobby, or available by cable for your laptop in the water bungalows only (also charged).

If you're not looking for luxuries but an unpretentious beach and diving holiday, Embudu Village is an excellent and enjoyable resort.

Fihalhohi Resort (Fihaalhohi island; ☎ 6642903; www.fihalhohi.net; half board s/d/wb US$190/210/370; airport transfer 75min, US$120; 150 rooms; ✗), open since 1981, is a charming budget place that retains an unpretentious appeal, a world away from the necessity of having your own butler or private plunge pool. Its dual attractions are its low prices and fantastic reef, making it a great budget diving resort.

The island itself is lovely, with white beaches almost all the way around it and a gorgeous lagoon in front. The house reef is very good for snorkelling, and is also used for night and individual dives. The dive centre charges US$42 for a single boat dive with tank and weights, or US$55 with all equipment, plus a US$13 boat fee. Open-water courses are US$430.

Meals at the Palm Grove restaurant are mostly buffet, and for variety there's a fun theme meal almost every night, from Middle Eastern to Mexican, flambé to fish and chips. Accommodation is in pleasant four-room, two-storey white painted blocks with thatched roofs. All have hot water, but a few have no air-con. Deluxe rooms, in two-storey blocks, have extras like a hairdryer and minibar. A set of 12 perfectly OK, midrange water bungalows was added in 2006. Despite the lovely beaches, erosion is a major problem here and sandbags are in evidence in many places. Fihalhohi is a fun resort, and a good choice for families, FITs and divers.

An attractive diving island, **Biyadhoo** (Biyadhoo island; ☎ 667171; www.biyadoo.com.mv; full board s/d/wb US$202/261; airport transfer 35min, US$120; 96 rooms; ✗ ▭) has thick foliage, high palms and lovely beaches in parts. Soft renovations in 2006 have stopped it showing its age too much, and it's a pleasant, laid-back budget option with some great nearby diving. The in-house dive operation charges guests at the end of their stay for the best overall package based on the number of dives they did, so there's no need to book anything in advance.

All 96 rooms are standards, housed in 16-room blocks. All have air-con and a minibar. There's paid internet access in the lobby from a PC. Request a room on the west side of the island for beach proximity – beaches on the east side have been badly affected by erosion and as such are not good for sunbathing, often visibly covered in sandbags. While the main beach on the west side is wide and flat, it can feel crowded.

Most people here are on full-board deals, with buffets served up for each meal in the resort's one restaurant. Other facilities include a football pitch, badminton and volleyball facilities and a spa. The resort has a friendly and relaxed feel and won't disappoint anyone looking for a good base for diving.

MIDRANGE

Kandooma (Kandoomafushi island; ☎ 6640511; www.kandooma-maldives.com; r/wb US$261/580; airport transfer 50min, US$140; 160 rooms; ✗ ▭ 🛜 ▣ 🚶), which reopened in 2008 after a long refurbishment that saw the entire place rebuilt following terrible tsunami damage, is a funky, fun resort that feels more like Ibiza or Miami than your typical Maldivian honeymoon bunk hole. The most noticeable feature is the cluster of buildings around reception that from the landing dock look like giant coconuts (apparently they're inspired by barnacles!). Inside, however, the reception area sets the tone for the re-vamped place – light, bright and with avant-garde light fittings.

The rooms are just as luminous: all white with the odd splash of tropical colour, they are definitely some of the coolest in the country in this price range. We especially love the duplex villas, with a bedroom, bathroom and balcony upstairs and an open-air downstairs sitting room with a sand floor facing the beach. There are 19 very smart water villas too, ideal for romantic sojourns.

There's an impressive COMO Shambhala spa, complimentary wi-fi in the rooms and free PC use above reception. The wide choice of food ranges from excellent buffets in the main restaurant to à la carte dining elsewhere. As the island is on the atoll edge the sea can be very rough here and beaches are relatively rocky by local standards. This is where the huge pool comes in handy. Children are well catered for, with a kids club and plenty of activities, including all water sports and a dive school. The local island of Guraidhoo is so close that you can walk to it across the lagoon at low tide.

Overall, this is a young and friendly resort that makes a great choice for people who want all the usual Maldivian treats in a sociable and outgoing atmosphere.

On the western edge of the atoll, **Adaaran Club Rannalhi** (Rannalhi island; ☎ 6642688; www .clubrannalhi.com; half board s/d/tr US$270/335/450; airport transfer 45min, US$125; 128 rooms; ✖ ♿ 🖳) is an Italian club-style resort popular with both Italians and Russians who favour all-inclusive, animation-heavy 'club'-style resorts. If that's not your thing, back away slowly. There are reasons to visit – the island itself is attractive, with tall palm trees, fine beaches and good snorkelling on the house reef, but it's built up and feels rather overdeveloped, not least since the recent addition of some two-storey water bungalows in 2008.

The rooms on dry land are in two-storey blocks, modern and well finished with all the amenities. The big, airy restaurant serves all buffet meals, featuring among other things all the Italian staples. There was no pool at last pass, but there were vague plans to build one.

Many of the guests dive, sometimes commuting to the dive sites in South Ari Atoll. Snorkelling is good on the house reef,

especially the excellent coral growth on the thila 100m off the service jetty. The main attraction, though, is the programme of activities, which start with morning aerobics, continue with volleyball and dance competitions, and finish late at night with amateur theatrics and karaoke.

Olhuveli Beach & Spa (Olhuveli island; ☎ 6642788; www.olhuveli.com; s/d/wb US$280/590; airport transfer 50min, US$190; 129 rooms; ✖ 🖳 📶 🖳) is a big upmarket resort that somehow manages to feel very intimate. This is largely due to a stylish post-tsunami refit that has kept the place looking stylish and smart several years on.

The main market here is Italian, followed by German and a smattering of Japanese and British visitors. The rooms are spread out along the beach in two-level blocks, but they are extremely tastefully done, furnished throughout with dark-wood four-poster beds and all featuring balconies or patios that lead straight out to the gorgeous beaches on either side of the island. There are also two rings of swish but rather identikit water bungalows stretching over the lagoon.

Although they're narrow in places, the beaches are attractive, and the wide lagoon is good for sailing and windsurfing. This is one of the first resorts to offer kitesurfing lessons and equipment. Snorkelling is excellent off the end of the jetty, at the edge of the reef, where turtles are common. The dive school runs drift dives in nearby channels, as well as wreck and night dives. Food is excellent, served at the main restaurant buffet, but with several alternatives such as Japanese restaurant Sakura. The Sun Spa is popular.

Overall, Olhuveli offers excellent value. It's the perfect compromise between budget prices and high standards, between romance and diving.

our pick Rihiveli Beach Resort (Mahaana Elhi Huraa island; ☎ 6643731; www.rihiveli-maldives.com; full board s/d/tr US$321/498/700; airport transfer 1hr, US$170; 48 rooms; 📶) is the personal creation of a Frenchman who lived here for 20 years. While he has now moved on, his legacy remains, and this almost exclusively French and Swiss resort retains its eco-friendly, laid back credentials. Indeed, this was the resort that coined the phrase 'no news, no shoes' – now used across the country – and you'll get funny looks if your shoes remain on for long after arrival!

Consisting of just 48 little bungalows, all built in a rustic style from now-illegal coral stone and with traditional thatched roofs, they have all the basics for comfort such as hot water but nothing considered superfluous, such as air-con, fridges, phones or a TV. This is the secret of its success and as such Rihiveli (silver sand) will never be overrun with your run-of-the-mill package group.

The open-air bar has a sand floor and shady trees overhead, while the restaurant is built over the lagoon and has a lovely view as well as excellent food. A conch-shell is blown to call guests to meals, and everyone is invited to take tea with the staff daily at 5.30pm. The usual water sports and tennis are all included in the room price, as is a daily excursion, so there's no chance of boredom here. You can wade across to two other, uninhabited islands where the resort organises regular barbecue lunches. Frequent boat trips to other reefs make up for the lack of snorkelling sites next to the resort. The main diving destinations are around nearby Hathikolhu Kandu, and there's a small wreck to explore. Wi fi is available at the lobby for a flat one-off payment of US$40 for your entire stay.

With its relaxed ambience, French style and natural appeal, Rihiveli is a unique and special resort for those who appreciate the simple things.

TOP END

our pick **Cocoa Island** (Makunufushi island; ☎ 6641818; www.cocoaisland.como.bz; wb from US$880; airport transfer 45min, US$200; 30 rooms; ✖ 🖥 🛜 🅿) is one of very few resorts that manage to get everything so right with such little fuss. This wonderful place is one of the most unique Maldivian resorts, and since its lavish refit at the hands of the COMO group, Cocoa has consistently impressed.

First of all, the small island has no rooms on it at all – they're all built over water in a shape that mirrors that of the island itself. And what rooms they are – built in the shape of traditional Maldivian dhoni boats, their interiors straight out of a glossy magazine spread – all clean lines, white cotton and dark wood. Newer two-floor loft villas are furnished with

white timbers and are even more stunning. Other great touches include outdoor showers, direct sea access from the rooms, free wi-fi and gorgeous COMO Shambhala bathroom products.

On the island proper there is nothing superfluous. A large infinity pool, cracking beaches, a superb restaurant with a large range of dishes, a smart cocktail bar, the sumptuous spa, a gym and the dive centre. Everything is luxurious, but nothing over the top. All in all, a top recommendation for low-key luxury.

Anantara Dhigu & Anantara Veli (Dhighufinolhu & Bodu Huraa islands; ☎ 6644100; www.anantara.com; Dhigu r/wb US$1045/1225, Veli wb US$950; airport transfer 40min, US$165; 160 rooms; ✖ 🖥 🛜 🅿 🚲) is a high-end Thai-owned resort is draped over three islands. All are officially their own resorts, and while in reality they're all centrally managed, we've listed Naladhu separately below as that 'six star' property is out of bounds to guests staying at the lowlier two resorts. Not that Dhigu or Veli could ever exactly be considered budget destinations.

Dhigu is the main resort, where guests arrive and where the majority of the facilities, such as diving school and water sports centre, are housed. It's a relatively crowded island featuring beach villas and large, very glamorous water villas with large decks and decorated in classic Asian styles. There's a big pool by the beach, a kids club, and a gorgeous over-water spa.

Crossing the lagoon to next-door Veli by a shuttle boat, there's more of the same. Veli, where all the accommodation is over water, nevertheless has the lowest-priced rooms at the resort, though even in the bottom category they're a good size – 62 sq metres each. Veli feels slightly over-developed in places, with seemingly endless over-water pathways to yet more water bungalows – despite the minimalist aesthetic in some of the rooms, the architects here clearly didn't agree that less really is more.

Veli has its own large pool, restaurants and spa, and is connected by a walkway to Naladhu. There are a variety of eateries here – seven in total across the three islands, including an excellent Thai restaurant on a walkway between Naladhu and Veli. This means that you're unlikely to get bored of the food, or of the huge amount of activities available. There's free wi-fi at Dhigu's

---

ALSO IN SOUTH MALE' ATOLL

Velassaru (Velassaru island; ☎ 3332200; www.velassaru.com; 129 rooms) Due to open in mid-2009, Velassaru is the latest upmarket property from local giant Universal Resorts. We were unable to visit for this update, but it promises to be a large, luxurious property.

Bolifushi (Bolifushi island) This island is closed while total redevelopment is carried out. It's due to reopen in 2012 as Jumeirah Maldives, a five star resort.

Villivaru (Viligilivaru island) Another resort that has been closed for a long time. There is currently no scheduled reopening date.

Fun Island Resort (Bodufinolhu island; www.villahotels.com) This big, popular and well-run resort had been operating since the mid-1980s but was badly damaged in the tsunami and was still closed for a complete refit and upgrading at the time of research.

Adaaran Prestige Vadoo (Vaadhoo island; www.adaaran.com) This island was a building site when we visited, as it prepared to open in mid-2009 as another of the mushrooming Adaaran properties in Maldives. The theme here is that of a Japanese village, with all 50 rooms over water, including four honeymoon suites that are only reachable by boat from the main island. It's slated to be a very upmarket resort, though, just moments from Male'.

---

reception area, but elsewhere wireless access is charged.

Taj Exotica (Embudhu Finolhu island; ☎ 6642200; www.tajhotels.com; r from US$1210; airport transfer 20min, US$121; 62 rooms; ❄ 💻 🛜 🍴) was the only Taj resort functioning in the Maldives at the time of writing as the Taj Coral Reef (see the box p124) was being transformed during a luxury refit.

This elegant, understated resort is all about quiet luxury and indulgence. The resort was one of the original pioneers of fine à la carte dining in the Maldives – the main Asia-Pacific restaurant here wouldn't know a buffet if it hit it in the face. Everything here is ordered and individually cooked from a sumptuous and expensive menu. This is one place where full board would come in handy – the meals here are far from budget. One feature of the second restaurant, which is built out over the lagoon and is open in the evenings, is an open hole over the water, where fish flock in the evening, attracted by the light.

The island is long and thin, with a beach on the lagoon side and water villas on the atoll edge. Other public area features include a DVD and book library, a well-stocked games room, a gorgeous infinity pool and, at the far end of the island, the breathtaking Jiva Grande Spa. There's a gym and free yoga classes each morning.

All categories of rooms are very smart, many of them with their own plunge pools overlooking the beach. The bathrooms in the lagoon villas have wonderful bathtubs next to huge windows allowing you to contemplate the sea as you soak.

Naladhu (Veliganduhuraa island; ☎ 6641888; www.naladhu.com; villa from US$2200; airport transfer 40min, US$200; 19 rooms; ❄ 💻 🛜 🍴) is the third island around the lagoon at Anantara and is operated by the same management, but marketed as a completely separate resort. Its concept is simple – an exclusive place where the rich and famous can remain unseen and totally private living in one of 19 large villas. This place is popular with security-conscious Russian millionaires, and though it's linked by a bridge to Veli, there's no access for non-Naladhu guests to the island. The villas are sumptuous, with huge pools and either beach access in the six beach houses or views to the ocean in the ocean houses where there's no sand. The resort, unsurprisingly, has little community feel – a large pool and a smart restaurant are all there really are to the communal areas – this is a place to celebrate privacy in style.

Ari Atoll

Second only to North Male' Atoll as the centre of the Maldivian tourist industry, Ari Atoll sits to the west of the capital, a vast oval lagoon dotted with reefs and as sumptuously inviting as anywhere else in the country. Like Male' Atoll, Ari is known universally by its traditional name rather than its official name of Alif, a usage we have followed here.

While the atoll is one natural entity, it is large enough to have been split into two administrative districts – North and South Ari Atoll. North Ari administrative district includes tiny Rasdhoo and Thoddoo Atolls as well, which aren't naturally part of Ari, but just northeast of it.

To the east, Ari Atoll is separated from South Male' Atoll by a 40km-wide channel, perhaps 500m deep; to the west, the sea floor drops precipitously to over 2000m. Abundant marine life in the atoll creates nutrient-rich water that flows out through channels, attracting large creatures from the open sea and divers from all over the world.

Despite its importance for the tourism industry, Ari Atoll is not a particularly developed part of the country. The regional capital, Mahibadhoo, has a population of just 1780 and there are only 18 inhabited islands in the entire atoll.

The atoll plays host to some of the most famous and exclusive resorts in the country, including the Conrad Maldives Rangali Island, Dhoni Island and W Retreat & Spa, although its exceptional diving – southern Ari is the best place in the country to see hammerhead sharks and whale sharks – means that there are still a host of cheaper diving resorts to chose from as well.

THODDOO ATOLL

Though administratively part of Ari Atoll, Thoddoo is actually a single, separate, oval island about 20km from the northern edge of the main atoll. It's about 1km across, and has a population of 1200. The principal activity is fishing, but Thoddoo is also known for its market-garden produce (watermelons and betel leaf especially) and its troupe of traditional dancers, who sometimes perform in tourist resorts.

Thoddoo is believed to have been occupied since ancient times. A Buddhist temple here contained a Roman coin minted in 90 BC, as well as a silver bowl and a fine stone statue of Buddha, the head of which is now in the National Museum in Male'.

Safari boats can stop here, but usually don't because of the lack of sheltered anchorages. You could also arrange a day trip here from one of the Rasdhoo Atoll resorts.

RASDHOO ATOLL

The small atoll of Rasdhoo lies off the northeastern corner of Ari Atoll proper. The main island of the atoll, also called **Rasdhoo** (population 900), is the administrative capital of North Ari Atoll, despite not being within the natural atoll itself. Rasdhoo is an attractive little town with a junior secondary school, a health centre, four mosques and a score of souvenir shops – it's often visited as a day trip from the nearby resorts. The island has been settled for many centuries and there are traces here of a Buddhist society predating the arrival of Islam.

ARI ATOLL

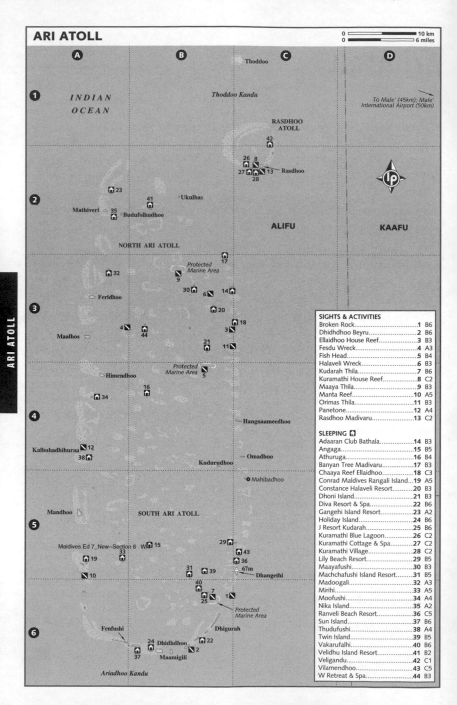

0 _____ 10 km
0 _____ 6 miles

INDIAN
OCEAN

Thoddoo

Thoddoo Kandu

To Male' (45km); Male'
International Airport (50km)

RASDHOO
ATOLL

42

26 8
27   13 Rasdhoo
28

23

41   Ukulhas

35   ALIFU   KAAFU

Mathiveri   Budufolhudhoo

NORTH ARI ATOLL

17

Protected
Marine Area

32
9

30 6 14
Feridhoo

20

4   18
44   3
Maalhos

21
11

Protected
Marine Area   5

16

34

Hanguaameedhoo

12
38   Omadhoo

Kalbuhadhihuraa

Kudurudhoo

Mahibadhoo

Mandhoo   SOUTH ARI ATOLL

29

15
Maldives Ed 7_New--Section 6 W   33   43
19   36
10   67m Dhangethi
31 39
40
7
25 1

Protected
Marine Area

Dhigurah

Fenfushi

24 Dhidhdhoo   22
37   2
Maamigili

Ariadhoo Kandu

ARI ATOLL

Sights & Activities

DIVING

The medical centre at Kuramathi has a decompression chamber and trained hyperbaric specialists.

Accessible from the shore, **Kuramathi House Reef** is good for beginning divers and snorkellers. A small dhoni and a 30m freighter have been sunk off the island to provide an attraction for divers. Sea fans and featherstars decorate the reef wall, and sharks, stingrays and turtles are also frequent visitors.

Also known as Hammerhead Point, **Rasdhoo Madivaru** is a more demanding dive on an outer reef where hammerhead sharks, mantas and other large pelagics are frequent visitors. Outside this reef the depth drops rapidly to over 200m and the water is exceptionally clear. It's a fine snorkelling site if conditions permit.

Resorts

Kuramathi Maldives (Kuramathi island; ☎ 6660527; www.kuramathi.com; airport transfer by speedboat 2hr, US$140; 290 rooms; ❄ ▯ ☎ ▣) is a unique island in the Maldives, as it houses no less than three resorts, in contravention of the government's beloved 'one island, one resort' policy. In fact, Kuramathi's three resorts are all run by the same management team and are all owned by Universal Resorts, but the island's size has allowed three separate entities aimed at different crowds to spring up here. Kuramathi island itself was once inhabited but population decline led to the mass relocation in 1970 of the remaining islanders to next-door Rasdhoo, leaving Kuramathi ripe for development.

Kuramathi Village (s/d US$300/310), the largest and least expensive Kuramathi resort, is where the younger, party crowd (comprising mainly Brits and Germans) come to stay. Rooms are basic, high-ceilinged affairs with hot showers and air-con but little else in the way of comforts. The superior and deluxe rooms offer some improved comforts although they're still fairly average.

Kuramathi Cottage & Spa (s/d/wb US$398/411/473), in the middle of the island, is a spa resort whose guests come for treatments, pampering and total relaxation. There are an incredible 50 water bungalows here, which are beautifully attired.

Kuramathi Blue Lagoon (s/d/wb US$435/460/580), at the more secluded end of the island, is

quieter and more upmarket. It features 20 water bungalows (favoured by honeymooners) and 36 beach cottages, which are popular with families.

The three resorts share all facilities and so these are great choices if you want a huge amount of activities and facilities. There's a marine biology centre here that provides guided snorkelling and diving as well as informative introductions to various aspects of the natural underwater world, from coral formation to reef structure.

Rasdhoo Atoll Divers (www.rasdhoodivers.com) serves all three resorts, charging US$77 for a boat dive with all equipment, US$62 with tank and weights only, and US$490 for an open-water course. There's a four-berth decompression chamber on the island too.

The lagoon is the perfect place for learning windsurfing and sailing. Motorised water sports, including wakeboarding, are available. Stingrays come into the shallows on the beach every evening. All in all, Kuramathi has a lot to offer and it's particularly good for a group of people who might want different things, as you can easily combine diving, spa treatments and partying here in a way that few other resorts can provide.

A charming island fringed with white beaches and featuring a huge 80m sandbank at one end, **Veligandu** (Veligandu island; ☎ 6660519; www.veligandulsland.com; s/d/tr/wb US$365/430/580/430; airport transfer by seaplane 20min, US$220; 74 rooms; ❄ ▯ ☎) is a great midrange option now that it's undergone a full refit, with attractive and stylish rooms for this price range that run from Jacuzzi Beach Villas in the lower category to the very smart Jacuzzi Water Villas. All rooms have flat screen TV, air-con and a rain shower. The resort is built in a traditional Maldivian style, although the rather modern rooms smash any genuine shipwreck fantasies before they can fully set in.

The island is rightly famous for its great beaches and is located on a beautiful lagoon within Rasdhoo. There are a couple of excellent dive sites nearby, with very common hammerhead shark sightings. The Swiss-run **Ocean-Pro dive base** (www.oceanpro-diveteam.com) charges very reasonably. The edge of the house reef is not very accessible and is not great for snorkelling. But Veligandu isn't primarily a diving or water sports resort – the main attractions are the stylish accommodation and fine beaches.

ARI ATOLL

The geographic entity of Ari Atoll (as opposed to the administrative regions of North and South Ari) is about 80km from north to south and 30km wide. The most populous island is **Mahibadhoo**, the capital of South Ari, with some 1780 people. Fishing and fish processing are the main industries – there's a cold storage and processing plant here. Safari boats might stop here, but there are no resorts nearby.

Other inhabited islands, typically with a population of a few hundred, are dotted around the edges of the atoll. Few of them are accessible from resorts, but safari boats may be able to stop at some of these islands, which are little visited by tourists. Quite a few islands have ruins or artefacts of ancient Buddhist and Hindu settlements.

Maamigili, in the south of the atoll, has over 1600 people, many of whom work in nearby resorts, or in tourist shops that cater to island-hopping visitors. The island of **Fenfushi** (population 560), on the southwest corner of the atoll, is noted for coral carving.

Sights & Activities
DIVING

All of the resorts have diving operations and Ari is a top pick for those who love underwater activities, being the best place in Maldives to see large pelagics such as whale and hammerhead sharks. During peak season some sites may have several groups diving on them at one time, but good divemasters will know how to avoid the crowds at popular sites and where to find equally attractive but less-popular sites. The following is a brief description of some well-known sites (from north to south), to give an idea of the possibilities.

Maaya Thila is a classic round thila known for the white-tip reef sharks that circle it. Caves and overhangs around the thila have lots of gorgonians, soft corals and schools of reef fish. It's a Protected Marine Area.

The well-known **Halaveli Wreck** was created in 1991 when a 38m cargo ship was deliberately sunk. It's famous for the friendly stingrays enticed here by regular feeding – keep your fingers away from their mouths.

Fesdu Wreck is a 30m trawler with a good covering of corals at a depth of 18m to 30m. Moray eels and groper live inside the hull, which is easily entered and has good growths of soft corals and sponges. Divers can also check the adjacent thila, which has hard and soft corals as well as lots of fish.

Only accessible to Ellaidhoo's guests, the excellent **Ellaidhoo House Reef** has a long wall just 25m from the beach. It has a row of caves with sea fans, whip corals, schools of bannerfish, Napoleons, stingrays and morays, and even a small wreck. This reef is popular with night divers.

Overhangs, caves, crevices, canyons and coral heads make **Orimas Thila** an exciting dive. Marine life includes good growths of soft corals, sea fans, anemones and clown fish. The top of the thila is only 3m down, and can be easily enjoyed by snorkellers if the conditions are calm. It is a Protected Marine Area.

Also called Mushimasmingali Thila, **Fish Head** is one of the world's most famous dive sites. Its steep sides are spectacular, with multi-level ledges, overhangs and caves supporting many sea fans and black corals; its top is heavily encrusted with anemones. Beware of stonefish. The prolific fish life at this Protected Marine Area includes fusiliers, large Napoleons, trevally and schools of hungry barracuda. The main attractions, however, are the numerous grey reef sharks, which can be seen up close. Strong currents can make this a demanding dive, and extreme care should be taken not to damage the superb but heavily used site.

The north side of Kalhuhadhihuraa Faru is subject to strong currents, so the caves and overhangs of **Panetone** are thick with soft coral growth. As well as the many reef fish, there are giant trevally, sharks, barracuda and turtles. From December to April, mantas feed around the outside of the channel; March to November are the best months to see sharks. There's excellent snorkelling in light currents.

Also called Madivaru, **Manta Reef** is at the end of a channel where powerful currents carry plankton out of the atoll during the northeast monsoon (December to April) – fast food for manta rays. Mantas also come to be cleaned. Reef fish include Napoleon wrasse, snapper and parrotfish, while pelagics such as turtles, tuna and sharks visit the outer reef slope. It's for advanced divers only, and great for snorkellers in the right conditions.

Kudarah Thila is a very demanding but exciting dive – if there is a current running, this is strictly for experienced divers. There are gorgonians, whip corals, black corals and a whole field of sea fans swaying in the current, surrounded by sharks and trevally from the open sea. In the gaps between large coral blocks, bluestriped snapper, tallfin, batfish, goby and other unusual small fish can be seen. It's a Protected Marine Area.

In the mouth of the Dhigurashu Kandu, **Broken Rock** is bisected by a canyon up to 10m deep and only 1m to 3m wide. Swimming through the 50m canyon is unforgettable, but extreme care is needed not to damage the coral formations on either side. Rock formations around the thila are decorated with sea fans and superb corals, and are inhabited by abundant marine life.

From May to September, whale sharks cruise almost continually along the 10km-long **Dhidhdhoo Beyru** on the southwestern edge of the atoll, which extends from Ariyadhoo Kandu north to the tip of Dhigurah island. There's plenty of fish life on the reef, and mantas also cruise the area. The reef drops off steeply into deep water, and it's quite exposed and subject to ocean currents.

Resorts

While some resorts nearer to Male' operate speedboat transfers to and from the airport, the majority of resorts use seaplane transfers due to the distances involved. These take anything from 20 to 45 minutes, and are more expensive than speedboat transfers. Bear in mind that as seaplanes do not fly at night, if you arrive after 4pm at Male' airport you'll have to stop over in Male' until the next morning for your seaplane transfer. This is usually done at the airport hotel, which is a good international-standard business hotel. However, it's not the ideal start to a holiday, so it's always best to land in good time before dusk.

BUDGET

Maayafushi (Maayafushi island; ☎ 6660588; maaya@dhivehinet.net.mv; s/d US$160/185; airport transfer by seaplane 25min, US$235; 60 rooms; ✗ 🖳) is a largely German and Italian resort that offers good-value diving holidays. The island is small

and quite intensively developed; soft sandy beaches surround it, and the house reef is a beauty. Rooms all have basic furnishings, air-con, hot water, TV, phone and beach frontage. Most of the guests are divers from Germany, Switzerland or Austria, but there are a few families with young children who get on well here. Most meals are set menu (with Indian dishes and lots of fresh fish), but there are a couple of buffet nights each week.

The dive school offers a wide range of courses, night dives and trips to the famous dive sites nearby, all for average prices. The excellent Maaya Thila dive site is very close (see p134) and a great place to see sharks.

our pick Chaaya Reef Ellaidhoo (Ellaidhoo island; ☎ 6660586; www.chaayahotels.com; s/d/wb US$180/200/280; airport transfer by seaplane 20min, US$225; 112 rooms; ✗ 🖳 🔊) has a reputation as the most hard-core diving destination in the Maldives, with over 100 dive sites within a half-day trip, making it one of the top choices in the country for keen divers. It has what many consider to be the country's finest house reef (quite an accolade given the competition!) with a 750m wall, lots of caves, corals, rich marine life (turtles, sharks, mantas and eagle rays) and even a small shipwreck.

Indeed, it's hard to choose a much better base for divers, not least since a 2008 refit by the Chaaya Hotel group, which has seen smart villa-style accommodation and large two-storey water bungalows on the lagoon replace the older, budget rooms. Yet despite this, prices have remained comfortably low.

The island isn't the most picturesque in the country by a long shot, but it offers enough of an all-round holiday to attract non-divers as well as divers.

One of the best resorts in the country for diving, **Adaaran Club Bathala** (Bathalaa island; ☎ 6660587; www.adaaran.com; full board s/d/tr US$190/230/295; airport transfer by seaplane 20min, US$190; 46 rooms; ✗) is a small, pretty island with a loyal tribe of repeat guests from all over Europe. This was the first Adaaran resort in the country, opening in 1992.

The cabana-style cottages are simple and rustic, but with all the essentials such as air-con and warm running water in their outdoor bathrooms. The style is very much Robinson Crusoe – you won't be in danger of any over-attentive pampering here

ARI ATOLL

(although there is a small spa) and most people come for the superb diving.

The attitude towards diving is extremely passionate here – the dive school actively encourages beginners to take one of their full open-water courses, which are spread out over five days and limited to a maximum of three students per group.

Dive costs are relatively low, but more costly if you need to rent full equipment, again making this a good choice for divers who have their own. Multi-dive packages are available. Bring your own wetsuit if possible. The edge of the house reef drops off steeply all around, and is accessible from the beach or more readily from the jetties – it's a good dive site in itself.

An immaculate beach goes right around the island, as does the house reef. The good mix of clientele gives the whole resort a very laid-back feel.

MIDRANGE

our pick **Angaga** (Angaagau island; ☎ 6660510; www .angaga.com.mv; s/d US$250/270; airport transfer by seaplane 25min, US$210; 70 rooms; 🔀) was Ari Atoll's first resort and has been operating since 1989. It's a gorgeous and obvious-choice island. White beaches fringe the island, and the house reef is great for diving and snorkelling – the corals have recovered from the bleaching well here. The thatch-roofed bungalows, with a traditional *undholi* (swing seat) out front, show a little more character than many of the midrange resorts available. Twenty new water villas are good quality for this price range.

The spacious sand-floored bar and restaurant also show some style – they are built in a distinctive fish shape. All meals are buffet, and include a good selection of Asian and European dishes – seafood barbecues are a regular event. The house wines are inexpensive, but all-inclusive packages are still good value if you indulge. Entertainment is nothing elaborate, but there are plenty of water sports and excursions on offer. Nearby Angaga Thila is a top dive site, but others are some distance away on the edge of the atoll. The dive centre charges reasonably for a range of diving packages and courses. Angaga is popular with Germans, Swiss, Brits and other Europeans, many of whom are repeat visitors.

Another almost implausibly perfect island, **Madoogali** (Madoogali island; ☎ 3327443; www .madoogaliresort.com; full board s/d/tr US$255/335/395; airport transfer by seaplane 35min, US$280; 50 rooms; 🔀 🖳) is richly verdant, has gorgeous beaches all the way around its circular shore and is set on a stunning lagoon – a real postcard favourite and rightly so. The ethos here is rustic Maldivian relaxation – the coral-walled architecture with thatched roofs and wooden interiors may have aircon, but that's one of the few concessions to the modern world.

The large majority of guests are Italian, but the resort has slowly moved from being an Italian-only place to having a large range of European guests, many of whom are repeat visitors.

The house reef is excellent for snorkelling, and as Madoogali is the only resort in this part of the atoll, there is easy access to lots of little-used dive sites. The dive centre charges reasonable rates.

Ranveli Beach Resort (Viligilivaru island; ☎ 6680825; www.ranvelivillage.com; s/d US$260/315; airport transfer by seaplane 25min, US$215; 56 rooms; 🔀 🖳) seems distinctly overbuilt, with too many rooms on a small island. The main restaurant is offshore, in a pavilion on a pier over the lagoon, and serves a rich variety of quality meals. The house reef is good for snorkelling, excellent dive sites are nearby, and there's a lot of white sandy beach as well as a spa. The guests are all from Italy, and Ranveli offers lots of animation and club-style activities.

Vilamendhoo (Vilamendhoo island; ☎ 6444487; www.vilamendhoomaldives.com; s/d US$275/350; airport transfer by seaplane 25min, US$280; 154 rooms; 🔀 🖳) is a very lush, well-vegetated island that still has some sense of space. The beaches are narrow around most of the island, but there's a big sandy area at one end, or both ends, depending on the season. The house reef is particularly good for snorkelling, and marked channels make it easy to reach the reef edge.

The rooms are divided into three categories; all are air-conditioned, spacious, clean and comfortable, with a thin toupee of thatch as a concession to natural style. The restaurant has a tiled floor, a timber ceiling and no walls, so it's cool and breezy. All meals are buffet style, and offer a wide choice of dishes, with theme nights for variety and several options for vegetarians. The main bar is the heart of the resort, and the guests on all-inclusive packages make sure it keeps beating.

There are over 40 accessible dive sites in the area, including some of the very best in the Maldives. For non-divers there are numerous excursions, a tennis court, windsurfing and waterskiing, but no pool.

Vilamendhoo is efficiently managed, but friendly and informal, and it attracts a good mix of visitors, mostly from Germany, Italy and the UK. It's recommended for divers.

Sun Island (Nalaguraidhoo island; ☎ 6660088; www .sunislandmaldives.com; half board s/d/tr US$277/287/ 387; airport transfer by speedboat 2½hr, US$274, by seaplane 35min, US$260; 426 rooms; ✷ ☐ ⌨) is the most massive of resorts (the largest in the country), and no place for re-enacting Swiss Family Robinson fantasies. Indeed, Sun Island is a modern, rather downmarket and not particularly charming place.

The rooms themselves are large and have decent indoor-outdoor bathrooms, bidets and minibars. Everything is very modern although it's hardly cutting-edge style and has none of the deeply considered charm of much of the Maldives resort market.

The Sun Island Diving School is quite a big operation with reasonable prices. Most dives are done at nearby sites, and groups can be pretty big. Snorkelling is doable at the reef edge off the end of the main jetty. Elsewhere the lagoon is wide, and only good for swimming and water sports.

If it's an activities-packed holiday you want, though, with endless choice, Sun is a good option. There are 11 bars, five restaurants and the fullest possible choice of water sports, diving, spa treatments, excursions and sports (including a putting range and tennis court), a video arcade and a good gym.

Villa Hotels have a habit of naming their resorts with such corny names that they seem naff before you even arrive, which is a real pity as **Holiday Island** (Dhiffushi island; ☎ 6680011; www.villahotels.com; full board s/d/tr US$313/323/336; airport transfer by speedboat 2½hr, US$150, by seaplane 35min, US$260; 142 rooms; ✷ ☐ ⌨) is beautiful – wide beaches, lush vegetation and a gorgeous lagoon make this every bit the picture-perfect Maldivian island. Like most of Villa Hotels' resorts this is a mid-level resort but the accommodation is very basic despite some recent attempts to upgrade the mustier rooms. Perhaps more of a gripe is that the whole place can feel rather crowded – the main buffet restaurant at dinnertime is quite a sight!

The rooms are in blocks of two (some with interconnecting doors for families), surrounded by cultivated gardens and fitted out with TV and hot water. Meal selection can be limited, but the quality is generally OK. The entire place is geared towards people who want to have fun, meet others and party. It's certainly not a place to escape from life and the omnipresent loud music may annoy you unless you're looking for it.

Recreational activities such as table tennis, badminton, billiards, tennis and use of the gym are free. Windsurfing, catamaran sailing and motorised water sports are available too. The beaches are lovely around most of the island, but snorkelling is not good in the lagoon, and boat trips out to the reef edge and beyond are charged as an extra. Diving is well catered for by the Villa Diving dive school; there are lots of good dive sites around and costs are average to low. While Holiday Island is relatively cheap for the quality of its accommodation and meals, it's still a place for a bog-standard package break. However, if so-called animation and its adherents frighten you like they do us, avoid.

Velidhu Island Resort (Velidhoo island; ☎ 6660551; www.velidhu.com.mv; half board s/d/tr/wh US$322/ 348/455/487; airport transfer by seaplane 20min, US$280; 100 rooms; ✷ ☐) is a sizeable island with some great beaches and a good house reef. While its architecture is not by any means stunning, the rooms are fine, despite their ordinary interiors, and the newer water bungalows are of a much higher standard, with their charming conical thatch roofs.

The **Euro-Divers dive centre** (www.eurodivers .com) is very professional and enthusiastic about the diving in this part of the atoll. A single boat dive is US$62 with tank and weights. To do an open-water course costs about US$375. The six-day, no-limit package is a good deal if you dive a lot. Velidhu could be a good choice for keen divers who are not looking for luxury, and its low-season prices can be great value.

Athuruga (Athuruga island; ☎ 6660508; www.plan hotel.com; rates unpublished; airport transfer by seaplane

25min, US$230; 46 rooms; ⓧ ▣) is one of two Planhotel properties in Ari Atoll (Thudufushi is the other one). It's an all-inclusive resort, including most drinks, excursions and nonmotorised water sports in the daily rate. Rooms here are only available through travel agencies – FITs look away now.

The air-con rooms are spacious and comfortable and all face onto the superb beach. Guests are mostly from Italy, Switzerland, Germany and the UK, and the atmosphere is casual. The meals are consistently good. Other facilities include the Serena Spa, water sports and animation areas.

The house reef offers easy snorkelling and a lot to see, and there are some good dive sites nearby, though it's an hour by boat to the exciting dives on the western rim of the atoll. The **Crab dive base** (www. thecrab.com), which also runs the diving on Thudufushi, charges about US$70 for a boat dive with tank and weights, and also offers packages.

Athuruga is quite densely developed, but it still has lots of palm trees and an excellent beach all round – it's a good-value resort with a mainly Italian ambience.

The second Planhotel resort in Ari Atoll, **Thudufushi** (Thudufushi island; ☎ 6660583; www .planhotel.com; rates unpublished; airport transfer by seaplane 25min, prices vary; 49 rooms; ⓧ) was given a complete refurbishment in 2007 and has a more rustic and low-key feel than its nearby sister hotel. The island is just beautiful, especially the beaches, with thick, mature foliage and a great house reef. However, like all Italian-dominated resorts, expect to see overly chatty animators and lots of loud tour groups in the main restaurant at all meals, which incidentally, can be very cramped, although food looked good when we visited.

In high season the majority of guests are Italian, but at other times there are also Germans and Brits. The dive centre management and prices are the same as at Athuruga, but Thudufushi may be better placed for dives on the atoll edge. Be aware that Thudufushi is closed to FITs.

J Resort Kudarah (Kudarah island; ☎ 6660549; www.jhotelsandresorts.com; s/d $485/580; airport transfer by seaplane 30min, $275; 50 rooms; ⓧ ▣ 🛜 🍽) is a small, elegant luxury resort on an attractive island. Redeveloped by J resorts, this former Italian package tour destination is now a

sleek tropical resort with quality furnishings and gorgeously designed rooms.

Of the rooms here, our favourites are the beach suites – fantastic two-floor villas surrounded by trees for privacy and with private plunge pools in the garden. Other facilities include good tennis courts, a full water sports centre, a marine education programme and a professionally-run dive school.

The resort is superbly located just minutes from superb diving at Kudarah Thila, which makes this a popular choice with divers. The beaches are not great, however – there is only one decent stretch that does get very busy, though this doesn't seem to bother any of the numerous repeat visitors.

TOP END

Gangehi Island Resort (Gangehi island; ☎ 6660505; www.gangehi.com; full board s/d/wb US$580/465/785; airport transfer by seaplane 25 min, prices vary; 40 rooms; ⓧ ▣) is an intimate, upmarket place that is looking better than ever after a renovation in 2008. Its new Swiss owners have doubled the number of water bungalows available with the addition of eight new 'deluxe' villas.

Stays are all-inclusive and the previous buffet restaurant has been replaced by the new à la carte Lagoon Restaurant. Other new additions include a beautiful new spa, where the treatments are carried out in 19th-century Keralan style, a brand new dive school and a new gym.

The island is pretty, with lots of palm trees, but unfortunately has suffered from sand movements, so the seafront rooms have very limited beaches and the overwater bungalows are sometimes surrounded by a sandbar. This is a great choice for a relaxed, upmarket resort with excellent diving nearby.

Nika Island (Kudafolhudhoo island; ☎ 6660515; www.nikamaldive.com; full board s/d/wb US$595/690/835; airport transfer by seaplane 25min, US$250; 37 rooms; ⓧ ▣ 🛜) is a majority Italian resort and one whose innovative approach to environmentally friendly and back-to-nature tourism has influenced resorts throughout the country. While Nika is now booked exclusively by a Milanese company, there is still an international clientele here, many of whom have been regulars since the 1980s.

Individual villas are spacious and imaginatively designed in a seashell shape. This is utter luxury, but genuinely eco-friendly (no pool and no air-conditioning outside some of the bedrooms – just the sea and natural ventilation) to the point that it looks spookily like a traditional Maldivian fishing village populated by well-heeled Europeans.

Tastefully decorated with thatched roofs and handcrafted timber furniture, the large villas have private gardens and preserve a rustic image – cooling is by natural ventilation through wooden louvre windows. The meals are Italian/international style and of high standard, served in the sand-floored dining room or outside on a seaside deck. Sadly, you aren't able to walk around the island, as beach villas have 'private beaches', which is a shame – though no doubt nice for those in beach villas! Water villas are a recent addition and are innovatively designed over three split levels.

Dive costs here are much higher than at other resorts, but groups are small and the attention is personal. Fishing, windsurfing, tennis and most other activities are included. Guests are mostly European or Japanese, and value the privacy that Nika provides. Though several new luxury resorts are more sumptuous and have fancier features, Nika is still doing the designer desert island thing to perfection.

Tiny **Mirihi** (Mirihi island; ☎ 6680500; www.mirihi .com; s/d/tr/wb US$640/670/740/700; airport transfer by seaplane 25min, US$280; 36 rooms; 🅿 💻 🛜) seems to go from strength to strength if rave traveller feedback is anything to go by. This gem of a resort takes its name from the yellow flower that grows around the island, and its philosophy is keeping it simple and natural. The wonderful beach that rings the thick vegetation in the centre of the island and the fantastic house reef beyond are both first class. Redeveloped in classy, contemporary style, Mirihi is a tiny island, but 30 of the rooms are built over the water so it's not too crowded – in fact, if anything, it feels positively spacious.

The beach villas have eye-catching decor, polished timber finishes, white linen furnishings, rich red and brown accents and every facility, including a CD player, TV and espresso machine. The over-water rooms have all this plus water views and very private sun decks. The main restaurant presents a lavish gourmet buffet for nearly every meal, usually eaten on a sun deck or on the sand. Some nights feature à la carte specials or theme dinners.

The Muraka restaurant, on a jetty over the water, specialises in grills and seafood.

In addition, there's a gym, a small spa, and activities such as board games, windsurfing and kayaking. Divers come here for access to sites all over South Ari Atoll. The **Ocean-Pro dive centre** (www.oceanpro-diveteam.com) charges US$85/65 per dive with/without equipment and US$732 for an open-water course.

Mirihi is remarkable for making the most of a small island without overdeveloping it. It's equally attractive as a stylish resort, romantic retreat or quality dive island.

Sumptuous barefoot luxury is the name of the game at the **Conrad Maldives Rangali Island** (Rangalifinolhu & Rangali islands; ☎ 6660629; www.conrad hotels1.hilton.com; r/wh US$850/1220; airport transfer by seaplane 35min, US$400; 150 rooms; 🅿 💻 🛜 💥), the Hilton Group's long-standing Maldivian resort, which was rebranded into a Conrad, one of the groups most exclusive brands, in 2007. As status symbols go, the Conrad doesn't have a bad one – its own gold-coloured logo-branded seaplane, which shuttles guests to and from the airport: no en-route drop offs for this crowd!

The property occupies two islands. The heart of the resort, with the main lobby, restaurants, bars, water sports, dive centres and 100 beach villas, is on Rangalifinolhu; on the second island, Rangali, are two other restaurants plus a bar, a separate reception area, and 52 water villas in their very own class of exclusivity. A walkway bridge connects the two islands across a broad lagoon.

With seven restaurants running the whole gamut of cuisines from local Maldivian to Japanese and European, you have plenty of choice. Most amazing is the Ithaa Undersea Restaurant, where diners eat in a glass-domed restaurant underwater, an experience quite unlike any other in the country. There's also a resident sommelier whose climate-controlled cave contains some 5000 bottles of selected wines.

The rooms are varied and beautifully conceived; the standard beach villas are up to 150 sq metres, all are set on the beachfront with sea views; they have outdoor terraces and outdoor bathrooms as well as sea views from the bath. The spectacular water villas all enjoy their own private terraces, gorgeous wooden interiors and, in the more luxurious ones, glass floors.

Diving, water sports, excursions and light entertainment are all on offer, but the real attraction at the Conrad is the unobtrusive, efficient and friendly service and the incredible food and wine.

Diva Resort & Spa (Dhidhdhoofinolhu island; ☎ 6982222; www.naiade.com; r/wb US$865/1405; airport transfer by seaplane 20min, US$350; 192 rooms; 🅧 🛜 🅡) was transformed from White Sands Resort & Spa to reopen as a posh Naïade resort in 2007. It's not quite as luxurious as its name would suggest – this is no place for hissy fits and Mariah Carey-esque demands. Instead, it's a solid, top end choice where stylish rooms compliment an already beautiful island.

At 2km long the island is one of the bigger ones in the Maldives, but Diva doesn't feel crowded despite the large number of rooms.

Rooms range from junior suites, which at 65 sq m are a good size, and go up to a giant presidential villa. The water villas do not have plunge pools, but the cheaper beach pool villas do. All rooms have the usual luxuries, including free wi-fi and outdoor showers. The rest of the island is equally well equipped for entertainment and activities, featuring no less than six restaurants, multiple bars, a great spa, a PADI-five star diving school, a full water sports centre and the usual host of excursions.

The island itself is long and narrow with natural, somewhat scrubby, vegetation and long white sandy beaches. The lagoon is wide on all sides, and a good place to learn windsurfing or catamaran sailing. For snorkelling, take one of the free boat trips to the reef edge – these go every afternoon. The island has always been popular with divers, especially for the whale sharks that cruise the outside edge of the atoll here from May to November, and the mantas on the west side of the atoll from December to May – since this resort became a diva, however, it's patronised by a different class of diver, but a no-less-passionate one!

After a total refit **Lily Beach Resort** (Huvahendhoo island; ☎ 6660013; www.lilybeachmaldives.com; d/wb US$910/1610; airport transfer by seaplane 25min, US$300; 119 rooms; 🅧 🛏 🛜 🅡) reopened in March 2009 as a novel concept: an upmarket all-inclusive resort. This is a first for the

Maldives and we're intrigued to see how it works. Unfortunately, we were unable to visit for this edition as the resort was still putting the finishing touches to its revamp, but it's a great idea.

Here you'll pay for few or no extras as everything is included in your room price – from unlimited cocktails to free snorkelling and even (weirdly) free cigarettes! Not a new concept, you say? Well, here instead of your usual all-inclusive crowd drinking cheap vodka and ersatz coffee, Lily Beach offers 'quality' brand names, good wines and decent food. It's hard to guess how genuinely upmarket the resort will be if it's not allowed to charge US$120 for a bottle of wine, but it looks like the rooms will be very elegant and understated, ranging from the beach villas at 68 sq m to the sunset water suite at 182 sq m.

The house reef is very good (turtles are common) and easily accessible for snorkelling. Keen divers come for the many South Ari dive sites such as the famous Kudarah Thila, especially in the whale shark season. The **Ocean-Pro dive base** (www.oceanpro-diveteam.com) offers competitive rates and has always been extremely friendly in the past. This is a great and exciting new departure for the resort, and will no doubt be a welcome addition to the all-inclusive market, while remaining a good deal more exclusive.

our pick **W Retreat & Spa** (Fesdhoo island; ☎ 6662222; www.whotels.com; r/wb US$1000/1700; airport transfer by seaplane 25min, US$362; 78 rooms; 🅧 🛏 🛜 🅡), in the middle of Ari Atoll, is sleek and imaginative, a boutique luxury venture loaded with more cool than any other in the country. W manages to get it right on all levels – staff are informal and friendly, the reception area is so efficient that you'll rarely see anyone even needing to be there and the resort itself is stunning.

To start with Fesdhoo island is gorgeous, with some lovely beaches and a great house reef packed with turtles, rays and reef sharks. On the island itself are the standard rooms – and even in the starting categories they're wonderful – each with its own private plunge pool and, perhaps their most charming feature, a thatched roof 'viewing deck' above the room, complete with daybeds. Higher categories are over water, culminating in four vast suites. All rooms are staggeringly cool, with clean lines, Bose surround sound system and huge private terraces.

The activities and facilities are just as good – from free nonmotorised water sports and an excellent diving school to a superb spa that looks a world away from any other in the Maldives and one of the very few (and definitely the best-looking) nightclubs in the country, open three times a week and complete with a dangerously wide-ranging vodka collection. Add to this three excellent restaurants, three glamorous bars, free in-room internet access, a vast swimming pool and even a private desert island for guests to use, and it's easy to see why this is the place of choice for the discerning, wealthy cool.

Dhoni Island (Mushimasmigili island; ☎ 6660751; www.dhoni-island.com; r US$2140; airport transfer by luxury dhoni 4hr $400, by seaplane 30min, $350; 6 dhoni & room pairings; ✂ 🖥 🛜) is certainly one of the more innovative top-end hotels, though its profile has rather dropped in recent years since it was sold by Per Aquum, the owners of other big-name resort Huvafen Fushi, and changed its name from Dhoni Migli to the more prosaic Dhoni Island.

The concept here is simple – on the island there are six luxury bungalows and each one is paired with a luxury customised dhoni. As well as your standard *thakuru* (butler; no longer such a status symbol in the Maldives) you get your own dhoni captain and two crew members on permanent 24-hour alert. You can sleep aboard your dhoni or in your beach bungalow – frankly, you can do whatever the hell you like at these prices.

Both the dhonis and the bungalows are incredible pieces of design and craftsmanship; 20m-long bespoke crafted sailboats fitted with an engine for longer trips (your dhoni can even meet you at Male' airport so you can step off the plane and straight into your hotel room!), they include all possible amenities from king-sized beds to Smeg kitchens and Philippe Starck bathroom fittings. They are definitely rather different to the Male' airport ferry.

On the island the beach bungalows are spread out generously to ensure total privacy. Of the six, four have plunge pools, but all are stunning – featuring private courtyards, incredible outdoor showers, bathrooms decked out in metallic slate and every luxury from Bose surround sound to espresso machines.

The island itself is charming, with gorgeous wide beaches, a luxurious spa, dive centre, DVD and CD library and a full suite of excursions and entertainments that can be arranged whenever a guest snaps their fingers.

Banyan Tree Madivaru (Beyrumadivaru Island; ☎ 6660760; www.banyantree.com; r US$2700; airport transfer by seaplane 20min, US$380; 6 tented villas) is the exciting second venture for the famous luxury chain in the Maldives (its first resort in North Male' Atoll is one of the best in the country). This latest ingenious addition to the scene has captured our hearts with a simple concept that works so well.

ARI ATOLL

ALSO IN ARI ATOLL

Constance Halaveli Resort (Halaveli island; ☎ 6667000; www.halaveli.com) was closed at the time of research but reopened in mid-2009 as a high-end Constance five-star property following a long closure and a total refit. Expect 57 water villas, three restaurants and a big spa.

Moofushi (Moofushi island; ☎ 6680517; www.moofushi.com) was closed for total refurbishment by the Constance group and is due to reopen in 2011.

Twin Island (Maafushivaru island; ☎ 6660596; www.tclub.com; 38 rooms) is entirely booked through the Italian package travel company TClub. This is a modern-style resort crowded onto a rather small island.

Machchafushi Island Resort (Machchafushi island; www.machchafushi.com) has a fantastic array of dive and snorkelling sites nearby including the extraordinary Kudarah Thila, but was closed for a total refurbishment at press time.

Vakarufalhi (Vakarufalhi island; ☎ 6680004; www.vakaru.com) was closed at the time of research as it renovates itself into a higher category of resort with the addition of the inevitable water bungalows. Due to reopen by 2010.

Beyrumadivaru island is tiny even by local standards and here Banyan Tree has created a mini-resort that manages to combine simplicity with utter fabulousness. The six residences on the island are 'tented pool villas', large, beautifully appointed collections of three tents, all with timber floors, wooden furniture and gorgeous design features, surrounding a large private swimming pool. Other features include an outdoor shower, a vast indoor bathroom and even two twin beds for spa treatments in your own room.

With fleets of staff hidden away far from your eye line in the island's thick foliage, you'll want for nothing. For those who actually wish to leave their tented villa for food (in-villa dining is the norm here) there's a choice of sandbank dining, the main restaurant, Boa Keyo, or the Madi 'Dining Experience', which is dinner on a yacht that sails around nearby islands. More traditionally, diving (with a choice of excellent local sites) can be arranged, as well as almost any excursion or activity. Overall, a great place for a romantic, totally secluded escape.

Northern Atolls

The least developed region of the Maldives, the Northern Atolls are pure tropical island escapism territory. While traditionally the tourism zone has only ever included the three atolls directly to the north of North Male' Atoll, there are another six even further north that have been gradually opening up to tourism as new islands are earmarked for development by the government. These atolls remain almost totally unknown by foreigners, and this is a great place to visit for a taste of untouched, traditional Maldivian life.

Maldivian history owes much to this part of the country – Mohammed Thakurufaanu, the man who drove the Portuguese out in the 16th century, was born on the island of Utheemu in Haa Alif Atoll, which remains a place of historical pilgrimage today for Maldivians who come to see his small wooden mansion.

There's also huge diving potential throughout the region; there are wrecks along the western fringe of the atolls, but these are only now being properly explored and documented.

In the Northern Atolls there are only 16 functioning resorts at present, making this an uncrowded and truly remote part of the country to visit. Tourism is slowly set to expand here, with a number of islands earmarked for development in previously tourist-free Haa Dhaal and Shaviyani Atolls.

About 200km beyond Ihavandhippolhu Atoll, at the country's northern tip, lie the Lakshadweep Islands, which have had a long association with the Maldives. Formerly known as the Laccadives, these islands are now Indian territory, but geologically they are part of the mostly submerged Laccadive-Chagos ridge that underlies all of the Maldives and extends down to the Chagos Archipelago.

HAA ALIF

Traditionally known as Ihavandhippolhu and North Thiladhunmathee Atolls, the very northern tip of the Maldives is generally known to one and all as Haa Alif Atoll, even though this refers to an administrative district that actually comprises the small, trapezoid-shaped Ihavandhippolhu Atoll and the northern tip of North Thiladhunmathee Atoll, which together have 16 inhabited islands and a population of just under 14,000. On Minicoy, the largest island of the Lakshadweep Islands, people speak a language very similar to Divehi and readily understand the Maldivian language themselves.

The second northernmost island, **Uligamu** (population 267) is the 'clear-in' port for private yachts – it has health and immigration officers as well as National Security Service (NSS) personnel, so yachts should be able to complete all formalities here (see p181). Following a feasibility study, the government has decided to establish a yacht marina in the Northern Atolls, but Uligamu has been ruled out for financial and environmental reasons.

The capital island is **Dhidhdhoo** (population 2500), which offers good anchorage for passing yachts. **Huvarafushi**, the next largest island (population 2200), is noted for its

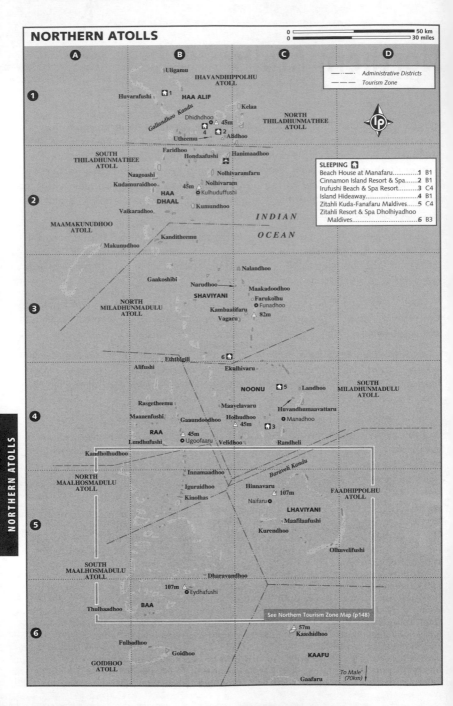

NORTHERN ATOLLS

0 ————————— 50 km
0 ————————— 30 miles

A   B   C   D

— · — · — Administrative Districts
— — — — Tourism Zone

SLEEPING

Beach House at Manafaru.............**1**	B1
Cinnamon Island Resort & Spa......**2**	B1
Irufushi Beach & Spa Resort.........**3**	C4
Island Hideaway..........................**4**	B1
Zitahli Kuda-Fanafaru Maldives.....**5**	C4
Zitahli Resort & Spa Dholhiyadhoo	
Maldives..................................**6**	B3

1

Uligamu

IHAVANDHIPPOLHU ATOLL

Huvarafushi **1**

HAA ALIF

Kelaa

Galandhoo Kandu

Dhidhdhoo 45m
4 **2**
Utheemu Abidhoo

NORTH THILADHUNMATHEE ATOLL

SOUTH THILADHUNMATHEE ATOLL

Faridhoo

Hondaafushi Hanimaadhoo

Naagoashi Nolhivaramfaru

Kudamuraidhoo 45m Nolhivaram

HAA DHAAL Kulhuduffushi

Vaikaradhoo Kumundhoo

2

INDIAN OCEAN

MAAMAKUNUDHOO ATOLL

Makunudhoo Kanditheemu

Nalandhoo

Gaakoshibi Narudhoo Maakadoodhoo

SHAVIYANI Farukolhu

NORTH MILADHUNMADULU ATOLL Kambaalifaru Funadhoo
Vagacu 82m

3

Ethtbigili

6

Alifushi Ekulhivaru

NOONU **5** Landhoo

SOUTH MILADHUNMADULU ATOLL

Rasgetheemu Maayelavaru

Maanenfushi Gaaundoodhoo Holhudhoo Huvandhumaavattaru
45m Manadhoo

RAA 45m **3**

Lundhufushi Ugoofaaru Velidhoo Randheli

4

Kandholhudhoo

NORTH MAALHOSMADULU ATOLL Innamaadhoo

Baraveli Kandu

FAADHIPPOLHU ATOLL

Iguraidhoo Hinnavaru 107m

Kinolhas Naifaru

LHAVIYANI

Maafilaafushi

Kurendhoo

Olhuvelifushi

5

SOUTH MAALHOSMADULU ATOLL

Dharavandhoo

107m
Eydhafushi

Thulhaadhoo BAA

See Northern Tourism Zone Map (p148)

57m
Kaashidhoo

6

Fulbadhoo

Goidhoo KAAFU

GOIDHOO ATOLL

Gaafaru To Male' (70km)

NORTHERN ATOLLS

music, dancing and sporting activities, and it also has a fish-freezing plant.

The island of **Utheemu** (population 520) is the birthplace of Sultan Mohammed Thakurufaanu, who, with his brothers, overthrew Portuguese rule in 1573. A memorial to this Maldivian hero, with a small museum and library, was opened in 1986. Thakurufaanu's wooden palace has been restored and Maldivians come to pay homage to their national hero.

Kelaa (population 1200) was the northern British base during WWII, mirroring Gan at the other end of the archipelago. The mosque here dates from the end of the 17th century. Yams and *cadjan* (mats made of coconut palm leaves) are the island's products.

Resorts

If you're arriving after a long-haul flight in the Maldives, bear in mind that selecting a resort in the far north of the country will add on at least two hours to your journey each way – often more, depending on flight timings. Many travellers have complained that this made all the difference to their moods on arrival and suggested we mention it here!

Cinnamon Island Resort & Spa (Alidhoo island; ☎ 6501111; www.cinnamonhotels.com; s/d/wb US$370/390/490; airport transfer by plane then speedboat total 80min, $330; 100 rooms; ❄ 🖥 🛎 🛜) opened in 2007 as a flagship hotel for the Sri Lankan Cinnamon Hotels group. Alidhoo is an almost perfectly circular island, with heavy foliage in its centre and a dazzling beach in parts, meaning that it certainly looks the part from afar. However, the island itself has no lagoon, with the result that it is particularly vulnerable to shifting sands at any time of the year and so the beach moves and can sometimes be a little small and disappointing.

The accommodation is of high standard, though, ranging from smart and spacious beach villas that have their own outdoor jacuzzis to duplex water villas, all decked out in bright tropical colours and with some terrific ocean views. The lack of a lagoon means that swimming in the sea is not always the experience it should be, though the resort does have a fantastic and large infinity pool.

The food gets rather mixed reports – the mainstay is a decent buffet, while the à la carte restaurants get better feedback. Other facilities include a dive school, water sports centre, library, sumptuous Mandara Spa and the usual host of excursions.

This is a decent upper- to mid-level place with serious top-end aspirations. Given the long journey up to the north, however, consider carefully if you want to come all this extra way.

Island Hideaway (Dhonakhli island; ☎ 6501515; www.island-hideaway.com; r/wb US$1110/1830; airport transfer by plane then speedboat total 80min, $340; 43 rooms; ❄ 🛁 🖥 🛎 🛜) is certainly true to its name – located about as remotely as you can imagine in the Maldives' most northerly atoll. But while some resorts might blanche at the idea of being so far removed from Male' and the busy international airport, Island Hideaway has effortlessly capitalised on it, after all many guests arrive here by private jet at the nearby Hanimaadhoo airport, or by yacht, which can be berthed at the resort itself (there are 30 berths for yachts up to 80m – all state of the art and installed by Walcon Marine).

When Island Hideaway opened in 2005 it was a sensation and has remained a much talked-about benchmark in Maldivian luxury since then. Set on a gorgeous crescent-shaped island with beaches 1.5km long on both sides, this is without a doubt one of the most beautiful resorts in the country.

The five categories of rooms start with the standard Funa Pavilions on the beach – which at 176 sq metres are still rather large. These white-walled houses have separate bedrooms and living rooms, teak floors throughout, slate and onyx finished outdoor bathrooms, all possible conveniences from DVD players to espresso machines, and feature their own gardens. The astonishingly grand water villas and the incredible two Hideaway Palaces (1420 sq metres of faintly ridiculous exclusivity coming in at around US$4000 per night) make up the top end of the resort's accommodation.

The pampering extends to the Mandara Spa, the infinity pool, a range of restaurants and boutiques. The pristine reefs around the island and the untouched sites further afield make another great reason to come here, while the **Meridis Diving School** (www.meridis.de) is exceptionally smart with luxury boats and tiny groups, but inevitably expensive. Some visitors have complained that there are a lot of kids here – unusual perhaps for a resort in this category; it's certainly fair to say that the resort is child-friendly and has a great (free) kids club.

So there you have it: this resort is one of the most exclusive and reclusive in the country (discretion and understatement being its unofficial slogan). So if having a handmade soap menu seems normal to you, you'll fit right in.

Beach House at Manafaru (Manafaru island; ☎ 6500400; www.beachhousecollection.com; r/wb US$1400/1250; airport transfer by plane then speedboat total 120min, $370; 68 rooms; ⊠ 🔲 🔲 🐛 🛜) is the most northerly resort in the country. It opened in late 2007, clearly with an eye to trumping nearby Island Hideaway as the luxury resort everyone was talking about. It hasn't quite worked out like that, however.

We've heard quite a few complaints from people who've paid these prices (the rack rates are slightly higher here than at Island Hideaway) and felt the place wasn't really up to scratch, though in fairness management does seem determined to overcome these teething problems and fix what's wrong. Bear in mind that due to its location this resort takes longer to reach from Male' International Airport than any other in the country, and so guests should rightly expect everything to be top notch once they arrive.

The rooms are without a doubt gorgeously designed, with the starting category alone being an enormous 152 sq metres, going up to the 693 sq metre Grand Beach Pavilion. The look is minimal but stylish with Asian touches such as dark wood fittings and rattan chairs. The resort also has all the facilities you'd expect at these prices – three restaurants, three bars, a gorgeous spa, dive centre and butler service 'to anticipate your needs'.

There is no house reef, however, meaning that the sea can be rather rough and that there's little to see for snorkellers. Another eyebrow raiser is that wi-fi is an incredible US$27.50 per day. Service and food have been said to be hit and miss in the past, and while this can be said for many resorts, it's unusual to hear such a complaint about a place in this price bracket.

HAA DHAAL

Haa Dhaal is an administrative district comprising some 16,000 people spread over 16 inhabited islands and made up of South Thiladhunmathee Atoll (the central section of an elongated reef and lagoon formation extending over 150km north to south) and the far smaller Maamakunudhoo Atoll (a narrow oval of reefs, about 20km to the west).

Kulhuduffushi is the capital island and also the most populous, with 7000 people. It has been chosen by the government as the Maldives' northern regional centre, and has a hospital, secondary school and all basic services. The traditional specialities here are rope making and shark fishing, though a national ban introduced in 2009 by the Maldivian government has forced local shark fishermen to hunt for other fish. The regional airport is on Hanimaadhoo (population 1200). Maldivian has flights to and from Male' on most days – and this is the only runway in all the Northern Atolls, so flights are busy. There was a hotel being built on Hanimaadhoo at the time of writing, which will provide FITs with the opportunity to stay over in a medium-sized Maldivian town en route to their resort if they'd like to see more of the local culture.

The highest natural point in the Maldives, at about 3m above sea level, is on **Faridhoo** (population 87), where there are ancient Buddhist ruins. On **Kumundhoo** there's a stone circle that seems to be the base of Buddhist stupa, and *hawitta* (artificial mound) remains can still be seen on **Vaikaradhoo**.

The area around Haa Dhaal suffers severe storms, and quite a few vessels have gone down in these waters. Maamakunudhoo Atoll is the graveyard of several ships, including the English ships *Persia Merchant*, wrecked here in 1658, and the *Hayston*, which ran onto a reef in 1819. In each instance, survivors were rescued by local people and treated with kindness, a source of great local pride.

The islands of **Hondaafushi**, **Naagoashi** and **Kudamuraidhoo** have been allocated as resorts and building is currently underway.

SHAVIYANI

Looking at a modern map, the Shaviyani administrative district, made up of Miladhunmadulu Atoll and Thiladhunmathee

Atoll, appears to be part of one elongated atoll enclosing a single, very long lagoon. Shaviyani administrative district comprises 15 inhabited islands with a total of 11,940 people. This atoll is most famous today as a major breeding ground for turtles, which breed successfully on its pristine beaches.

The capital is **Funadhoo** (population 1520), a pretty island with the ruins of an ancient mosque and 13th-century tombstones. **Narudhoo** (population 426) is a tiny island with a natural freshwater lake on it – one of the very few places in the whole country where water collects above ground.

The main mosque on the island of **Kanditheemu** (population 1150) incorporates the oldest known example of the Maldives' unique Thaana script – it's an inscription on a doorframe, which notes that the roof was constructed in 1588. Another famous island is uninhabited **Nalandhoo**, where the Thakurufaanu brothers hid their boat between guerrilla battles with the Portuguese.

The beautiful crescent island of Dholhiyadhoo was due to open as the 100-room luxury **Zitahli Resort & Spa Dholhiyadhoo Maldives** (www.zitahlidholhiyadhoo.com) in 2010, the first resort in the atoll.

A further four islands in the atoll have been earmarked for development into resorts. These are **Gaakoshibi, Farukolhu, Kambaalifaru** and **Vagaru** – the latter will be a very posh 35-room Per Aquum spa resort called Maakaana when it is completed.

NOONU

The southern end of the Miladhunmadulu-Thiladhunmathee Atoll complex is called South Miladhunmadulu, and it forms the Noonu administrative district, comprising 13 inhabited islands with a combined total of just over 10,000 people. The capital island, **Manadhoo**, has 1200 people, but **Holhudhoo** (population 1500) and **Velidhoo** (population 1700) are more populous.

On the island of **Landhoo** (population 580) are the remnants of a *hawitta* supposedly left by the fabled Redin, a people who figure in Maldivian folklore. The *hawitta* is a 15m-high mound known locally as *maa badhige* (great cooking place). Thor Heyerdahl writes extensively about the tall, fair-haired Redin in his book *The Maldive Mystery*. He believes them to have been the first inhabitants of the Maldives, as long ago as 2000 BC.

There are now two brand-new resorts open in Noonu, with a further four in the pipeline.

Irufushi Beach & Spa Resort (Medhafushi island; ☎ 6560591; www.irufushi.com; r/wb US$545/641; airport transfer by seaplane 45min, US$355; 180 rooms; ❌ ♨ ☐ ⌨ 🖭) opened in 2008. This enormous development is impressive, from beach villas with charming thatched roofs to water bungalows with their own private pools. Decor is in a minimalist tropical-Asian style, with lots of black wood, rattan furniture and brightly coloured accents.

As with many new resorts there have of course been teething problems – we've heard some fairly unimpressed reports about the food and service in the restaurants. While there is a range of restaurants, all inclusive guests can only eat at the main buffet, which doesn't seem to change much. Other facilities include a great spa, an expensive diving school and water sports centre. The house reef is perfectly OK without being spectacular, although there are some good dive sites nearby.

Zitahli Kuda-Fanafaru Maldives (Kudafunafaru island; ☎ 6561010; www.zitahlikudafanafaru.com; r/wb US$740/800; airport transfer by seaplane 45min, US$375; 50 rooms; ❌ ☐ ⌨ 🖭) is Noonu's similarly new but far smaller and more exclusive-feeling resort, and the first of three Zitahli properties to open in the Maldives. The island itself is a real stunner, with wide powder-white beaches and thick foliage on a perfect lagoon.

The rooms are similarly impressive – all are massive, from the 175 sq metre Deluxe Beach Villas to the Super Deluxe Beach Villa with its own pool at a massive 220 sq metres – you won't feel crowded here! The design of the rooms is as fabulous as you'd expect at these prices, with higher categories coming with their own large private pools and featuring every amenity you can think of – from espresso machines to rain showers to DVD players. The resort offers a full range of facilities from a dive school (very expensive) to a spa, freshwater swimming pool and water sports centre. Again, we've heard guests talk about bad service here, which seems to be typical for non-global brands opening in the Maldives, but otherwise reports of this resort's beauty and excellent rooms have been universally positive.

NORTHERN TOURISM ZONE

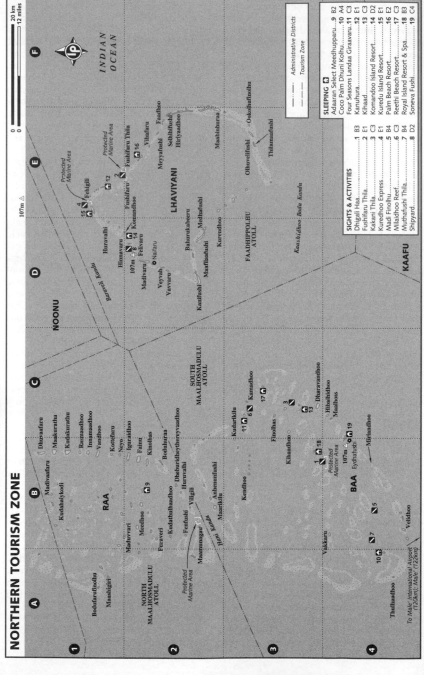

20 km
12 miles

INDIAN
OCEAN

Administrative Districts
Tourism Zone

SIGHTS & ACTIVITIES

Dhigali Haa	**1** B3
Fushifaru Thila	**2** E1
Kakani Thila	**3** C3
Kuredhoo Express	**4** E1
Madi Finolhu	**5** B4
Miladhoo Reef	**6** C3
Muthafushi Thila	**7** B4
Shipyard	**8** D2

SLEEPING 🛏

Adaaran Select Meedhupparu	**9** B2
Coco Palm Dhuni Kolhu	**10** A4
Four Seasons Landaa Giraavaru	**11** C3
Kanuhura	**12** E1
Kihaad	**13** C3
Komandoo Island Resort	**14** D2
Kuredu Island Resort	**15** E1
Palm Beach Resort	**16** E2
Reethi Beach Resort	**17** C3
Royal Island Resort & Spa	**18** B3
Soneva Fushi	**19** C4

RAA

NOONU

LHAVIYANI

NORTH
MAALHOSMADULU
ATOLL

SOUTH
MAALHOSMADULU
ATOLL

FAADHIPPOLHU
ATOLL

BAA

KAAFU

Bodufulhudhoo
Maashigiri

Madivaafaru
Kudahalykodi

Dhuvaafaru
Maakurathu
Kudakurathu
Rasmaadhoo
Innamaadhoo
Vandhoo

Maduvvari
Meedhoo
Furaveri
Kudathuladhoo

Iguraidhoo
Faini
Kinolhas

Kottefaru
Neyo

*Protected
Marine Area*

Fenfushi
Viligili

Dhebaridheythereyvaadhoo
Huravalhi
Anhenunfushi
Maarikilu

Boduhuraa

Kendhoo

Kihaadhoo

Finolhos

Kudarikilu
Kamadhoo

Dharavandhoo
Hithaadhoo
Maalhos

Mirandhoo

Eydhafushi

Vakkaru

Thulhaadhoo

Velidhoo

Hinnavaru
Huravalhi
Madivaru
Veyvah
Yavaru

Fehligili

Komandhoo
Fedivaru
Naifaru

Fushifaru

Bahurukeeru
Kanifushi
Maafilaafushi
Medhafushi

Kurendhoo

Fushifaru Thila
Vihafaru
Meyyafushi
Sehhihfushi
Hiriyaadhoo

Faadhoo

Olhuvelifushi

Maabinhuraa

Oeoihufinolhu

Thilamaafushi

*Protected
Marine Area*

*Protected
Marine Area*

*Protected
Marine Area*

Kashidhoo Badu Kandu

Baareli Kandu

Iloni Kandu

107m △

107m △

107m △

107m △

To Male' International Airport
(120km); Male' (122km)

Four further islands – **Maavelavaru, Randheli, Ekulhivaru** and **Huvandhumaavattaru** – have been allocated for development as resorts.

RAA

Raa administrative district, with around 15,000 people dispersed throughout 15 inhabited islands, is made up of North Maalhosmadulu Atoll and the island of Alifushi. Development has been slow to get going here, but there is now one resort here, and several more on the way. Its isolation has made it popular with diving safari boats, and new dive sites are being documented all the time.

The sea to the west of Raa has some of the best fishing areas in the country. The capital island **Ugoofaaru** (population 3000) has one of the largest fishing fleets in the country.

Tragedy struck Raa in 2004, when the tiny but crowded island of **Kandholhudhoo** was totally destroyed by the tsunami. The 3600 people who lived there are now dispersed around other islands in the atoll. The previously uninhabited island of Dhuvaafaru is currently being developed for the displaced population, though until the island is ready, the resources of the atoll will remained strained, particularly in Ugoofaaru, where many of the refugees now reside.

The island of **Alifushi** (population 2000), which is actually in a small, separate atoll to the north of Raa proper, is reputedly the home of the finest dhoni builders in the country. The government-owned Alifushi Boat Yard continues the tradition, producing a modern version of the dhoni. **Iguraidhoo** (population 1300) and **Innamaadhoo** (population 540) are also boat-building and carpentry centres that are accessible for excursions from Meedhupparu Island Resort.

According to local legend, the now uninhabited island of **Rasgetheemu** is where Koimala Kaloa and his princess wife landed after being exiled from Sri Lanka before moving to Male' to found a ruling dynasty. Another important visitor to the atoll was the Arab seafarer Ibn Battuta, who landed at **Kinolhas** in 1343 and then moved on to Male'.

The channel between Baa and Raa, locally known as Hani Kandu, is also named Moresby Channel after the Royal Navy officer Robert Moresby, who was responsible for the original marine survey of the Maldives made from 1834 to 1836. There's good diving on both sides of the Moresby Channel, as it funnels water between the atolls, bringing pelagic fish and promoting coral growth. Mantas abound in October and November. The channels entering the atoll are studded with interesting thilas, and reefs dot the inside of the atoll.

Resorts

Raa Atoll is currently home to just the one resort. Elsewhere, the islands of **Maanenfushi**, **Gaaundoodhoo**, **Eththigili** and **Lundhufushi** have all been approved for development, though given the global economic downturn their futures are not entirely certain.

our pick **Adaaran Select Meedhupparu** (Meedhupparu island; ☎ 6587700; www.meedhupparu.com; full board s/d/tr US$195/240/325; airport transfer by seaplane 45min, US$285; 215 rooms; ✗ ☐ ☒) is the place to go to truly get away from it all. You are truly remote here: it's the only island resort in the whole of Raa Atoll, which also has extra resorts within a resort scattered about other parts of the island. Lookswise, Meedhupparu does not disappoint, with its gorgeous, wide white beaches sloping down to the perfect turquoise lagoon. While once colonised by the Italian market, Meedhupparu today is the biggest Maldivian resort in the Adaaran chain's group of properties and it attracts many British, German, Russian and Italian visitors.

The resort also features an Ayurvedic Village made up of 24 houses, popular with German guests, as well as an area known as the 'Water Villas' that functions as a resort within a resort, aimed at wealthier clients. The Water Villas complex is marketed separately and non-Water Villa guests are not allowed into the Water Villa area of the island, which includes an exclusive Balinese spa and a charming garden full of Sri Lankan flowers. The rooms elsewhere in the resort are perfectly fine if lacking in character, and the rooms in the Ayurvedic Village are identical, featuring thatched roofs.

Water sports and diving are big attractions here – the water sports activities available include two catamarans, and the diving is so diverse due to the remote location of the resort that new diving spots are constantly being discovered. Over 27 dive sites are visited regularly by the resort's dive boats and there's a huge variety of species to see. However, the diving isn't as cheap as it is at most resorts. On the plus side, there's a huge pool, gym, tennis and badminton courts and a big choice of bars and restaurants to keep people entertained.

BAA

The Baa administrative district includes South Maalhosmadulu Atoll and the small Goidhoo Atoll, 10km further south. Its inhabitants number roughly 10,000 people in 13 inhabited islands and a variety of large resorts. Fishing is the most important activity, but Baa is also famous for its lacquer work and the fine woven-cotton sarong, called a *feylis*. **Eydhafushi**, the capital and principal island (population 2400), is also the *feylis* centre. **Thulhaadhoo** (population 1750) is the second-largest island and the main centre for the production of lacquered boxes and jars. Both of these islands can be visited on excursions from nearby resorts.

Because of its isolation, **Goidhoo** has traditionally been a place for castaways and exiles. In 1602 Francois Pyrard, a French explorer, found himself on the island of **Fulhadhoo** after his ship, the *Corbin*, was wrecked. Incredibly, in 1976 a German traveller was banished here from Male' for the murder of his girlfriend – he refused offers of extradition, converted to Islam and later married a local woman.

Sights & Activities

DIVING

Strong currents flowing through the Kamadhoo Kandu provide an environment for soft corals, which thrive on **Milaidhoo Reef**, on the north side of an uninhabited island. The reef top, at 2m, is great for snorkelling, and it drops straight down to about 35m. This cliff has numerous caves and overhangs with sea fans and sponges.

The north side of **Kakani Thila**, at 25m to 30m, retains coral formations in excellent condition, and colourful soft corals fill the overhangs. It's also home to lots of fish, including Napoleons, jackfish and Oriental sweetlips.

The small **Dhigali Haa**, though well inside the atoll, commonly attracts pelagic species (barracuda) and grey reef sharks. Other fish include jacks, batfish and trevally. It's

also a good place to see nudibranchs, yellow and orange soft corals and anemones (with clown fish).

The sandy **Madi Finolhu** has large coral blocks on which black corals grow. Stingrays can be seen on the sand, and mantas also pass through. This is a good beginners' dive (20m).

Overhangs at **Muthafushi Thila** are home to soft corals and anemones. Many hard corals are in good condition and very colourful, soft corals can also be seen. There are large schools of blue-striped snapper.

Resorts

MIDRANGE

The **Reethi Beach Resort** (Fonimagoodhoo island; ☎ 6602626; www.reethibeach.com; rates via travel agents; airport transfer by seaplane 35min, rates vary; 100 rooms; ✹ ✹) is a budget resort with plenty of charm. The island has lots of natural vegetation, soft white beaches, an accessible house reef and an expansive lagoon. The buildings, all with thatched roofs, are designed to blend with the environment, and also incorporate some Maldivian design elements like the deep horizontal mouldings used on the old Friday Mosque in Male'. Rooms are standard and have air-con, TV, minibar and decent bathrooms. The deluxe villas are more spacious and have better beach frontage, while the water villas are decent but nothing show-stopping.

Guests are mostly British, German and Swiss, many on half-board packages that let them try the weekly barbecue and the two speciality restaurants (Chinese and Maldivian) as well as the selection in the main buffet. No direct bookings are taken here, so apply to travel agents to get a room.

For the sporting guest, there's a swimming pool, gym, squash, badminton and tennis. Windsurfing, sailing and other water sports are popular here because of the wide lagoon. Kitesurfing is also on offer here, as are parasailing, wakeboarding and jet skiing. The spa offers a full range of massage and beauty treatments. The **Sea-Explorer dive centre** (www.sea-explorer.net) is very professional and reasonably priced. Qualified divers can make dives off the house reef, and with few resorts in the area you'll probably have good dive sites to yourself.

Kihaad (Kihaadhuffaru island; ☎ 6606688; www.valtur.com; rates via travel agents; airport transfer by seaplane 35min, incl in package; 100 rooms; (🍴 🏊 🖥 🛜) is exclusively booked out by Italy's Valtur travel agency, meaning its almost entirely Italian clientele are on all-inclusive one-week packages. The island is not open to FITs.

The island is gorgeous and enjoys lots of vegetation and some great sand spits out into the lagoon. The restaurant serves a rich selection of Italian and international dishes: buffet for breakfast and lunch, table service for dinner. The resort has a first-class swimming pool, disco, spa, kids club and water sports centre, and the island itself has shady palm trees, perfect beaches, a lovely lagoon for sailing and a house reef that's accessible for snorkelling and diving.

Royal Island Resort & Spa (Horubadhoo island; ☎ 6600088; www.royal-island.com; half board s/d/tr US$395/405/545; airport transfer by seaplane 35min, US$300; 150 rooms; 🍴 🛜) is Villa Hotels' flagship upmarket resort (its others, such as Paradise Island, Sun Island and Holiday Island, are distinctly lower down the food chain). Though the style here is much more natural than at other Villa properties, it doesn't have the character of smarter or smaller resorts. This is a place for activities and socialising rather than a get-away-from-it-all, shipwreck chic kind of place.

The island is long and narrow, with magnificent long stretches of white beach and a brilliant house reef. Most of the natural vegetation has been preserved, including many coconut palms, pandanuses, screw pines and seven big banyan trees. An old bathing pool and some mosque ruins have also been preserved.

The modern-looking rooms front onto the beach. Inside they have pine walls, hardwood floors and all the gadgets from air-con and IDD phone to kettle and satellite TV. They're nothing special, but functional and comfortable.

The busy main restaurant is a buffet where you sit at the same table every day and are served by the same waiter. Food is decent, though the restaurant is not exactly intimate. A second restaurant specialises in à la carte Mediterranean meals, though it's generally underused.

TOP END

Coco Palm Dhuni Kolhu (Dhunikolhu island; ☎ 6600011; www.cococollection.com.mv; s/d/wb US$546/594/1082;

airport transfer by seaplane 30min, US$320; 100 rooms; 🍴 🖥 🛜) is a favourite with honeymooners and counts an enormous number of its guests as repeat visitors. The island is a stunner, with a wide beach on one side, thick vegetation, and an architecturally interesting space with a tent-like thatched pavilion for reception, restaurant and bar areas.

The beach villa rooms are circular with high, thatched, conical roofs, quality furnishings and open-air bathrooms, while the deluxe rooms have, in addition, an individual plunge pool, though these are now looking a little tired. These island rooms are value for money as the 14 over-water bungalows now feel somewhat antique, and though nice enough are very overpriced. A full refurbishment is planned in the near future.

One definite highlight is the food. All meals are buffet in the main restaurant, but they are of very high quality, while the à la carte Thai restaurant is excellent. Other nice touches include an outdoor cinema, which couples can hire to watch a movie on the beach, a lovely spa and an Ocean-Pro dive centre.

Coco Palm has developed a well-deserved reputation for being an ideal honeymoon and couples' hideaway and we'll be curious to see how things look after its full revamp brings it up to the standards of sister resort Coco Palm Boduhithi (p122).

Further islands that are earmarked for development include **Kihavahuravalhi**, which will be the site of another resort from Thailand's Anantara group, as well as **Vakkaru** and **Mudhdhoo**.

Rightly one of the most famous resorts in the country, eco-fabulous **Soneva Fushi** (Kunfunadhoo island; ☎ 6600304; www.sixsenses.com/soneva-fushi; r from US$662; airport transfer by seaplane 30min, US$360; 65 rooms; 🍴 🏊 🖥 🛜) is a place to get back to nature in some serious style. The personal creation of hoteliers Sonu and his wife Eva, it's an incredibly impressive island where rustic private houses are scattered about in the thick vegetation of one of the Maldives' largest resort islands.

Each villa here is like a small (and in many cases not-so-small) house built with natural materials, fitted with designer furnishings and finished in rustic style. All the deluxe features are included (air-con,

CD player, etc) but most of them are concealed – no plastic is visible. Villas are well spaced around the edges of the island, affording complete privacy – they're reached by sandy tracks that wind through the lush vegetation, which is kept as natural as possible. Given the island's large size, guests get around by bicycle and after a couple of days you really get to know the initially complex pathways that lead you to the various amenities hidden away in the thick foliage.

There's a big range of villas as well as prices, and even if the 15 'standard' Rehendi Rooms come in comfortably below four figures a night, prices quickly rise as you move up the categories. With the choice of five superb restaurants (including the wonderful treehouse-style Fresh in the Garden, where you cross a rope bridge to get to your table), the food is a real highlight of the resort, with as much of it as possible grown here.

This is a resort that takes its eco-credentials and social responsibility seriously. You can take a tour of the resort's recycling area and see the ingenious ways many things are reused on the island, while across the lagoon on Baa's capital Eydhafushi, the resort has built a school. It's hard not to be impressed.

There is a full range of resort recreations, many of them complimentary. The **Soleni dive school** (www.soleni.com) has years of experience diving the sites around Soneva, while the excellent Six Senses spa is the perfect place to indulge yourself. More unusual (free) activities include watching an outdoor film at the lovely Cinema Paradiso and observing the stars in the only resort observatory in the Maldives.

For back-to-nature meets haute couture, you'll find nowhere better than Soneva Fushi.

our pick Four Seasons Landaa Giraavaru (Landaa Giraavaru island; ☎ 6600888; www.fourseasons.com /maldiveslg; r/wb from US$1200/1300; airport transfer by seaplane 30min, US$395; 102 rooms; ✄ ♿ ▢ ☀ ☎) is simply extraordinary. It's a palace of a hotel in the grand style whose combination of brilliantly designed, vast rooms, great beaches and Four Seasons standard of service make it one of the absolute top resorts in the country.

This resort opened in late 2006 on an island that was converted from a coconut plantation (which accounts for the fantas-

tically dense vegetation and high palms). The style fuses traditional Maldivian village with designer minimalism to a stunning degree – bright blue doors, recycled coral stone walls and yellow door frames give way to sleek, industrial-style concrete floors, and traditional dark wood Asian furniture. Rooms in nearly all categories have huge private lap pools and those on land have big gardens with an outdoor sitting room, day bed and direct access to the beach.

With a choice of three vast pools, four great restaurants, a one hectare over-water spa, a kids club, a teenagers club, free water sports and a marine biology lab, it's not a place you can be easily bored. A luxurious diving school runs trips morning and afternoon with a maximum of 12 participants in each group – 20 dive sites are nearby and whale sharks and mantas are very common in September. The Russians have now overtaken the Brits as the biggest nationality here, but being a Four Seasons it attracts a classy international crowd.

LHAVIYANI

The single atoll of Faadhippolhu makes up the administrative district of Lhaviyani, where fishing is the main industry and tourism is gradually becoming more important. It has a population of about 9000 living on just five inhabited islands. On the capital island, **Naifaru** (population 3680), the people have a reputation for making attractive handicrafts from coral and mother-of-pearl, and for concocting local medicines. Nextdoor Madivaru is the site for a new regional airport. **Hinnavaru** (population 3000) is also densely settled, and the central government is promoting the development of **Maafilaafushi** as an alternative, but so far only about 130 people have settled there. Maafilaafushi had a much greater population in the 17th century, but it was later abandoned, though remnants of the old mosque can still be seen. Day trips from the resorts visit all these islands, as well as **Felivaru**, which has a modern tuna-canning plant.

Sights & Activities
DIVING

Usually done as a long drift dive through the channel next to the Kuredu resort, **Kuredhoo Express** is a demanding dive in strong currents, but it also offers brilliant snorkelling on the eastern side. Napoleon wrasse, grey reef sharks and trevally frequent the channel entrance, while inside are overhangs dripping with soft corals. Look for morays, turtles and stingrays. It's a Protected Marine Area.

Shipyard is another demanding dive, with two wrecks within 50m of each other. Strong currents around these ships have promoted rapid growth of soft and hard corals, which now form a habitat for many types of reef fish. Moray eels and sweepers live inside the wrecks, while nurse sharks cruise around the bottom.

When the current is strong, **Fushifaru Thila** is no place for beginners, but when the currents are slow the top of the thila is superb for snorkelling. The thila, with lovely soft corals, sits in the centre of a broad channel and attracts mantas, eagle rays, sharks, groper, sweetlips and turtles. Cleaner wrasse abound on the thila, which is a Protected Marine Area.

Resorts

Though Kuredu has been open for over 25 years, the other resorts are more recent (late 1990s), and reflect the upmarket trend in Maldives tourism. One big new development here is a proposed luxury resort on the island of Hudhufushi, to be managed by Ritz Carlton.

BUDGET

Kuredu Island Resort (Kuredhoo island; ☎ 6620337; www.kuredu.com; s/d/wb US$140/160/340; airport transfer by seaplane 40min, US$260; 330 rooms; ✖ ▢ ☎) is about as close as you can get to a resort city in the Maldives – this truly is the resort that has everything, and people will love it or loathe it in equal measure for this very reason. Since a comprehensive refit several years ago, Kuredu has managed to go impressively upmarket while retaining its very reasonable prices and it's now a great chance to enjoy a midrange style resort at distinctly budget prices.

Established as a diving camp in 1976, Kuredu is favoured by British and German visitors – the former make up some two-thirds of the guests. You can effectively have whatever kind of holiday you're after here – the sheer number of activities and facilities available is mind-boggling. From the only golf course in the Maldives (six holes and a 250m driving range) and kite-

boarding to a decompression chamber and a football pitch, Kuredu has it all.

The beach bungalows all have air-con, phone, hot water and minibar, but are still very affordable. The new, all-wood beach villas face the best beach, have an open-air bathroom, a stereo and coffeemakers, and cost up to US$50 more. Spa beach villas are more expensive again, and the spacious Sangu water villas, made with the honeymooners in mind, are suitably grand. In fact, the Sangu Resort is an exclusive resort within a resort: the restaurant here does first-class buffet meals with live cooking stations as a special attraction and 'wedding' ceremonies or renewal-of-vows services are held here.

The main reception, restaurant, bar, swimming pool, shops and dive centre are all near the centre of the island, and cater for the generally younger, livelier crowd in the less-expensive rooms. The buffets in the main restaurant are pretty good, with a fair selection of Asian and international dishes. In addition there are three à la carte restaurants. Recreation facilities include a gym, tennis courts, a well-used beach volleyball court and the aforementioned golf course. The palatial spa offers Swedish, Thai and Oriental massages as well as lessons. Excursions go to a variety of local fishing villages, resorts and uninhabited islands. There's a day cruise on a traditional wooden yacht (US$75) and a choice of fishing trips. Excellent dive sites are accessible from Kuredu and just a few other resorts.

All in all, Kuredu is a well-run resort with a lively, sociable atmosphere. If you want high-style luxury or intimate island atmosphere, it may not be for you. But for activities such as diving and snorkelling, plus relaxation, recreation, families and fun, Kuredu is hard to beat.

MIDRANGE

Famous throughout the atoll for being a particularly beautiful island, triangular **Palm Beach Resort** (Madhiriguraidhoo island; ☎ 6620087; www.palmbeachmaldives.com; full board s/d/tr US$270/395/535; airport transfer by seaplane 40min, US$340; 118 rooms; ✖ ▢ ☎) enjoys some of the best beaches in the atoll along its almost 2km length. The bungalows dotted along both sides of the island are spacious and have all mod cons, though the white walls, tiled floors and bamboo furniture aren't especially stylish. Most of the resort facilities (restaurant, bar, pool, spa, sports centre) are towards one end of the island, quite a way from some of the rooms. Electric carts and bicycles are available to help people get around.

The main restaurant serves all meals as buffets with an Italian bias, and they're very good. Seven bars are dotted around the island. Live music, discos and other entertainment happens in the pool bar. Tennis, squash and most water sports are free, as are some excursions and snorkelling trips (the lagoon isn't good for snorkelling). The diving school charges very reasonable diving rates and runs the full gamut of courses for beginners.

Most guests come from Italy, but it's not really a club-style resort, and the animation is low-key. In fact, the whole resort has a very casual atmosphere. It attracts all age groups, and quite a few families with children, so it's perfectly possible to stay here as a FIT (fully independent traveller), unlike at many Italian package resorts.

our pick Komandoo Island Resort (Komandhoo island; ☎ 6621010; www.komandoo.com; s/d/wb US$360/460/560; airport transfer by seaplane 40min, US$290; 65 rooms; ✖ ▣ 🛜), the smaller and more stylish sibling of Kuredu, shares the same management. The feel at this resort couldn't really be more different, though – instead of crowds of excitable holidaymakers going from activity to activity, at Komandoo the pace is far more relaxed and the resort ethos is one of pampering and relaxation. There are no children allowed here, making this a favourite spot for honeymooners and other couples enjoying a romantic break.

The round island is ringed by a strikingly beautiful beach, although the sea breaks that surround much of the island obscure the desert-island perfection somewhat. The visitors here are mainly British and German.

The hexagonal rooms, prefabricated in pine from Finland, come complete with air-con, phone, four-poster bed, minibar, safe and CD player, and they all front directly onto a pure white beach. Fifteen water bungalows were added in 2006 and they are suitably impressive.

The four reefs accessible through two channels from the island have a wide variety of marine life (256 fish species have been documented) and recovering corals, so are ideal for snorkelling from the beach.

Perhaps Komandoo's most charming feature is its own uninhabited island just a short boat ride across the lagoon. The island is not lush, but is impressively landscaped. The main restaurant and bar buildings have sea views, sand floors and an intimate feel. The food and service get rave reviews, and the Duniye Spa adds another opportunity for indulgence.

TOP END

Kanuhura (Kanahuraa island; ☎ 6620044; www.kanuhura.com; r/wb US$865/1400; airport transfer by seaplane 40min, US$390; 100 rooms; ✖ 🍴 ▣ 🛒 🛜) is a sumptuous, impressive place with magnificent beaches, stunning accommodation and top-notch food. This place manages to get it right on so many levels – it's classy and stylish without being too formal, it's romantic without being too quiet and it's welcoming to families without allowing the kids to run riot. If you want a laid-back, high-end beach holiday with considerable style, this may be for you.

The rooms combine classical luxury and elegant simplicity. The beach villas have four-poster beds, a separate dressing area, a fabulous indoor-outdoor bathroom, lots of polished timber and a frontage onto the perfect beach. They're equipped with the works – air-con, safe, stereo, satellite TV, DVD, espresso machine, minibar, bathrobes, umbrellas and even slippers. The more expensive suites and water villas are even bigger and feature several rooms, private spas, sun decks and direct sea access.

The resort's public areas, restaurants and spa are focused around the expansive infinity pool near the main jetty. There's also a gym, aerobics studio, karaoke bar, cigar lounge, games room and library with free internet access. Other facilities around the island include the Nashaa nightclub, several boutiques, a coffee shop, tennis and squash courts, and an excellent kids club. This is a complete resort.

At the other end of the island is the high-end outdoor dining option of the Veli Café – overlooking the resort's very own desert islet of Jehunuhura. A complimentary boat shuttles guests back and forth between the two. The main attraction of Jehunuhura being the gorgeous Cove's Beach restaurant, open for lunch, but there's also the beds scattered about the undergrowth for lovers to lounge in while pretending to be in an upmarket version of Lost.

Kanahuraa is a big island, about 1km long, and assiduous landscaping is augmenting the natural vegetation with local species. Lovely, squeaky beaches go right around the island, and the wide lagoon makes for smooth sailing – you can follow the reef for 5km and make your own stops at several tiny uninhabited islands along the way.

The house reef is not suitable for snorkelling, so take one of the special snorkelling excursions run by the dive school. Over 40 dive sites are accessible.

Southern Atolls

The southern atolls of the Maldives have been busy over the past few years providing the country with new resorts in ever more atolls. With far better transport infrastructure than the north of the country – there are three regional airports with daily connections to the capital and a new international airport at Gan, which has helped to open up a brand-new region to direct flights from Europe – this is where some of the most exciting resorts are soon to be seen.

Indeed, development here is set to be huge over the next decade, with each atoll hosting at least one resort development. Already, safari boats are regularly exploring dive sites as far south as the Huvadhoo Kandu (famously known as One-and-a-Half-Degree Channel), and surfing trips are going to the remotest breaks of Gaaf Dhaal. Despite this, the region is almost totally pristine and a wonderful place to visit.

Until recently the southern atolls had retained a traditional way of life for the most part and development had been minimal. The exception was Gan, in the far south of the country, where the British had established military facilities in WWII and an air-force base that operated from 1956 to 1976. Even 30 years after the British departed, Gan still has an unusually British feel. Today, staying at the former RAF base, now the budget Equator Village resort, remains one of the best ways to experience real life in the Maldives, as a road now connects Gan to three other inhabited islands that tourists are free to explore by bicycle or taxi, without the usual restrictions.

VAAVU

The Vaavu administrative district is made up of Felidhoo Atoll (also spelled Felidhe and Fulidhoo) and the small, uninhabited Vattaru Falhu Atoll. This is the least populous area of the country, with around 1600 inhabitants spread over just five inhabited islands.

The main industry is fishing, and there is some boat building as well as two budget tourist resort islands. The capital island is **Felidhoo**, which has only about 450 people, but visitors are more likely to go to its neighbouring island, **Keyodhoo** (population 510), which has a good anchorage for safari boats. At the northern edge of the atoll, **Fulidhoo** (population 330) is an attractive island, regularly visited on day trips from the resorts – you may see some impressively large boats under construction here. **Rakeedhoo** (population 160), at the southern tip of the atoll, is used as an anchorage by safari boats taking divers to the nearby channel.

Sights & Activities

DIVING

There are at least 24 recognised dive sites in the atoll and only two resorts in the area. Some of them are not readily accessible, even from the resorts, and are mostly visited by safari boats. The following sites are rated as among the best in the Maldives, and they all offer superb snorkelling.

A not-too-demanding drift dive in a channel divided by a narrow thila, **Devana Kandu** is a great snorkelling area too. There are several entrances to the channel, which has overhangs, caves, reef sharks and eagle rays. The southern side has soft corals and lots of reef fish. Further in, the passages join up and there is a broad area of hard corals, the deeper parts being less affected by bleaching. The whole channel is a Protected Marine Area.

Fotteyo is a brilliant dive and snorkelling site in and around a channel entrance – it's worth making several dives here. There are numerous small caves, several large caves and various arches and holes, all decorated with colourful soft corals. Rays, reef sharks, groper, tuna, jackfish, barracuda, turtles and even hammerhead sharks can be seen. Inside, the channel floor is known as 'triggerfish alley'.

Rakeedhoo Kandu is a challenging dive in a deep channel – the east and west sides are usually done as separate drift dives. Broad coral shelves cover overhangs and caves, which have sea fans and black corals. Turtles, Napoleon wrasse, sharks and schools of trevally are often seen and the snorkelling on the reef top is brilliant.

A remote channel dive on the southern edge of Vattaru Falhu, **Vattaru Kandu** is now a designated Protected Marine Area. It is not too demanding unless the currents are running at full speed. The reef next to Vattaru is a fine snorkelling area. Around the entrance are many caves and overhangs with soft corals, sea fans and abundant fish life – barracuda, fusilier and white-tip reef sharks. Turtles are sometimes seen here, and manta rays from December to April.

Resorts

As its name suggests, **Alimatha Aquatic** (Alimathaa island; ☎ 6700575; www.alimatharesort.com; s/d US$275/320; airport transfer by seaplane 20min, US$210, by speedboat 1¾hr, US$150; 102 rooms; 🔀) is a resort devoted to the pleasures of diving, snorkelling and water sports. Like its sister resort Dhiggiri, Alimatha was completely renovated in the late 1990s. It's also an Italian-dominated, club-style resort with the guests on inclusive packages. The lagoon is quite wide and more suited to sailing and windsurfing (included in the package price) than snorkelling.

Dhiggiri (Dhiggiri island; ☎ 6700593; www.dhiggiriresort.com; s/d US$340/365; airport transfer by seaplane 20min, US$210, by speedboat 1½hr, US$150; 45 rooms; 🔀) caters largely to the Italian market and so its general style is that of an all-inclusive resort, with all guests on packages that include activities, a couple of excursions, all meals, drinks and nonmotorised water sports. The rooms have air-con, phone, minibar and TV; 10 of them are rather unimpressive water bungalows. It's a small island, a little bit cramped, but splendidly isolated, with pristine dive sites nearby and a house reef that's accessible for snorkellers.

MEEMU

Meemu administrative district (traditionally called Mulaku) has only about 4700 people living on its eight inhabited islands. **Muli** (population 750) is the capital island, and gets a few day visitors from nearby resorts. Nearby **Boli Mulah** and **Kolhuvaariyaafushi** islands, in the south, are more populous, with about 1120 and 800 people, respectively. Both these islands grow yams, which are an important staple in more fertile islands, and an alternative to rice, which must be imported.

The atoll was opened up to tourism with the first resorts built here in the 1990s, and has lots of relatively newly logged dive sites both in the kandus on the edges of the atoll, and inside the atoll around the numerous thilas and giris.

Sights & Activities
DIVING

Shark's Tongue is east of Boli Mulah, in the mouth of the Mulah Kandu. White-tips sleep on the sandy plateau, and grey reef sharks hang around a cleaning station at 20m. In strong currents, black-tip, grey and silver tip sharks cruise through the coral blocks: this is no place for beginner divers.

Giant Clam is an easy dive around two sheltered giris, where several giant clams are seen between 8m and 15m, even by snorkellers. Numerous caves and overhangs are rich with anemones and home to lobsters, groper and glassfish. Colourful butterflyfish and clown triggerfish are easily spotted, but look hard for well-camouflaged stonefish and scorpionfish.

Resorts

Chaaya Lagoon Hakuraa Huraa (Hakuraahuraa island; ☎ 6720014; www.chaayamaldives.com; wb from US$290; airport transfer by seaplane 45min, US$275; 80 rooms; 🔀 🖥), which reopened in 2005 after a posttsunami refit, is now a well-designed resort combining romance and water sports. With nearly all its unusual villas over water (they have tented white roofs and are quite unlike the typical water villa by numbers you'll see in other places), some stunning beaches and plenty of activities, this is a great place to combine activity and indolence.

Catering mainly to British and German guests on all-inclusive packages, Hakuraa offers only over-water bungalows in a massive

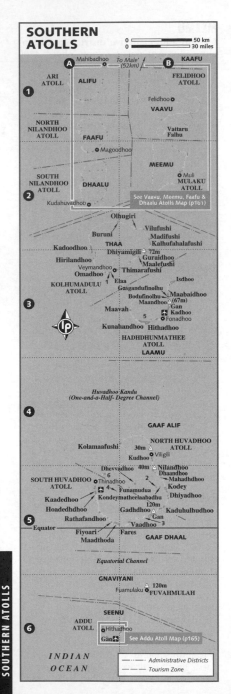

swathe of construction spread out over the lagoon. The lagoon is not good for snorkelling, though snorkelling gear and twice-daily snorkelling trips are included in the package. The dive school is good value and offers what so few centres in the Maldives can these days – access to truly pristine dive sites. With so many little-visited dive sites in the area, diving might be the best reason to stay at Hakuraa.

Medhufushi (Medhufushi island; ☎ 6720026; www .aaaresorts.com.mv; r/wb US$290/390; airport transfer by seaplane 45min, US$280; 120 rooms; ✄ ☐ ☐ ☐) re-opened in 2008 after a full refit by its parent group (which also owns Filitheyo), this quality place is getting good feedback from recent visitors, even if a lot of them ended up here after being bumped from Filitheyo!

Medhufushi is perfect for romance and tranquillity without an enormous price tag. Rooms are reasonably priced for what you get – stylish wooden cabins on the beach with thatched roofs, and even better water villas.

The main activities are water sports and diving in this pristine atoll, where some fantastic new sites are being logged. There's also an excellent spa, a great selection of beaches and a pretty house reef.

Elsewhere in Meemu, the three tiny islands of **Gasveli**, **Dhekunuboduveli** and **Kudausfushi** are earmarked for development into one 60-bedroom resort.

FAAFU

The administrative district of Faafu, also known as North Nilandhoo Atoll, has about 3800 people living on its five inhabited islands. The capital island, **Magoodhoo** (population 520), is a small fishing village with a very traditional Islamic community.

Sights & Activities

On the southern edge of the atoll, **Nilandhoo** (population 1500) has the second-oldest mosque in the country, Aasaari Miskiiy, built during the reign of Sultan Mohammed Ibn Abdullah (1153–66). It is made of dressed stone and the interior is decorated with carved woodwork. It's possible that the stones were recycled from the ruins of earlier, pre-Islamic structures.

Thor Heyerdahl's book *The Maldive Mystery* has an entire chapter about this island. His expedition unearthed many phallic stone carvings, like the lingam associated with the Hindu god Shiva in his manifestation as the creator. Some of these images can be seen in the National Museum in Male'. Heyerdahl's expedition also found ruins apparently from an ancient gate, one of seven surrounding a great pagan temple complex. You can visit Nilandhoo on a full-day excursion from Filitheyo resort, but the ruins are mostly unexcavated. As Heyerdahl wrote:

Five teams of archaeologists could dig here for five years and still make new discoveries. The magnitude of this prehistoric cult centre seemed quite out of proportion to the size of the island.

The diving in the area is the other main attraction.

Filitheyo Reef, the kandu south of Filitheyo resort, is now a Protected Marine Area and has several diving possibilities. Only accessible by boat, the house reef on the southeast corner of the resort descends in big steps, where great clouds of fish school. Swarms of batfish and several Napoleons are resident, while grey reef sharks, rays and trevally are frequent visitors.

The **Two Brothers** are two thilas located in a narrow channel. The big 'brother' (north) tops out at 3m and is covered with soft corals and sponges, and attracts snorkellers. Many turtles reside here. Big pelagics cruise around both 'brothers' and there are lots of nudibranchs, pipefish, gobies and other small marine life.

Resorts

Filitheyo (Filitheyo island; ☎ 6740025; www.aaaresorts .com.mv; s/d/tr/wb US$218/242/315/427; airport transfer by seaplane 35min, US$290; 125 rooms; 🍽 🖥 🏊) is a beautifully designed and finished resort on a large, well-vegetated, triangular island. The public buildings are spacious, open-sided Balinese-style pavilions with palm-thatch roofs and natural touches.

Most rooms are comfortable timber bungalows facing the best beach, nested among

the palm trees, and equipped with amenities including open-air bathrooms and personal sun decks. Deluxe villas provide extra space and style, while the water villas have sea views and private balconies. Resort facilities include a gym, small spa, infinity pool, reading room and shops. Some low-key evening entertainment is organised, and there's an interesting programme of excursions and fishing trips.

Beaches are pretty all around, but the lagoon is shallow on the south side, and not suitable for swimming on the east side. The north side has it all – soft sand, good swimming and an accessible house reef that's great for snorkelling. Qualified divers can do unguided dives off the house reef too.

The atoll is also home to the faintly ridiculous **Rania Experience** (Maafushi island; ☎ 6740555; www.raniaexperience.com; island all-inclusive per night US$12,000; 🍽 🖥 🏊 🛁), currently the most sumptuous resort in the country. Here you get the island of Maafushi to yourself, a staff of 25, a private yacht and basically anything you damn well please. There's a minimum three-night stay, and frankly, you probably can't afford it.

DHAALU

The administrative district of Dhaalu is made up of the South Nilandhoo Atoll and has about 5000 people living on its seven inhabited islands.

The biggest and most interesting island is the capital, **Kudahuvadhoo** (population 1600), which has an ancient and mysterious mound. The mound is now just sand, but originally this was the foundation of a structure made of fine stonework. The building stones were later removed to build part of the island's mosque. Heyerdahl said the rear wall of this mosque had some of the finest masonry he had ever seen, surpassing even that of the famous Inca wall in Cuzco, Peru. He was amazed to find such a masterpiece of stone-shaping art on such an isolated island, although the Maldivians had a reputation in the Islamic world for finely carved tombstones. Kudahuvadhoo is a long way from the resorts on this atoll, so visiting is difficult, but worth enquiring about. The waters around Kudahuvadhoo have seen several shipwrecks, including the 1340-ton *Liffey*, which went down in 1879, and the *Utheem*, which hit the same reef in 1960.

In the north of the atoll are the so-called 'jewellers islands'. **Ribudhoo** (population 210) has long been known for its goldsmiths, who are believed to have learnt the craft from a royal jeweller banished here by a sultan centuries ago. Another possibility is that they developed their skills on gold taken from a shipwreck in the 1700s. The nearby island of **Hulhudheli** (population 560) is a community of traditional silversmiths. Most of the gold and silver work on sale in Male' now seems to be imported, though the gold chains and medallions worn by many children may be made in these islands. Many of the craftspeople here are now making jewellery, beads and carvings from black corals and mother-of-pearl. Both islands are quite accessible from the nearby resorts.

Sights & Activities
DIVING
A big attraction of these resorts is the access to infrequently explored dive sites.

A channel on the northern edge of the atoll, **Fushi Kandu** is a Protected Marine Area. Steps on the east side have eagle rays and white-tip reef sharks. Thilas inside the channel are covered with hard and soft corals, and are frequented by turtles, Napoleon fish and schooling snappers. Look for yellowmouth morays and scorpionfish in the crevices.

Macro Spot, a sheltered, shallow giri, makes a suitable site for snorkellers, novices and macrophotographers. Overhangs and nooks shelter lobsters, cowries, glassfish, blennies and gobies.

Resorts
our pick **Vilu Reef** (Meedhuffushi island; ☎ 6760011; www.vilureef.com; half board d/tr/wb US$470/635/900; airport transfer by seaplane 35min, US$350; 122 rooms; ✕ ▣ ⊠) is something of a closely guarded secret for its many repeat visitors. It's small, with huge palms and great beaches almost all the way around the island, which are especially good on the lagoon side. The island itself is thick with trees and bushes and, despite being quite crowded, has been developed with considerable care.

The style is traditional on the outside (white walls, thatched roofs) and modern convenience inside. The rooms range from the attractive but simple semi-detached beach villas to the far more sumptuous water villas. They are all equipped with mod cons as well as decent outdoor bathrooms.

On one side, a wide beach faces a lagoon that's perfect for sailing and sheltered swimming, while on the other side a nice but narrower beach fronts a house reef that offers excellent snorkelling. Divers are well catered for by the reasonably priced diving school that runs a full range of courses.

Vilu Reef is a good choice – combining friendly informality with some class and style – and it's a great place to come for people looking for well-priced diving without having to go to a very basic resort.

Angsana Velavaru (Velavaru island; ☎ 6760028; www.angsana.com; r/wb US$505/1260; airport transfer by seaplane 35min, US$320; 84 rooms; ✕ ▣ ⊠) This ultra-chic resort is Angsana's second Maldivian property and a welcome international brand in the southern atolls. Taking over from a far more midrange resort following the tsunami, the redeveloped island enjoys classy accommodation with a strong Asian feel. The deluxe beachfront villas with pools are sumptuous.

Instead of over-water bungalows, the new 'InOcean' villas are stand-alone structures a kilometre out from the main island, connected by boats to the mainland across the lagoon. While they're dazzling, with every possible feature, including vast swimming pools, terraces, day beds and outdoor bathrooms, surely we can't be alone in wondering why you'd want to be so far from the main island?

The island itself is a real stunner – it has wide sandy beaches where turtles once nested (Velavaru means 'turtle island') – and while the wide lagoon is no good for snorkelling, there are free snorkelling trips every day. Dive sites in this atoll are not well documented, but the Velavaru Marine Centre is working on changing that.

Elsewhere in the far south of the atoll, the islands of **Maafushi**, **Embudhoofushi** and **Olhuveli** have been put for tender as resort islands. A regional airport is also mooted for Kudahuvahoo, which will massively increase the atoll's appeal for holidaymakers.

THAA
Thaa administrative district, or Kolhumadulu Atoll, is a large, slightly flattened circle about 60km across, and one of the major fishing regions of the country. It

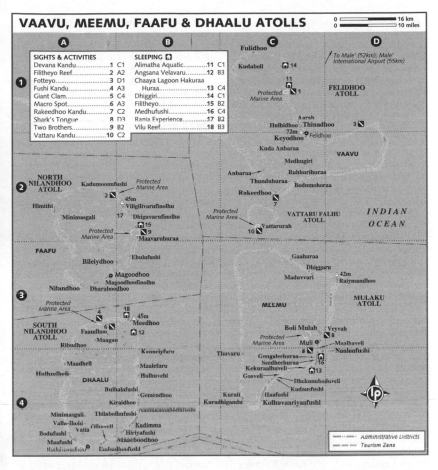

VAAVU, MEEMU, FAAFU & DHAALU ATOLLS

0   16 km
0   10 miles

SIGHTS & ACTIVITIES		
Devana Kandu	1	C1
Filitheyo Reef	2	A2
Fotteyo	3	D1
Fushi Kandu	4	A3
Giant Clam	5	C4
Macro Spot	6	A3
Rakeedhoo Kandu	7	C2
Shark's Tongue	8	D3
Two Brothers	9	B2
Vattaru Kandu	10	C2

SLEEPING		
Alimatha Aquatic	11	C1
Angsana Velavaru	12	B3
Chaaya Lagoon Hakuraa		
Huraa	13	C4
Dhiggiri	14	C1
Filitheyo	15	B2
Medhufushi	16	C4
Rania Experience	17	B2
Vilu Reef	18	B3

consists of 13 inhabited islands and is home to about 8500 people. The capital island is **Veymandhoo** (population 920). All the islands are on the edges of the atoll, mostly clustered around the kandus, and they're quite densely settled. **Thimarafushi** (population 1250), near the capital, is the most populous island, and with two other islands makes up a sizable community. Ruins of a 25m-wide mound on the island of **Kibidhoo** show this group of islands has been populated for centuries.

On **Guraidhoo** (population 1150), in another island group, is the grave of Sultan Usman I, who ruled the Maldives for only two months before being banished here. On **Dhiyamigili** (population 450) there are ruins of the palace of Mohammed Imaaduddeen II, a much more successful sultan who ruled from 1704 to 1721 and founded one of the Maldives' longest-ruling dynasties.

The northern island of **Buruni** (population 570) is a centre for carpenters, many of whom work elsewhere, building boats and tourist resorts. The women make coir rope and reed mats. Around the mosque are an old sundial and tombstones that have been dated to the late 18th century. The island of **Vilufushi** was abandoned by its inhabitants following the 2004 tsunami.

There are currently no operational resorts in Thaa, but the islands of **Elaa, Kalhufahalafushi, Maalefushi** and **Olhugiri** are all in various stages of becoming resorts.

LAAMU

Geographically known as Hadhdhunmathee Atoll, Laamu administrative district has about 12,000 people living on its 12 inhabited islands, and it's one of the major fishing centres in the country. Freezer ships anchor near the former capital, **Hithadhoo** (population 830), collecting fresh fish directly from the dhonis.

The island of **Kadhoo** has an airfield (airport code KDO) that has regular flights from Male'. Kadhoo is linked by causeways to the large island of **Fonadhoo** (population 1760) to the south, which is now the atoll capital. The causeway also goes north to the islands of **Maandhoo** (population 490) and **Gan** (population 2500), forming one of the longest stretches of road in the country – all of 12km. Maandhoo has a government-owned STO (State Trading Organisation) refrigeration plant and a fish-canning factory.

There are numerous archaeological sites in Laamu, with evidence of pre-Muslim civilisations on many islands. At the northeastern tip of the atoll, on **Isdhoo** (population 1550), a giant, black dome rises above the palms. Who built the ancient artificial mound, known as a *hawitta*, and for what reason, is not really known. Buddha images have been found on the island, and HCP Bell believed such mounds to be the remains of Buddhist stupas, while Heyerdahl speculated that Buddhists had built on even earlier mounds left by the legendary Redin people. For many years the mound was a landmark for boats navigating between the atolls, but it didn't save the British cargo ship *Lagan Bank*, which was wrecked here on 13 January 1938. The **Friday Mosque** on Isdhoo is around 300 years old. It was probably built on the site of an earlier temple because it faces directly west, rather than towards Mecca, which is to the northwest.

Bell also found quite a few mounds on Gan (also known as Gamu) island, which he also believed to be Buddhist stupas, and he found a fragment of a stone Buddha face, which he estimated was from a statue over 4m high. Almost nothing remains of these structures because the stones have been removed to use in more modern buildings. There are mounds on several other islands in Laamu, including Kadhoo, Maandhoo and Hithadhoo – one is over 5m high.

The **Six Senses Latitude Laamu** (Olhuvelhi island; ☎ 6800800; www.sixsenses.com; 100 rooms) is due to open in late 2009 as Laamu's first resort, and as it's a venture of the same company that gave us Soneva Fushi and Soneva Gili, it's definitely going to be something fairly spectacular – stay tuned.

Elsewhere in the atoll, the twin islands of **Bodufinolhu** and **Gasgandufinolhu** have been allocated for a 200-bed resort.

GAAF ALIF

The giant Huvadhoo Atoll, one of the largest true coral atolls in the world, is separated from Laamu by the 90km-wide Huvadhoo Kandu. This stretch of water is also called the One-and-a-Half-Degree Channel, because of its latitude, and it's the safest place for ships to pass between the atolls that make up the Maldives.

Because Huvadhoo is so big, and perhaps as a response to the 'southern rebellion' (see p164), the atoll is divided into two administrative districts. The northern district is called Gaaf Alif, and it has 10 inhabited islands and about 8300 people. **Viligili**, the capital island, is also the most populated, with about 2000 people. Just south, the island of **Kudhoo** has an ice plant and fish-packing works. The atoll also has some productive agriculture, much of it on **Kodey** (population 215). This island also has four *hawittas* – evidence of Buddhist settlement. Heyerdahl discovered a limestone carving here, which he believed to be of the Hindu water god Makara. The statue must have been here before the Islamic period and is thought to be over 1000 years old. Its significance, Heyerdahl believed, lay in the fact that it demonstrated that other religions aside from Buddhism permeated the Maldives before Islam took hold in 1153.

In the centre of the atoll, **Dhevvadhoo** (population 500) is not well placed for fishing or farming, but the islanders are famous for their textile weaving and coir-rope making. There are also mosques from the 16th and 17th centuries.

At the time of writing, two resorts were nearing completion: Per Aquum's 'destination spa' **Soul Salus Fushi** (www.peraquum.com) on the island of Meradhoo and **Alila Villas Hadahaa** (www.alilavillas.com) on the island of Hadahaa. Both should be open by 2010.

The islands of **Kondeymatheelaabadhu**, **Mahadhdhoo** and **Funamudua** were under tender for development at press time.

GAAF DHAAL

Geographically isolated from Male', but strategically located on the Indian Ocean trade routes, Gaaf Dhaal – or Huvadhoo Atoll, to use its geographical name – had independent tendencies dating back many years. It had its own direct trade links with Sri Lanka, and the people spoke a distinct dialect almost incomprehensible to other Maldivians. The island of **Thinadhoo** was a focal point of the 'southern rebellion' against the central rule of Male' during the early 1960s. So much so that troops from Male' invaded in February 1962 and destroyed all the homes. The people fled to neighbouring islands and Thinadhoo was not resettled until four years later. It now has a population of 4450. Huvadhoo Atoll was divided into two administrative districts, the southern part being Gaaf Dhaal, which now has over 11,000 people on 10 inhabited islands and Thinadhoo as its capital.

Though remote from any resorts, Gaaf Dhaal has a small but growing number of foreign visitors who make boat trips around the southeastern edge of the atoll to surf the uncrowded waves that break around the channel entrances (see p91). On the island of **Kaadedhoo**, near Thinadhoo, a small airport (airport code KDM) has daily connections to Male' with Maldivian, and the surfing safari boats meet clients there.

On **Gadhdhoo** (population 1450), women make superb examples of the mats known as *tundu kunaa*, which are woven from special reeds found on an adjacent island. Souvenir shops in Male' and on some resorts sell these mats – those from Gadhdhoo are the softest and most finely woven.

Just southwest of Gadhdhoo, the uninhabited island of **Gan** has remnants of one the most impressive *hawittas*, originally a pyramid with stepped ramps on all four sides, like many Mexican pyramids. The ruin was 8.5m high and 23m square. Heyerdahl also found stones here decorated with sun motifs, which he believed were proof of a sun-worshipping society even older than the Buddhist and Hindu settlements.

In the south of the atoll, only about 20km from the equator, the island of **Vaadhoo** has two *hawittas*, and a mosque that dates from the 17th century. The mosque is elaborately decorated inside and has a stone bath outside, as well as ancient tombstones carved with three different kinds of early Maldivian script.

Gaaf Dhaal is about to see its first resort, **Raffles Konottaa** (www.raffles.com), which will be the first venture of the Singapore-based Raffles hotel group in the Maldives, while **Alila Villas Lonudhuahutta** (www.alilavillas.com) is to be the second Alila property in the country. Opening dates were uncertain at press time.

GNAVIYANI

Gnaviyani administrative district is made up of just one island, intriguing **Fuvahmulah** (confusingly often called Foahmulah or Fuamulaku as well). It's not an atoll, but rather a solitary island stuck in the middle of the Equatorial Channel with a population of around 7600. About 5km long and 1km wide, it's the biggest single island in the country and one of the most fertile, producing many fruits and vegetables such as mangoes, papayas, oranges and pineapples. Yams grow so well here that they were once a dietary staple, though rice is now preferred. The natural vegetation is lush, and there are two freshwater lakes.

A beach goes around most of the island, but the fringing reef is quite narrow and is pounded by big waves on whatever side is exposed to the prevailing swells. The lack of a safe anchorage has always limited fishing activity and made it difficult to get passengers and goods ashore. With help from the national government, a new harbour was completed at the eastern tip of the island in 2003, allowing Fuvahmulah to join the modern world by enabling goods and equipment to be brought in easily and making development of some light industry feasible.

A new road links the harbour and the main village at the island's heart. New roads, wetland reclamation and infrastructure improvements are planned. A 120m-high telecommunications tower in the island's centre is visible from miles away. It makes the microwave connection north to Gaaf Dhaal and south to Addu Atoll, and has reduced the island's isolation, which now has an internet cafe and well-used mobile-phone service.

Fuvahmulah is officially divided into seven districts, but most of the people live around the north side and across the centre of the island in villages that appear to be a continuous settlement. Sandy roads crisscross the island, and there are lots of motorcycles and small pick-up trucks. Many of the people work in resorts in the tourism zone, and the money they send home partly accounts for the apparent affluence of the island.

Despite Fuvahmulah's apparent isolation, navigators passing between the Middle East, India and Southeast Asia have long used the Equatorial Channel. Ibn Battuta visited in 1344, stayed for two months and married two women. Two Frenchmen visited in 1529 and admired the old mosque at the west end of the island. In 1922 HCP Bell stopped here briefly, and noted a 7m-high *hawitta*. Heyerdahl found the *hawitta* in poor condition, and discovered remnants of another nearby. He also investigated the nearby mosque, the oldest one on the island, and believed it had been built on the foundations of an earlier structure built by skilled stonemasons. Another old mosque, on the north side of the island, had expertly made stonework in its foundations and in an adjacent stone bath.

Fuvahmulah is not an easy destination for modern travellers, although there's a new hotel under construction here. To get to Fuvahmulah you go by boat via Gan, which has several scheduled flights a day from Male'. From Gan it's 50km and you'll need to charter a launch, unless you're able to get a place on the passenger boat that carries about 20 people and takes just over an hour if the weather is OK. Unfortunately, until the Maldives opens up to independent tourism, visiting fascinating places like Fuvahmulah will be more trouble than it's worth to most people.

ADDU ATOLL

Definitely one of the best places for independent travellers to come, heart-shaped Addu Atoll is the most southern extreme of the country and has a very different feel to it for a number of reasons. It's good for so-called FITs (fully independent travellers), as from Equator Village, the charming budget resort on the former British naval base of Gan, you can cycle to three inhabited islands via a causeway – the only resort in the country where you have such access and freedom.

Addu Atoll is the main economic and administrative centre in the south of the country, and the only place to rival Male' in size and importance. Its 18,000 people spread out over seven inhabited islands is a huge number for the Maldives. Now the location of the Maldives' second international airport and the huge, luxury Shangri-La resort being built on the nearby island of Viligili, the re-

gion will play an important role in the future development of the Maldives' travel market.

There is an independent streak in the Addu folk – they even speak differently from the people of Male'. Tensions came to a head in the 1960s under the leadership of Abdulla Afif Didi, who was elected president of the 'United Suvadiva Islands', comprising Addu, Fuvahmulah and Huvadhoo. Afif declared independence from the Maldives, but an armed fleet sent south by Prime Minister Ibrahim Nasir quashed the short-lived southern rebellion. Afif fled the country, but is still talked about on his home island of Hithadhoo. He went to live in the Seychelles, where he ultimately rose to the position of foreign minister.

The biggest influence on Addu's modern history has been the British bases, first established on Gan during WWII as part of the Indian Ocean defences. In 1956, when the British could no longer use Sri Lanka, they developed a Royal Air Force base on Addu as a strategic Cold War outpost. The base had around 600 personnel permanently stationed here, with up to 3000 during periods of peak activity. The British built a series of causeways connecting Feydhoo, Maradhoo and Hithadhoo islands and employed most of the population on or around the base. In 1976 the British pulled out, leaving an airport, some large industrial buildings, barracks and a lot of unemployed people who spoke good English and had experience working for Westerners. When the tourism industry took off in the late 1970s, many of the men of Addu went to Male' to seek work in resorts and tourist shops. They have never lost their head start in the tourism business and to this day, in resorts all over the country, there's a better than even chance that the Maldivian staff will be from Addu.

Tourism development in Addu itself has been slow to start, due to bad transport links. The Shangri-La resort, finally due to open by 2010, has been years in the making. Now there are several flights a day to Male' and a few direct charter flights to Gan from Europe.

Sights & Activities
DIVING

A particular highlight of Addu is the magnificent coral here, much of which escaped the widespread coral bleaching of 1998. If you go diving elsewhere in the Maldives

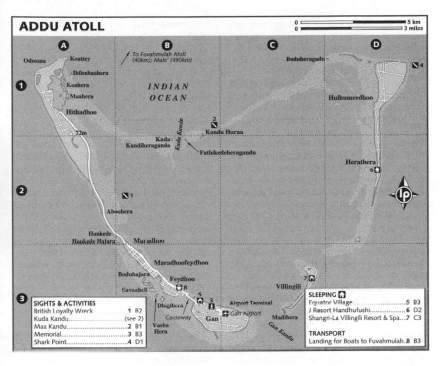

ADDU ATOLL

SIGHTS & ACTIVITIES
British Loyalty Wreck	**1** B2
Kuda Kandu	(see 2)
Maa Kandu	**2** B1
Memorial	**3** B3
Shark Point	**4** D1

SLEEPING 🏠
Equator Village	**5** B3
J Resort Handhufushi	**6** D2
Shangri-La Villingili Resort & Spa	**7** C3

TRANSPORT
Landing for Boats to Fuvahmulah	**8** B3

and then come here you'll be amazed. On the northern edge of the atoll you can see huge table corals that might be hundreds of years old, and fields of staghorns that have all but disappeared in most parts of the country. It's not all good, though – corals inside the lagoon suffered as badly as anywhere else from coral bleaching.

The **British Loyalty Wreck** has a good covering of soft corals, and turtles, trevally and many reef fish inhabit the encrusted decks. This oil tanker was torpedoed in 1944 by the German submarine U-183, which fired through an opening in the antisubmarine nets at the entrance to Gan Kandu. The disabled ship stayed in the atoll until 1946 when it was towed to its present location and used for target practice by another British ship. The 140m wreck lies in 33m of water with its port side about 16m below the surface.

The northeastern edge of **Maa Kandu** has a wide reef top, between 5m and 7m, covered with live acrophora corals – big brain corals, long branching staghorns and table corals 3m across. White-tip reef sharks, eagle rays and sometimes mantas can be spotted,

along with turtles and numerous reef fish. It's an excellent site for snorkelling.

Kuda Kandu is another superb sight near to Maa Kandu, where a huge array of coral thrives between 5m and 15m. Currents can be strong here, so it's not for novices.

Off the northeast corner of the atoll **Shark Point**, sometimes called the Shark Hotel, is a plateau at about 30m. Grey reef sharks cruise around here, white-tip reef sharks lie on the sand and other sharks can be seen in deeper water further out.

GAN

Gan (also known as Gamu) is atypical of the Maldives: it has a far more colonial feel and a refreshingly different atmosphere from anywhere else in the country. Even though you'll be staying at a resort here, there's much more to do and see here than at your standard Maldivian desert island.

Inhabited since ancient times, Gan was the site where HCP Bell excavated a large 9m-high mound. He believed it to be the ruins of a Buddhist stupa. His expedition made careful measurements of the site, took photos and made precise drawings that are published in his monograph. This was fortunate, as the archaeological sites and almost everything else on Gan were levelled to create the air-force base in 1956.

The British took over the entire island and constructed airport buildings, barracks, jetties, maintenance sheds, a Naafi (Navy, Army and Air Force Institutes) canteen, a golf course, tennis courts and a 2600m concrete runway. For more information about RAF Gan, go to www.gan.philliptsmall.me.uk. Many of these structures remain, some picturesquely run-down, others used for various purposes. Most of the island's lush native vegetation was cleared, but the British then landscaped with new plants – avenues of casuarinas, clumps of bougainvillea, swaths of lawn and even roses. It's much more spacious than most resort islands and it has a slightly weird and eerie atmosphere, but it's very peaceful and relaxed – like an old, abandoned movie set.

One sight is a low-key **memorial** to those who served on the base, including Indian regiments such as the 13th Frontier Force Rifles and the Royal Bombay Sappers & Miners. Dozens died here 'in the service of their country', though the atoll saw no action at all apart from the 1944 attack on the British Loyalty. Big guns, which were part of the WWII defences, now guard the memorial. Across the road are the post office, some telephones and a branch of the Bank of Maldives. The old Astra cinema, a fixture at all RAF bases, has a few nifty 1950s architectural touches. Several times a week it shows Indian and Sri Lankan movies to entertain the Sri Lankan garment workers who now work on the island and live in some of the former barracks. There are several pleasant cafes scattered around the island.

West of the Equator Village resort is a complex of buildings that used to be the officers' mess and living quarters. It's now the 'Dhoogas', a facility providing accommodation for visiting government officials, and off-limits to foreigners. A small and unimposing building here was once a chapel, but has been converted to a mosque. You can walk or cycle right around the island on narrow dirt roads, crossing the airport runway at each end. You'll see lots of trees and greenery, a couple of graveyards and a few incongruous buildings. There are no decent beaches and no surfable waves – just the Indian Ocean crashing on a broad, shallow reef.

FEYDHOO, MARADHOO & HITHADHOO

The causeways and the new road go from Gan to the atoll capital Hithadhoo via Feydhoo and Maradhoo as well as some other tiny islands that are now joined together. There are no spectacular attractions along the way, but the smaller villages are an absolute delight. Local teashops serve tea, cakes and 'short eats', and some will have a more substantial fish curry. Remember that these villages are inevitably very conservative, so dress modestly.

Like most Maldivian villages they are laid out on a rectangular grid with wide, straight, sandy streets and white coral-stone houses. A few vehicles will be seen, but for most of the day the streets are empty. In the early morning, and especially the evening, locals will be out walking or cycling, sitting outside their houses or leaning against the low front walls. Shady trees overhang the streets and you can usually catch a glimpse of the sea at one end of the street or the other.

Most of the houses have corrugated iron roofs, but are otherwise traditional. Older buildings are made of coral-stone while newer ones are made of concrete blocks. There's usually a courtyard or an open space with a shady tree and a *joli* or *undholi* providing a cool place to sit in the heat of the day. Notice the big, square chimney blocks – there are wooden racks inside them, where fish are hung to be smoked. Another distinctive feature can be seen at street junctions, where walls and buildings all have rounded corners.

You can easily walk from Gan to Feydhoo (population 2724), which has several mosques – a large, new white one, a small, pretty blue one, and several old ones on the sandy back roads that look a little like tiny churches. On the new lagoon-side road are several new buildings, like the modern petrol station, a big store and a teahouse/cafe offering great short eats. Boats to Fuvahmulah use the small harbour here.

When the British took over, the villagers from Gan were resettled on Feydhoo, and some of the people from Feydhoo were then moved to the next island, Maradhoo, where they formed a new village. Maradhoo now has a population of 2000 in two villages that have run together – the southern one is called Maradhoo-Feydhoo. The first thing you'll see as you approach up the road is the boat-building activity on the lagoon side.

Further north, the road follows an isthmus that was once three narrow, uninhabited islands. One island used to house an ammunition bunker. After a few kilometres of palm tree lined road you pass a recycling zone and a sports ground with several football pitches and a grandstand. You're on Hithadhoo, the Maldives' largest town outside Male', with a population of 9500. The Dhiraagu office near the tower has pay phones and an internet cafe. Further up the road are a new mosque and several schools – the high school is one of two outside Male' that teaches up to A level (matriculation). There's nothing in particular to see here, but there are a few shops and just wandering and seeing a real Maldivian town is quite something.

Near the main road there are several light-industry buildings and a power station, while a grid of streets with traditional houses extends to the western seashore. Beyond the built-up area, the tip of the island bends to the east, and is covered with coconut plantations, swampy lakes and a surprising amount of woodland. The coast is mostly too rocky or shallow for bathing, but there are some narrow beaches. Rough roads go right to the tip of the island at Koattey, also called Demon Point. It's said there was once a fort here, and later a British gun emplacement, but there's nothing left to see now. It feels like the end of the earth.

HULHUMEEDHOO

At the northeast corner of the lagoon, this island has two adjoining villages, Hulhudoo and Meedhoo, both known as Hulhumeedhoo, with a total population of about 2600. Local legend says that an Arab was shipwrecked here in about 872, and converted the islanders to Islam 280 years before the people of Male'. The cemetery is known for its ancient headstones, many of which are beautifully carved with the archaic Dhives Akuru script. The southern half of Hulhumeedhoo is now the enormous J Resort Handhufushi, which is the second-largest resort in the country, and unusual for being on the same island as Maldivian settlements. Guests at the resort are of course free to visit Meedhoo and Hulhudhoo.

Resorts

our pick **Equator Village** (Gan island; ☎ 6898721; www.equatorvillage.com; all-inclusive s/d/tr US$130/188/240; flight from Male' to Gan 1½hr, US$300, three-minute bus transfer from airport US$8; 78 rooms; ✗ ☐ ☎) is, for our money, one of the best-value resorts in the country. The additional expense of flying to Gan from Male' is quickly offset by the low, low room rates and the all-inclusive packages they come with. More than anywhere else, though, staying here gives you the unique opportunity to see something of 'normal life' in the Maldives – this is no picture-perfect Maldivian desert island resort, and all the better for it.

Formerly a British RAF base, Gan revels in its heritage. Neat lines of rooms (former barracks!) fan out from the main reception building, and are surrounded by extremely mature and well-tended gardens that overflow with exotic flowers and plants.

The rooms are modern, basic and thoroughly unromantic – this is not a honeymooners' destination. They are also spacious and have everything you need (although no TV or phone), including an en-suite bathroom and air-con.

The reception, bar and dining areas have been created from the old mess, thoroughly redecorated in very unmilitary pink, white and grey. These open-sided spaces with their cane furniture and ceiling fans look out onto a sizable swimming pool and through palm trees to the blue sea beyond. The full-size billiard table is a handsome inheritance from the Brits, as are the first-class tennis courts.

The meals are all buffet with a limited selection and a British bias and are rather a low point – expect curry, roast beef, mashed potatoes and tinned fruit for dinner, and sausages, eggs and cereal for breakfast. The Maldivian barbecue buffet is the best meal of the week. Most guests are on an all-inclusive package, and can wash it down with beer or house wine. There's not a lot of organised evening entertainment, but the bar is one of the friendliest and most fun in the Maldives.

Despite the British slant to the food, most of the guests are actually from Germany, although Brits make up the second-biggest group, along with a mix of other Europeans. More than half are divers, and from time to time ex-RAF personnel who were once stationed here come back for a nostalgic holiday. An RAF visitors book at reception has more than 50 signatures, and some books and photo albums are also kept here (available on request).

Bicycles can be hired to explore the neighbouring islands at US$5/10 per half-/full day, although they're free with the all-inclusive deal, along with an island-hopping excursion, night fishing trip and twice-daily boat to Viligili for snorkelling and beach time.

The only beach on Gan is a few hundred metres east of the resort, and it's not great – don't come here if you want to re-enact the Bounty advert. It's one of the few resorts in the country that doesn't provide the fabulous turquoise-water and whitesand combo. However, divers take note: the coral here is flabbergasting – and this should definitely be high on your list of top diving resorts. The dive centre is a small but friendly operation run by **Diverland** (www .diverland.com) and includes the great dive sites in the area at very reasonable prices.

FITs and anyone else wanting to see something of the real Maldives will really appreciate Equator Village as it allows you to see much more of daily Maldivian life; you can cycle to Hithadoo via the new road and you generally enjoy a much higher level of freedom here.

We can't quite say the same for **J Resort Handhufushi** (Hulhumeedhoo island; ☎ 6897766; www .jhotelsandresorts.com; half board r US$274; flight from Male' to Gan 1½hr, US$307, speedboat transfer from Gan 20min, included in flight cost; 273 rooms; ☒ ☐ ☒), which opened in 2007 as Herathera and immediately caused controversy when several tour operators decided to pull their clients as the resort wasn't ready to receive guests. Since then, the resort has been completed and rebranded as yet another of the Sri Lankan J Resort's properties. It's a big place – 273 rooms at last count, with plans (and enough space) for even more. Accommodation is excellent – beach villas and jacuzzi beach villas are the two room categories, both modern, simple but very comfortable with all mod cons. Food is said to be very good on the whole too, and bikes can be hired, which makes exploring the island easy and fun. Other facilities include a great pool, a spa, water sports centre and plenty of eating and drinking options.

But common to many new resorts run by non-global hotel chains in the Maldives, the biggest failing is said to be a familiar one of poorly trained staff with no service ethic. As the staff make the holiday in any resort, this is a major drawback.

Furthermore, the beach, which effectively didn't exist until recently, is enhanced by compacted coral, which makes the sand very sharp indeed (bring beach shoes!). All in all, it's not a very attractive place, with rocky beaches and fairly barren foliage – a far cry from the postcards sold in the hotel gift shop. Of course, the diving here is excellent as it is anywhere in Addu Atoll, and this is one of the reasons to stay here. However, until things are brought up to an altogether higher level, we'd rather stay at Equator Village.

The third resort, due to open during the lifetime of this book (though we said that in the last edition too), is the **Shangri-La Villingili Resort & Spa** (Villingili island; www.shangri -la.com; 184 rooms; ☒ ☐ ☒). The Shangri-La group's first venture in the Maldives, it's a huge undertaking that has been bedevilled by construction problems and is now three years late in opening. Of course, it's likely to be magnificent when it does open, as any resort hoping to compete in the increasingly luxurious top-end hotel market here has to be. Watch this space.

Getting There & Away

Island Aviation flies from Male' to Gan and back two or three times a day. The standard fare for foreigners is US$300 return.

Private yachts should report by radio to the National Security Service (NSS) in Gan or Hithadhoo to arrange security and customs clearance, but may have to continue to Male' for health and immigration checks to complete the 'clear-in' process.

Getting Around

The best way to get around Gan and over the causeway to neighbouring villages is by bicycle. Equator Village includes bike hire in its rates, but they aren't too comfortable for tall people. Taxis shuttle between the islands and around the villages; from Gan to Hithadhoo should cost about Rf100. Taxis wait at the airport and you can order one from Equator Village. The buses you see on the main road are only for workers in the Gan garment factories. Equator Village picks up guests by free minibus from the airport, though you may need to call on arrival and remind them!

Directory

CONTENTS

ACCOMMODATION

Ouch. That's most people's reaction to Maldivian resort prices, and it's fair to say this is not and will never be a cheap place to stay. Even budget hotels cost more than a top-end place in India or Sri Lanka, but quality in general is superior to elsewhere in Asia.

In this book we list accommodation for each chapter, divided into three groups: budget, midrange and top end. For each option a bed-and-breakfast room rate is quoted for the height of the season (mid-Jan to April) unless otherwise stated. In Male', however, breakfast is only included in the room price where indicated. There are almost no single rooms in resorts, so singles are nearly always doubles for single occupation. Where there is a separate price for singles, we list this, otherwise we just list the standard room price in the starting category. As many travellers specifically want a water bungalow (a room on stilts over the water), we also list the starting category water bungalow price for two people in the height of the season.

Resorts

The vast majority of accommodation for travellers consists of the roughly 110 self-contained island resorts throughout the country. We list all the operating resorts in this book, as well as many that were refurbishing at the time of writing and those that are planned to open in the near future.

The long-standing 'one island, one resort' policy means that development is contained and nowhere in the country feels crowded. Each resort provides rooms, meals and activities for its guests, ranging from the most basic beach huts, with a buffet three times a day and a simple diving school, to vast water villas with every conceivable luxury in them, à la carte dining and all kinds of activities, from kiteboarding to big game fishing.

Most resorts have a range of room categories, so for the sake of ease we give the rate for the lowest category of room and for the lowest category of water bungalow (if available). However, be warned, these prices are nothing more than a guideline. They are rack rates, and so booking through a travel agent will get you access to far better deals and lower rates. The rack rates quoted are usually subject to an US$8 per person per night government bed tax and a 10% service charge.

Budget resorts (up to US$250 per double room per night) tend to be busier and more basic in their facilities and level of sophistication than more expensive resorts. Few budget resorts are being built these days so those that do exist tend to be dated from the 1980s or '90s, and are often in need of a lick of paint.

Midrange resorts (from US$250 to US$500 per night) make up the majority of the Maldives accommodation options. They are noticeably slicker, better run and have a better standard of facilities and accommodation, all carried off with some style.

Top-end resorts (more than US$500 per night) are currently what the Maldives is all

DIRECTORY

about. The world-class standards are uniform in this category and range from the very good to the mind-bogglingly luxurious.

Booking resorts through travel agents is nearly always cheaper than doing so directly. However, with the (slow) rise of independent travel in the Maldives, some resorts offer great deals via their websites.

For our pick of the Maldives' best ecofriendly resorts, see p16.

Hotels

The only hotels currently operating in the country are located in Male'. As these are far cheaper than the island resorts, we've used a separate price breakdown for the capital's hotels: budget (under US$50), midrange (US$50 to US$90) and top end (over US$90). The choice is not inspiring and the rooms are often cramped due to the shortage of space (see p103).

At the time of writing new 'city hotels' were planned for many of the inhabited islands throughout the country. When these are functioning it will open up many previously closed islands to tourism, part of a new government plan to diversify the country's tourism industry, particularly with an eye to attracting more independent travellers.

Safari Boats

Live-aboard safari boats allow you to travel extensively throughout the country, visiting great dive sites, desert islands and small local settlements usually too remote to see travellers. Live-aboards also range from simple to luxury. The advantage is that you can visit many places off-limits to resort travellers, dive in pristine waters and enjoy a very sociable atmosphere. Prices range from bargain basement to exorbitant depending on the facilities available (see p64).

Inhabited Islands

There's at present no commercial accommodation in the island villages, and visitors are not legally permitted to pay for a place to stay. If for whatever reason you do stay on an inhabited island, you'll be put up in the house of the *kateeb* (island chief) or a house maintained for the purpose of accommodating guests.

BUSINESS HOURS

Male' is really the only place you have to worry about business hours in the Maldives, the resorts being far more flexible as they have to cater to hordes of visitors.

The working week elsewhere in the Maldives runs from Sunday to Thursday. Friday and Saturday are rest days and it's advisable to avoid Male' and local islands on these days as they are ghost towns. On workdays, businesses operate from 8am or 9am until 5pm or 6pm, but this varies. Shops in Male' will often stay open until around 10pm or 11pm, and some will shut in the heat of the afternoon – from midday until 3pm or thereabouts. Nearly all Male' businesses stop several times a day for prayers, which can be frustrating for shoppers, as businesses suddenly close for 15 minutes to half an hour. Most banks in Male' are open from about 8am to 1.30pm, Sunday to Thursday, or 9.30am to 12.30pm during Ramazan.

Government offices are open Sunday to Thursday from 7.30am to 2pm. During Ramazan, hours are from 9am to 1.30pm.

Teashops can open very early or close very late. During Ramazan the places where locals eat will probably be closed during daylight hours, but will bustle after dark.

CHILDREN

Younger children will enjoy a couple of weeks on a Maldivian resort island, particularly if they like playing in the water and on the beach. Although exotic cuisine is sometimes on the menu, there are always some pretty standard Western-style dishes that kids will find edible.

Older children and teenagers could find a resort a little confining after a few days and they may get bored. Canoeing and fishing trips might provide some diversion, while a course in sailing or windsurfing could be a great way to spend a holiday. Table tennis, tennis, volleyball or badminton might also appeal. The minimum age for scuba diving is 16 years, but most resorts offer a 'bubble blowers' introduction for younger kids, which is very popular. Kids clubs for 12s and under and teen clubs are very common in bigger, smarter resorts. These are free and the kids clubs run activities all day long to keep the little ones busy, while teenagers are able to do what they want – even if it means playing computer games in a darkened air-conditioned room. Where resorts have good kids clubs or a generally very welcoming child-friendly policy we've included the child-friendly icon.

Be aware that young children are even more susceptible to sunburn, so bring sun hats and sunblock. Lycra swim shirts are an excellent idea – they can be worn on the beach and in the water and block out most UV radiation.

Practicalities

Note that some resorts do not encourage young children – check with the resort directly – and that children under five are often banned from honeymoon resorts. Where kids are welcome, it's no problem booking cots and organising high chairs in restaurants, and there's often a babysitting service and kids club in bigger, family-oriented resorts. Nappies are available in Male', but usually not in resorts, so bring all the nappies and formula you'll need for the duration of the holiday. Breast-feeding should only be done in private.

CLIMATE CHART

The Maldives has a tropical climate distinguished by two seasons, or monsoons: the dry northeast monsoon from December to March, and the wet southwestern monsoon from May to November, with more strong winds and rain. April is a transitional period noted for clear water and heat. The temperature remains remarkably consistent at around 30°C. For more on weather, see p13.

COURSES

Diving courses are a particular attraction for travellers to the Maldives. The standard learn-to-dive course is an open-water certificate, but the bigger dive centres offer a host of advanced and speciality courses, including advanced open water, divemaster, night diving and so on (see p72 for more information).

CUSTOMS

The immigration cards issued to you on your flight to Male' include a great list of items that are banned from the republic. Alcohol, pornography, pork, narcotics, dogs, firearms, spear guns and 'idols of worship' cannot be brought into the country and you're advised to comply. Baggage is always X-rayed and may be searched carefully, and if you have any liquor it will be taken and held for you till you're about to leave the country. This service will not extend to other prohibited items, and the importation of multiple Bibles (one for personal use is fine), pornography and, in particular, drugs, will be treated very seriously.

The export of turtle shell, or any turtle-shell products, is forbidden.

DANGERS & ANNOYANCES

It's hard to imagine anywhere much safer than the Maldives. Theft from resorts is very rare, given that only staff and guests have access to the resort island; but still, make use of the safes in the rooms, keep your doors locked and don't leave cash around, wherever you are.

The most likely danger is sunburn – don't ever underestimate the power of the equatorial sun at midday on a bright, cloudless afternoon. Sadly many people do, and receive bad burning and exposure to dangerous UV rays. Be sure to wear a high-factor lotion for at least the first couple of days and be particularly careful when snorkelling or travelling by boat (when the breeze can make it seem far cooler than it is).

Second to the sun is the water. While it's true most diving accidents happen on the diving boat, it's extremely important to take diving seriously. Don't touch coral, shells or fish. Beware of the possibility of

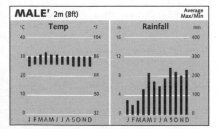

MALE' 2m (8ft)

DIRECTORY

strong currents and don't swim too far out from an island's fringing reef, or too far from a boat on a snorkelling trip. Don't try surfing unless you know where you are and what you're doing – the surf breaks over coral reefs and you could be badly grazed or knocked unconscious.

It would be unlucky to be hit by a falling coconut, but it does happen, more so in windy weather. Imagine a 2kg coconut falling 15m onto your head. Check if a coconut tree is laden with big coconuts before lying underneath it.

Crimes of violence are very unusual, but there are burglaries and theft in the capital. There are very few cases of theft from resort rooms. Nevertheless, it's wise to deposit your valuables with the resort office, to keep your room locked and not leave cash lying around.

EMBASSIES & CONSULATES

The foreign representatives in Male' are mostly honorary consuls with limited powers and often nobody in residence. In an emergency contact your country's embassy or high commission in Colombo, Sri Lanka.

Germany & Austria (Map p95; ☎ 3322971; Universal Enterprises, 38 Orchid Magu)
India (Map p98; ☎ 3323016)
Italy (Map p98; ☎ 3322451; Cyprea, 25 Boduthakurufaanu Magu)
New Zealand (Map p98; ☎ 3322432; 30 Boduthakurufaanu Magu)

GAY & LESBIAN TRAVELLERS

This is a grey area legally in the Maldives, where gay awareness can hardly be said to be very high. By Maldivian law all extramarital sex is illegal although such mores are not applied to the resorts, where in practice anything goes as long as it is low key or behind closed doors. Same-sex couples will be able to book a double room with no questions asked (from budget to luxury, Maldivian hotel staff are the model of discretion) and it's common to see same-sex couples enjoying Maldivian holidays, although no resort here actually markets itself to the gay market. Public displays of affection may embarrass Maldivian resort staff, but won't result in anything but blushes on their part. In Male' and on inhabited islands discretion is key and public displays of affection should not be indulged

in by anyone, gay or straight – the Maldives remains an extremely conservative place.

HOLIDAYS

If you're in a resort, Maldivian holidays will not affect you – service will be as normal. If you visit Male' or an inhabited island on a holiday, you might see some parade or public celebration, shops may not open or may open late in the day, and government offices and most businesses will be closed. Christmas, New Year, Easter and European school holidays will affect you more – they're the busiest times for tourists and bring the highest resort prices, although locals don't celebrate them, of course.

If a holiday falls on a Friday or Saturday, the next working day will be declared a holiday 'on the occasion of' whatever it was. Most Maldivian holidays are based on the Islamic lunar calendar and the dates vary from year to year.

Ramazan Known as Ramazan or *roarda mas* in the Maldives rather than Ramadan, the Islamic month of fasting is an important religious occasion that starts on a new moon and continues for 28 days. Expected starting dates for the next few years are: 11 August 2010, 1 August 2011, 20 July 2012 and 9 July 2013. The exact date depends on the sighting of the new moon in Mecca and can vary by a day or so either way.

Kuda Eid Also called Id-ul-Fitr or Fith'r Eid, this occurs at the end of Ramazan, with the sighting of the new moon, and is celebrated with a feast.

Bodu Eid Also called Eid-ul Al'h'aa, the Festival of the sacrifice, 66 days after the end of Ramazan, this is the time when many Muslims begin the pilgrimage (haj) to Mecca.

National Day A commemoration of the day Mohammed Thakurufaanu and his men overthrew the Portuguese on Male' in 1578. It's on the first day of the third month of the lunar calendar.

Prophet's Birthday The birthday of the Prophet Mohammed is celebrated with three days of eating and merriment. The approximate start dates for the next few years are: 26 February 2010, 15 February 2011, 4 February 2012 and 24 January 2013.

Huravee Day The day the Malabars of India were kicked out by Sultan Hassan Izzuddeen after their brief occupation in 1752.

Martyr's Day Commemorates the death of Sultan Ali VI at the hands of the Portuguese in 1558.

The following are fixed holiday dates:
New Year's Day 1 January
Independence Day Celebrates the ending of the British protectorate (in 1965) on 26 and 27 July.

Victory Day Celebrates the victory over the Sri Lankan mercenaries who tried to overthrow the Maldivian government in 1988. A military march is followed by lots of schoolchildren doing drills and traditional dances, and more entertaining floats and costumed processions on 3 November.

Republic Day Commemorates the second (current) republic, founded in 1968 on 11 November. Celebrated in Male' with lots of pomp, brass bands and parades. Sometimes the following day is also a holiday.

INSURANCE

A travel-insurance policy to cover theft, loss and medical problems is highly recommended. Some policies offer lower and higher medical-expense options; the higher ones are chiefly for countries that have high medical costs, and this would be a good idea for a Maldives trip. You may prefer to choose a policy that pays doctors or hospitals directly rather than your having to pay on the spot and claim later. If you have to claim later, make sure you keep all documentation. Some policies ask you to call back (reverse charge) to a centre in your home country where an immediate assessment of your problem is made.

Some policies specifically exclude 'dangerous activities', which can include diving, so check your policy carefully if you plan to dive. See p84 for information on insurance for divers.

INTERNET ACCESS

Most resorts have internet access available for guests. In the top-end resorts this will often (but extraordinarily not always) be free and will usually be both wireless and from a terminal at reception for those not travelling with laptops.

Midrange resorts usually offer wireless or terminal access, or both, and in some good midrange resorts access is free, but in most cases it's paid for.

In budget resorts wireless is currently very rare, and access is usually via a 'cyber-cafe' – usually a moulding 1990s PC in the lobby – if anything.

In Male' internet cafes are rare, while wi-fi hotspots (usually paid) are increasingly common.

LEGAL MATTERS

Alcohol is illegal outside resorts – you're theoretically not even allowed to take a can of beer out on a boat trip. Some foreign residents in the capital have a liquor permit, which entitles them to a limited amount per month, strictly for personal consumption at home.

Illicit drugs are around, but are not widespread. Penalties are heavy. 'Brown sugar', a semirefined form of heroin, has become a problem among some young people in the capital and even in some outer islands.

With a scattered island population and limited resources, the Maldivian authorities rely heavily on delegation. Apart from the police and the military, there is a chief on every atoll and island who must keep an eye on what is happening, report to the central government and be responsible for the actions of local people.

Resorts are responsible for their guests and for what happens on their island. If a guest goes swimming in the nude, the resort can be fined, as well as the visitor.

MAPS

Put simply, the Maldives is a nightmare to map. The islands are so small and scattered that the result is an extremely confusing one in which you're forever trying to distinguish between the tiny islands and the reefs that surround them. Another problem is scale – the country is over 800km from north to south, but the largest island is only about 8km long.

For anyone doing any serious amount of travel, especially diving, *Maps of the Maldives* (Water Solutions) is indispensable and in a very practical book form, alleviating the need to fold out a vast map. It includes everything from shipwreck sites to Protected Marine Area plans. It's on sale at the Novelty Bookshop (p94) in Male'.

MARRIAGE CEREMONIES

Despite being a favourite of honeymooners, it's actually impossible for non-Muslims to get married in the Maldives at present. This may change in the near future as the new government, conscious that the country is missing out to rivals Mauritius and Seychelles due to this legal technicality, has recently raised the possibility of legalising non-Muslim marriage for foreigners. Nothing is certain yet, but this could be implemented within the lifetime of this book. In the meantime the closest you can get are 'informal' weddings a 'renewal of vows'-type ceremony. Contact your resort well in advance of your trip to organise this.

MONEY

The currency of the Maldives is the rufiya (Rf), which is divided into 100 larees. Notes come in denominations of 500, 100, 50, 20, 10, five and two rufiya, but the last two are uncommon. Coins are in denominations of two and one rufiya, and 50, 25 and 10 larees. The value of the rufiya is pegged to that of the US dollar, so the exchange rate between the two currencies never changes. Most hotel and travel expenses will be billed in dollars. If you're staying in a resort, all extras (including diving costs) will be billed to your room, and you pay the day before departure. Resorts accept cash, credit cards or travellers cheques in all major currencies, although US dollars are preferred.

See the Quick Reference inside the front cover for other exchange rates. See also p13 for information on costs.

ATMs

There's a slowly growing number of ATMs in Male' – most of them (but not all) now allow you to withdraw funds from international accounts. Those that definitely do are the ones outside the major banks on Boduthakurufaanu Magu. Note that while you can do cash advances on credit cards over the counter at Male' airport and at most resorts, there are no ATMs outside Male'.

Cash

It's perfectly possible to have a holiday in the Maldives without ever touching cash of any sort, as in resorts everything will be chalked up to your room number and paid by credit card or travellers cheques on departure. However, it's a good idea to have some cash with you – small-denomination US dollars are most handy for tipping staff and buying sundries in transit. You won't need Maldivian rufiya unless you're using local shops and services. Even these will usually take dollars, but you'll be given change in rufiya.

There are no restrictions on changing money into rufiya, but there's no need to change a lot. Rufiya are not readily negotiable outside the country, so reconvert any leftovers at the bank counter in the airport when you leave.

Credit Cards

Every resort takes major credit cards including Visa, Amex and MasterCard. A week of diving and drinking could easily run up a tab over US$2000, so make sure your credit limit can stand it. The cashier may want 24 hours' notice to check your credit. Many resorts apply a surcharge of 5% to credit-card payments, so it may be best to have enough travellers cheques to cover the bulk of your extras bill.

International Transfers

Banks in the Maldives are not noted for their efficiency in international transactions. A transfer using the 'Swift' system seems to be the most efficient way to get money to the Maldives. Villa Travels is the agent for **Western Union** (Map p98; ☎ 3329990; moneytransfer@villatravels.com; Boduthakurufaanu Magu), a reliable but expensive way to transfer funds. The **HSBC Bank** (Map p98; Boduthakurufaanu Magu) might be your best bet. Try to have the money handed over to you in US dollars, not rufiya.

Tipping

Tipping is something of a grey area in the Maldives, where a 10% service tax is added to nearly everything from minibar drinks to room prices. In many places this would mean that you don't need to tip in addition, but it's still the case that people serving you personally will often expect something. It's good form to leave a tip for your room staff and in smarter resorts, your *thakuru* (butler). Give any tips to the staff personally, not to the hotel cashier – US dollars, euros and local currency are equally acceptable. A few dollars a day is fine for room staff, while anyone carrying your bags might expect US$1 or so per bag. There's no need to tip bar staff.

In Male' the fancier restaurants usually add a 10% service charge, so you don't need to tip. Tipping is not customary in local teashops. Taxi drivers are not tipped, but porters at the airport expect Rf10 or US$1.

Travellers Cheques

Banks in Male' will change travellers cheques and cash in US dollars, and possibly UK pounds, euros, Japanese yen and Swiss francs. Most will change US-dollar travellers cheques into US dollars cash with a commission of US$5. Changing travellers cheques to Maldivian rufiya should not attract a commission.

Some of the authorised moneychangers around town will exchange US-dollar or euro travellers cheques at times when the banks are closed. You can always try some of the hardware shops, souvenir shops and guesthouses. Most tourist businesses will accept US dollars in cash at the standard rate, and euros at reasonable rates.

POST

Postal services are quite efficient, with mail to overseas destinations delivered promptly; mail from overseas, especially packets and parcels, is subject to customs screening and can take considerably longer. The **main post office** (Boduthakurufaanu Magu; 8.15am-9pm Sun-Thu, 3-9pm Fri, 9.15am-9pm Sat) in Male' has a poste restante service.

A high-speed Express Mail Service (EMS) is available to many countries. Parcel rates can be quite expensive and will have to clear customs at the main post office, where a bored-looking customs official will be stationed to inspect any packages you're sending home.

At the resorts you can buy stamps and postcards at the shop or the reception desk. Generally there is a mailbox near reception.

SOLO TRAVELLERS

While travelling on your own through the Maldives can feel akin to spending Valentine's Day alone in a romantic French restaurant for two weeks, it's perfectly possible and many people do it. As there are almost no single rooms in the country's resorts and hotels, you'll find that you'll be paying much more than someone in a couple, as often the reductions for single occupation are tiny. However, if you can afford to, there's nothing stopping you, and if – like most single travellers in the country – you're here for a specific reason such as diving or surfing,

---

PRACTICALITIES

Newspapers & Magazines

The four Dhivehi daily papers are Aafathis, Mladhu, Haveeru and Jazeera. They are available from shops throughout the country, but not in resorts. They all have some pages in English, although there's nothing of much interest. Haveeru has a decent English edition online at www.haveeru .com. Far better for current affairs is Minivan News (www.minivannews.com), an English language web-based paper with sharp and well-researched local reporting. A smattering of international papers and magazines are available from bookshops in Male'.

Radio & TV

TVM, the national TV station, is broadcast from Male' during the day, with regular breaks for prayer and much religious content. The rest of the schedule is made up of political programmes, variety shows and Al Jazeera rebroadcasts in English. There's news in English at 9pm. Other local TV channels include DhiTV and VillaTV.

Nearly all resorts and most Male' hotels have satellite TV including BBC World News, CNN, Al Jazeera, Star Movies and HBO alongside Sri Lankan, Indian and European channels.

The Voice of Maldives Radio (www.vom.gov.mv) is broadcast to the whole country for 11 hours each day on medium wave, 1449kHz, and also at 89MHz. The news, in English, is read at 6pm for 15 minutes.

Electricity

Electricity supply is 220V to 240V, 50Hz AC. The standard socket is the UK-style three-pin, although there are some variations so an international adaptor can be useful (and is essential for non-UK travellers).

Weights & Measures

Although the Maldives is officially converting to the metric system, imperial measures are widely used. Metric measurements are used in this book.

you'll quickly meet up with kindred spirits in the resorts where these activities are most popular. Safari boats are likewise a great option as the sociable nature makes them good for making friends. Single women will find the Maldives a wonderful place to travel, completely free of the chauvinism that can so often be a deterrent. For more on independent travel, see p15.

TELEPHONE

There are two telephone providers operating in the Maldives: the relative old-timer Dhiraagu, a joint venture of the government and the British Cable & Wireless company; and the newer Wataniya, a Kuwaiti provider that introduced some much-needed competition to the market in 2005.

Both providers operate good coverage, although given the unique geography of the country there are still lots of areas out of coverage in the atolls. You can buy a local SIM card for around US$10 and use it in your own phone if it's been unlocked at home (check with your provider) – this becomes worth the price almost immediately if you're using your phone quite a lot.

All resorts have IDD phones, either in the rooms or available at reception. Charges vary from high to astronomical, starting around US$15 for three minutes; our advice is never to use them outside of an emergency.

The international country code for the Maldives is ☎ 960. All Maldives numbers have seven digits and there are no area codes. If you find you have a six-digit number for a Male' business, add a 3 to the start and it should work. Operator and directory inquiry numbers are ☎ 110 for the Maldives and ☎ 190 for international inquiries. To make an international call, dial ☎ 00, then the country code, area code and number.

TIME

The Maldives is five hours ahead of GMT, in the same time zone as Pakistan. When it's noon in the Maldives, it's 7am in London, 8am in Berlin and Rome, 12.30pm in India and Sri Lanka, 3pm in Singapore and 4pm in Tokyo.

The majority of resorts operate one hour ahead of Male' time to give their guests the illusion of extra daylight in the evening and a longer sleep in the morning. This can make it tricky when arranging pick-up times and transfers, so always check whether you're being quoted a time in Male' Time or Resort Time.

TOILETS

Male's public toilets charge Rf2. On local islands, you may have to ask where the *fahana* is. In general you're better off using toilets in cafes and restaurants in Male' – they're usually cleaner and free.

TOURIST INFORMATION

The official tourist office is the **Maldives Tourism Promotion Board** (☎ 3323228; www.visitmaldives .com; Boduthakurufaanu Magu, Male'). Its office on the 4th floor of the Bank of Ceylon building has maps and other printed material, and can answer specific inquiries.

The Maldives has only one official tourist office abroad: the **Maldives Government Tourist Information Office** (☎ 0 618 2993 4857; info@ visitmaldives.de; Aschaffenburgerstr 96G, 63500 Seligenstadt, Germany). Most tourism promotion is done by private travel agents, tour operators and resorts.

TRAVEL PERMITS

Foreigners must have an Inter-Atoll Travel Permit to visit or stay on any inhabited island other than Male', the islands around Male' and a resort island. The exception is if you're making a day trip, either from a resort or from Male', in which case you need to leave the island by sundown.

Permits are issued by the **Ministry of Home Affairs** (Map p98; Boduthakurufaanu Magu) in Male' and cost Rf10. Permits are issued only between 8.30am and 11am on all days except government holidays.

All foreigners must have a local sponsor who will guarantee their accommodation and be responsible for them. Note also that it is illegal for anyone to request payment for accommodation on an inhabited island.

Permit applications must be in writing and include the applicant's name, passport number, nationality, the name of the island/ atoll to be visited, dates of visit, name and address of sponsor, the name and registration number of the vessel to be used and the purpose of the visit. The stated purpose can be something like visiting friends, sightseeing, photography or private research.

Your sponsor should be a resident of the island you wish to visit, and must be prepared to vouch for you, feed you and accommodate you. This support must be given in writing, preferably with an OK from the *kateeb* (island chief) and submitted with your application. It's best to have the sponsor submit the application on your behalf.

The most straightforward way to visit the outer atolls is with a registered safari boat, but a reputable tour company, travel agent or guesthouse proprietor may be able to help you make the necessary contacts to get a sponsor. Many Male' residents have friends or family in various outer atolls, but as they will be responsible for you when you visit the island, a great deal of trust is involved. Getting a letter of support-cum-invitation back from the island can take a couple of weeks if it's isolated from the capital.

The permit will specify which atolls or islands you can visit. As soon as you land on an island you must go to the island office and present the permit. A foreigner travelling in the outer atolls without a permit, or breaching its conditions, can be fined Rf100.

This rather draconian policy is being reviewed at present by the new government. While some degree of institutionalised separation between tourists and the local population is likely to be continued, there are plans afoot to make the inhabited islands (particularly larger population centres) far more accessible to foreigners.

TRAVELLERS WITH DISABILITIES

At Male' International Airport, passengers must use steps to get on and off planes, so contact your airline to find out what arrangements can be made. The arrivals area is all at ground level, but departure usually involves going up and down stairs.

Transfers to nearby resorts are by dhoni or speedboat and a person in a wheelchair or with limited mobility will need assistance, which the crews will always be happy to provide. Transfer to more distant resorts is often by seaplanes, which can be more difficult to access, but staff are quite experienced in assisting passengers in wheelchairs or with limited mobility.

Most resorts have few steps, ground-level rooms and reasonably smooth paths to beaches, boat jetties and all public areas, but beware that some of the more rustic and 'ecofriendly' resorts have a lot of sand floors. Staff – something there's never a shortage of

in the Maldives – will be on hand to assist disabled guests. When you decide on a resort, call them directly and ask about the layout. It's usually a good idea for guests to advise their tour agency of any special needs, but if you want to find out about specific facilities, it's best to contact the resort itself.

Many resort activities are potentially suitable for disabled guests. Fishing trips and excursions to inhabited islands should be easy, but uninhabited islands may be more difficult to disembark on. Catamaran sailing and canoeing are possibilities, especially if you've had experience in these activities. Anyone who can swim will be able to enjoy snorkelling. The **International Association for Handicapped Divers** (www.iahd.org) provides advice and assistance for anyone with a physical disability who wishes to scuba dive. Resort dive schools should be able to arrange a special course or programme for any group of four or more people with a similar disability.

No dogs are permitted in the Maldives, so it's not a destination for anyone dependent on a guide dog.

VISAS

The Maldives welcomes visitors from all countries, issuing a 30-day stamp on arrival. Citizens of India, Pakistan, Bangladesh or Nepal are given a 90-day stamp. If you want to stay longer you'll either need to apply for an extension to the 30-day stamp or leave the country when your 30 days is up, then return.

While officially you're supposed to show US$30 for every day's stay, this is not usually enforced, and showing a credit card will usually placate concerns. However, you should know the name of your hotel and be able to show a return air ticket out of the country if asked by immigration officials.

Visa Extensions

To apply for an extension, go to the **Immigration Office** (Map p98; ☎ 3323913; ⏰ 8am-1pm Sun-Thu) in the Huravee Building next to the police station in Male'. You must first buy an Extension of Tourist Visa form (Rf10) from the ground-floor desk. You'll need a local to sponsor you. The main requirement is evidence that you have accommodation, so it's best to have your resort, travel agent or guesthouse manager act as a sponsor

DIRECTORY

and apply on your behalf. Have your sponsor sign the form, and bring it back to the office between 7.30am and 9.30am, along with your passport, a passport photo, the Rf750 fee and your air ticket out of the country. You have to have a confirmed booking for the new departure date before you can get the extension – fortunately, the airlines don't ask to see a visa extension before they'll change the date of your flight. Proof of sufficient funds (US$30 per day) or a credit card may also be required. You'll be asked to leave the documents at the office and return in a couple of days to pick up the passport with its extended visa (get a receipt for your passport).

Extensions are for a maximum of 30 days, but they give you only until the date on your ticket – the cost is the same, for one day or 30. Overstaying your visa (or extension), even by an hour, can be a major hassle as they may not let you board your flight, and you will have to go back to Male', book another flight, get a visa extension and pay a fine before you can leave.

WOMEN TRAVELLERS

Culturally, resorts are European enclaves and visiting women will not have to make too many adjustments. Topless bathing and nudity are strictly forbidden, but bikinis are perfectly acceptable on resort beaches.

Reasonably modest dress is appropriate in Male' – shorts should cover the thighs and shirts should not be very low cut. Women may be stared at on the street in Male', especially if their dress or demeanour is seen as provocative, but nothing more serious is likely to happen. Local women don't go into teashops in Male', but a foreign woman with a male companion would not cause any excitement.

In more out-of-the-way parts of the country, quite conservative dress is in order. It is very unlikely that a foreign woman would be harassed or feel threatened on a local island, as Maldivian men are conservative and extremely respectful. They are very closed, small communities and the fact that a foreign woman would be associated with a local sponsor should give a high level of security.

Transport

CONTENTS

GETTING THERE & AWAY

ENTERING THE COUNTRY

Entering the Maldives is simple and hassle-free. However, you must know the name of your resort or Male' hotel, and if you are travelling independently and don't have one arranged, then entering one at random is fine. If you tell them you haven't book accommodation then you'll be frog-marched to the nearest travel agency's airport desk and made to book something.

Passport

There are no restrictions on foreign nationals entering the country. Israelis and people who have Israeli stamps in their passports are perfectly welcome, which is rare in the Muslim world. Visas are not needed for visits of 30 days or less (see p177). Theoretically, travellers must have US$30 per day for the duration of their stay, though this is not usually enforced and producing a credit card is a perfectly good substitute if you're asked.

AIR
Airports & Airlines

There are two international airports in the Maldives, though you're far more likely to land at **Male' International Airport** (MLE; ☎ 3322075; www.airports.com.mv), than you are at **Gan International Airport** (GAN; ☎ 6898010), which currently only receives a few charter flights. Male' International Airport is on the island of Hulhule', 2km across the water from the capital. It's a decent airport due to undergo a full renovation in the coming years.

The national carrier is Maldivian (see p181; formerly the domestic airline Island Aviation), which connects the Maldives to India and Sri Lanka as well as flying to all domestic terminals from the capital. The international carriers serving Male' are a mixture of scheduled and charter airlines. Some airlines only fly in certain seasons and the list of charter airlines changes frequently.

SCHEDULED AIRLINES
Aeroflot (SU; www.aeroflot.com)
Air India (Map p98; IC; ☎ 3310111; www.airindia.com)
Austrian (OS; ☎ 3334004; www.aua.com)
Bangkok Airways (Map p98; OS; ☎ 3317117; www.bangkokair.com)
Emirates (Map p98; EK; ☎ 3315466; www.emirates.com)
Malaysia Airlines (Map p98; MH; ☎ 3332555; www.malaysiaairlines.com)
Qatar Airways (Map p98; QR; ☎ 3334777; www.qatarairways.com)
Singapore Airlines (Map pp98; SQ; ☎ 3320777; www.singaporeairlines.com)
SriLankan Airlines (Map p98; UL; ☎ 332002; www.srilankan.aero)
Transaero (UN; www.transaero.ru; Male' airport)

CHARTERED AIRLINES
Note that most charter airlines don't have offices in Male' and should be contacted via the home country.
Air Berlin/Belair/LTU (4T; www.airberlin.com)
Air Italy (I9; www.airitaly.eu)
Condor (DE; www.catchafly-t.com)
Edelweiss (EDW; www.edelweissair.ch)
Eurofly/Meridiana (GJ; www.meridiana.it)
First Choice (FCA; www.firstchoice.co.uk)

THINGS CHANGE...

The information in this chapter is particularly vulnerable to change. Check directly with the airline or a travel agent to make sure you understand how a fare (and ticket you may buy) works and be aware of the security requirements for international travel. Shop carefully. The details given in this chapter should be regarded as pointers and are not a substitute for your own careful, up-to-date research.

TRANSPORT

Monarch (MON; www.flymonarch.com)
Thomson (TOM; www.thomson.co.uk)
Neos (NO; www.neosair.it)

Tickets

If you're on a package, you'll usually have little or no choice about the airline you fly, as it will be part of the package. Fully independent travellers (FITs) should shop around for both scheduled and charter deals. More and more chartered airlines are selling flight-only seats and these can be good deals, so check their websites as well as those of scheduled carriers. The other advantage of charter flights is that you can fly direct from Western Europe to Male', without the usual change in the Middle East or Sri Lanka common for scheduled airlines.

Australia

Australians usually reach the Maldives via Singapore, Kuala Lumpur or Bangkok. The few Australian visitors to the Maldives makes this an expensive flight. There are no chartered flights currently operating between Australia and Male'.
Flight Centre (☎ 133-133; www.flightcentre.com.au)
STA Travel (☎ 134-782; www.statravel.com.au)

France

Charter flights operate between Paris and Male' during high season. The rest of the year Emirates, Qatar and SriLankan offer the best connections and prices.
Nouvelles Frontières (☎ 01 49 20 65 87; www.nouvelles-frontieres.fr)
Voyageurs du Monde (☎ 08 92 23 56 56; www.vdm.com)

Germany

Germany has a large number of charter airlines bringing visitors to resorts year-round. Direct flights from Düsseldorf, Frankfurt and Munich as well as from other cities are available on a number of chartered airlines.

Italy

There is an excellent charter choice available from Italy to Male' – most are nonstop flights, although some pick up in two or more Italian cities en route. For scheduled flights, Emirates followed by SriLankan and Qatar have the best connections from Rome and Milan. **CTS Viaggi** (☎ 06 4411166; www.cts.it) is a recommended travel agency.

Other Europe

There's a weekly flight on Austrian Airlines from Vienna, and irregular seasonal flights from Moscow on Aeroflot (via Colombo) and Transaero, and from Zurich on Edelweiss.

Japan

Japanese travellers usually fly on SriLankan, as there's a direct Tokyo–Male' flight that continues to Colombo. Alternatively, popular services from Japan include those via Singapore and Bangkok on Singapore Airlines and Bangkok Airways, respectively. Chartered flights are not in operation.

UK & Ireland

The direct scheduled twice-weekly flight on SriLankan between London Heathrow and Male' is the popular option. Other SriLankan flights go via Colombo. Other popular options include scheduled flights from London, Birmingham and Manchester via Doha (Qatar Airways) and Dubai (Emirates). Thomson and First Choice have some fantastically cheap seats on their charter flights to Male' from London Gatwick. These can be booked by independent travellers and are often less than half the price of scheduled flights.
Ebookers (☎ 0871-2235000; www.ebookers.com)
Opodo (☎ 0871-2770090; www.opodo.co.uk)
STA Travel (☎ 0871-2300040; www.statravel.co.uk)
Trailfinders (☎ 0845-0585858; www.trailfinders.co.uk)

USA & Canada

The sheer distance involved in travelling between North America and the Maldives makes the US and Canadian tourism market minuscule. People travelling from North America will usually fly via London and then continue by Qatar Airways, Emirates or SriLankan. From the West Coast travel via Singapore, Bangkok or Kuala Lumpur makes most sense.

SEA
Sri Lanka

Despite the obviousness of this route, there is currently no scheduled transport between Sri Lanka and the Maldives by boat, nor do cargo ships generally take paying passengers. You might be lucky if you ask around in Colombo, but it's unlikely.

Yacht

Yachts and super yachts cruise Maldivian waters throughout the year – this is after all one of many playgrounds for the rich and famous. However, with the Maldives being somewhat out of the way, this is not a standard port of call. The Maldives has not been a popular stop for cruising yachties, but more are coming through and official policy is becoming more welcoming. The negatives include: the maze of reefs that can make it a hazardous area; the high fees for cruising permits; the officialdom; the restrictions on where yachts can go; and the absence of lively little ports with great eating options and waterfront bars.

Recently, a 100-berth marina has been built at Island Hideaway in the far north of the country (see p145), and this is the only place currently set up for servicing yachts in a professional way. Addu, in the far south, has a sheltered anchorage, a tourist resort and refuelling and resupply facilities.

The three points where a yacht can get an initial 'clear in' are Uligamu (Haa Alif) in the north, Hithadhoo/Gan (Addu Atoll) in the south, and Male'. Call in on VHF channel 16 to the National Security Service (NSS) Coastguard and follow the instructions. If you're just passing through and want to stop only briefly, a 72-hour permit is usually easy to arrange. If you want to stay longer in Maldivian waters, or stop for provisions, you'll have to do immigration, customs, port authority and quarantine checks, and get a cruising permit. This can be done at any of the three clear-in facilities.

If you want to stop at Male', ensure you arrive well before dark, go to the east side of Viligili island, between Viligili and Male', and call the coastguard on channel 16. Officially, all boats require a pilot, but they don't usually insist for boats under 30m. Carefully follow the coastguard's instructions on where to anchor, or you may find yourself in water that's very deep or too shallow. Then contact one of the port agents, such as **Island Sailors** (☎ 3332536; www.islandsailors.com) or **Century Star** (☎ 3325353).

Port agents can arrange for port authority, immigration, customs and quarantine checks, and advise on repairs, refuelling etc. They'll charge about US$175 for a two-week stay, including all government charges – it would be a nightmare to do it all without an agent's help. After the initial checks

you'll be able to cross to the lagoon beside Hulhumale', the reclaimed land north of the airport. This is a good anchorage. The bigger stores, like STO Trade Center and Fantasy, have quite a good range of provisions at reasonable prices. The port agents can advise on other necessities such as radio repairs, water and fuelling.

The cost of a cruising permit for the first month is US$400, and the second month US$500. Customs, port and inspection charges increase with the size of the boat. You're nearly always able to stop at resorts to eat, drink, swim, dive and spend your money, but you should always call the resort first. Usually you have to be off the island by sunset.

Before you leave Maldivian waters, don't forget to 'clear out' at Uligamu, Hithadhoo or Male'.

GETTING AROUND

AIR
Domestic Air Services

Air transport is essential in the Maldives, given the large geographical spread of the islands and the total lack of roads. The domestic carrier is the national carrier **Maldivian** (Map p98; ☎ 3335544; Boduthakurufaanu Magu; www.island.com.mv), which offers several daily flights to the following four regional airports. Flights are on 37-seater Dash 8 jets and 16-seater Dornier 228 aircraft and fill up fast, so reserve in advance (booking online from home is possible) to ensure you can get the flight you want.

Gan (Addu, four to five flights daily, US$300 return, one hour 10 min)

Hanimaadhoo (Haa Dhaal, six flights daily, US$220 return, one hour)

Kaadedhdhoo (Gaaf Dhaal, two to three flights daily, US$260 return, one hour)

Kadhdhoo (Laamu, one flight daily, US$220 return, one hour)

Seaplane

Most travellers in the Maldives are far more likely to use the services of the two charter seaplane companies, **Trans Maldivian Airways** (☎ 3348400; www.transmaldivian.com) and **Maldivian Air Taxi** (☎ 3315201; www.maldivianairtaxi.com), both of which fly tourists from the seaplane port next to Male' International Airport to

TRANSPORT

resorts throughout the country. Both companies fly 18-seater DeHavilland Twin Otter seaplanes under contract to resorts throughout the Maldives, so you won't have any choice about who you fly with – each resort has a contract with just one of the carriers.

All seaplane transfers are made during daylight hours, and offer staggering views of the atolls, islands, reefs and lagoons. The cost is between US$150 and US$400 return, depending on the distance and the deal between the resorts, and it's generally included in the package price. If you are an FIT, the seaplane will be charged as an extra.

Charter flights for sightseeing, photography and emergency evacuation can also be arranged. Call both companies for rates and availability. Note that cargo capacity on the seaplanes is limited. All passengers and baggage are weighed before loading, and some heavy items may have to wait for a later flight or be transferred by boat.

BOAT
Dhoni Charters
In Male', go along the waterfront to the eastern end of Boduthakurufaanu Magu by the airport ferry jetty and you'll find many dhonis waiting in the harbour. Most of these are available for charter to nearby islands. The price depends on where you want to go, for how long, and on your negotiating skills – somewhere between Rf1000 and Rf2000 for a day is a typical rate, but if you want to start at 6am and go nonstop for 12 hours, it could be quite a bit more. You can also charter a dhoni at most resorts, but it will cost more (anything from US$300 to US$600 per day) and you'll only get one if they're not all being used for excursions or diving trips.

Ferries
Apart from regular passenger ferries between Male' and the airport, Hulhumale' and Viligili, ferry services in the Maldives are extremely slow, irregular and uncomfortable. Long-distance ferries do not generally accept foreigners for travel – enquire at the ferry terminal in Male' if you have a reason to travel to a distant inhabited island (you'll normally need a permit for such a trip (see p176). Plans for a new interisland ferry service open to foreigners have been announced by the new government, although will no doubt take several years to get up and running.

Speedboat
Resorts in North and South Male' Atoll, as well as some in Ari Atoll, offer transfer by speedboat, which costs anything from US$50 to US$300 return depending on the distance. This is generally included in the package price, but for independent travellers it's charged as an extra on leaving the resort.

The boats range from a small runabout with outboard motor to a massive, multi-deck launch with an aircraft-type cabin.

Most big travel agencies can organise the charter of launches from Male', which, if you can afford it, is absolutely the best way to get around. **Inner Maldives** (Map p98; ☎ 3315499; www.innermaldives.com.mv) has very good value launches for charter at around $400 per day, excluding the (substantial) fuel prices. For the price you'll get the services of the captain and a couple of crew members for a 10-hour day. If chartering a boat for the day, standard practice is for the client to pay for the tank to be refuelled on arrival back at Male'. Another well-priced and reliable company to hire launches from in Male' is **Nazaki Marine** (☎ 3324315; www.nazaki.com).

Vedhi
A *vedhi* is a large dhoni with a big, square-shaped wooden superstructure, and is used for trading between Male' and the outer atolls. Sail-powered *vedhis* once made trading trips to Sri Lanka, India, Myanmar (Burma) and Sumatra, but these days the *vedhis* are diesel powered and used only for interatoll transport.

No *vedhi* will take you as a passenger to an atoll unless you have a permit to go there. To get a permit, you must be sponsored by someone from that atoll, and it's best to have that person arrange transport. *Vedhis* use Inner Harbour in Male', west of the fishing harbour.

Travel on a *vedhi* is slow and offers basic food and no creature comforts. Your bunk is a mat on a shelf, the toilet is the sea and fellow passengers may include chickens. A trip down to Addu Atoll, the most southerly and distant atoll, will take at least two days and cost around Rf350.

CAR & MOTORCYCLE
The only places where visitors will need to travel by road are Male' and the southernmost atoll, Addu. Taxis are available in both places and driving is on the left.

Health

CONTENTS

The Maldives is not a dangerous destination, with few poisonous animals, no snakes and – by Asian standards – good health care and hygiene awareness. Staying healthy here is mainly about being sensible and careful.

BEFORE YOU GO

INSURANCE

Make sure that you have adequate health insurance and that it covers you for expensive evacuations by seaplane or speedboat, and for any diving risks. See p84 for details on diving insurance.

RECOMMENDED VACCINATIONS

The only vaccination officially required by the Maldives is one for yellow fever, if you're coming from an area where yellow fever is endemic. Malaria prophylaxis is not necessary.

IN THE MALDIVES

AVAILABILITY & COST OF HEALTH CARE

Self-diagnosis and treatment can be risky, so seek qualified help if you need it. Nearly all resorts have a resident doctor, but otherwise it may be necessary to go to Male', to the nearest atoll capital, or have a doctor come to you.

The Maldivian health service relies heavily on doctors, nurses and dentists from overseas, and facilities outside the capital are limited. The country's main hospital is the **Indira Gandhi Memorial Hospital** (Map p95; ☎ 3316647; Boduthakurufaanu Magu) in Male'.

Male' also has the **ADK Private Hospital** (Map p98; ☎ 3313553; Sosun Magu), which offers high-quality care at high prices. The capital island of each atoll has a government hospital or at least a health centre – these are being improved, but for any serious problem you'll have to go to Male'. Patients requiring specialist operations may have to be evacuated to Colombo or Singapore, or taken home.

Emergency evacuations from resorts are coordinated by the Coast Guard and the two seaplane companies. However, be aware that seaplanes can only do evacuations during daylight hours from a limited number of landing/take-off sites.

INFECTIOUS DISEASES
Dengue Fever

Mosquitoes aren't generally troublesome in Maldivian resorts because there are few areas of open fresh water where they can breed. However, they can be a problem at certain times of the year (usually after heavy rainfall), so if they do tend to annoy you, use repellent or burn mosquito coils, available from resort shops at vast expense (bring your own just in case).

Dengue fever, a viral disease transmitted by mosquitoes, occurs in Maldivian villages but is not a significant risk on resort islands or in the capital.

TRAVELLER'S DIARRHOEA

A change of water, food or climate can all cause a mild bout of diarrhoea, but a few rushed toilet trips with no other symptoms

---

DIVERS' MEDICAL CHECK

If you plan to do a diving course in the Maldives, you might want to get a diving medical check-up before you leave. There's a special form for this – a local diving club or dive shop will have the form and a list of doctors who can perform the diving medical check. In the Maldives, you can have it done at the ADK Hospital (p96) and the Indira Ghandi Memorial Hospital (p96), both in Male'.

is not indicative of a serious problem. Dehydration is the main danger with any diarrhoea. Fluid replacement and rehydration salts remain the mainstay in managing this condition.

ENVIRONMENTAL HAZARDS

Most of the potential danger (you have to be extremely unlucky or foolhardy to actually get hurt) lies under the sea.

Anemones

These colourful creatures are also poisonous and putting your hand into one can give you a painful sting. If stung, consult a doctor as quickly as possible; the usual procedure is to soak the sting in vinegar.

Coral Cuts & Stings

Coral is sharp stuff and brushing up against it is likely to cause a cut or abrasion. Most corals contain poisons and you're likely to get some in any wound, along with tiny grains of broken coral. The result is that a small cut can take a long time to heal. Wash any coral cuts very thoroughly with fresh water and then treat them liberally with antiseptic. Brushing against fire coral or the feathery hydroid can give you a painful sting and a persistent itchy rash.

Heat Exhaustion

Dehydration and salt deficiency can cause heat exhaustion. Take the time to acclimatise to high temperatures, drink sufficient liquids and don't do anything too physically demanding.

Salt deficiency is characterised by fatigue, lethargy, headaches, giddiness and muscle cramps; salt tablets may help, but adding extra salt to your food is better.

Heatstroke

This serious condition can occur if the body's heat-regulating mechanism breaks down and the body temperature rises to dangerous levels. Long, continuous periods of exposure to high temperatures and insufficient fluids can leave you vulnerable to heatstroke.

The symptoms are feeling unwell, not sweating very much (or at all) and a high body temperature (39°C to 41°C, or 102°F to 106°F). Where sweating has ceased, the skin becomes flushed and red. Severe, throbbing headaches and lack of coordination will also occur, and the sufferer may be confused or aggressive. Hospitalisation is essential, but in the interim get the victim out of the sun, remove their clothing, cover them with a wet sheet or towel and then fan continuously. Give fluids if they are conscious.

Sea Urchins

Don't step on sea urchins as the spines are long and sharp, break off easily and once embedded in your flesh are very difficult to remove.

Sharks

There is a negligible danger from sharks if they are not provoked. Many types of shark inhabit the Maldives, but they all have plentiful supplies of their natural food, which they find far tastier and more conveniently bite-sized than humans.

Stingrays

These rays lie on sandy sea beds, and if you step on one, its barbed tail can whip up into your leg and cause a nasty, poisoned wound. Sand can drift over stingrays so they can become all but invisible while basking on the bottom. Fortunately, stingrays will usually glide away as you approach. If you're wading in the sandy shallows, try to shuffle along and make some noise. If stung, bathing the affected area in hot water is the best treatment; medical attention should be sought to ensure the wound is properly cleaned. In rare instances stingray stings can be very serious, even, in the most extreme cases, resulting in death.

Stonefish

These fish lie on reefs and the sea bed, and are well camouflaged. When stepped on, their sharp dorsal spines pop up and inject a venom that causes intense pain and sometimes death. Stonefish are usually found in shallow, muddy water, but also on rock and coral sea beds. They are another good reason not to walk on coral reefs.

Bathing the wound in very hot water reduces the pain and effects of the venom. An antivenene is available and medical attention should be sought as the after-effects can be very long lasting.

Language

CONTENTS

The language of the Maldives is Divehi, also commonly written as 'Dhivehi'. It is related to an ancient form of Sinhala, a Sri Lankan language, but also contains some Arabic, Hindi and English words. On top of all this, there are several different dialects throughout the country.

English is widely spoken in Male', in the resorts, and by educated people throughout the country. English is also spoken on Addu, the southernmost atoll, where the British employed many of the islanders on the air base for 20 years. On other islands, especially outside the tourism zone, you'd be very lucky to find an adult who speaks anything other than Dhivehi.

Dhivehi has its own script, Thaana, which was introduced by the great Maldivian hero Thakurufaanu after he tossed out the Portuguese in the 16th century. Thaana looks like shorthand, has 24 letters in its alphabet and is read from right to left (their front page is our back page). See the box on this page for some examples of this unique writing system.

The Romanised transliteration of the language is a potpourri of phonetic approximations, and words can be spelt in a variety of ways. This is most obvious in Maldivian place names. For example: Majeedi Magu is also spelt Majidi, Majeedhee and Majeedee; Hithadhoo also becomes Hithadhu and Hitadhu; and Fuamulak can be Fua Mulaku, Foahmmulah or, thanks to one 19th-century mariner, Phoowa Moloku.

To add to the confusion, several islands have the same name (there are six called Viligili), and there are names for the 20 administrative atolls that do not coincide with the names used for the Maldives' 25 natural atolls.

THAANA – THE SCRIPT OF DHIVEHI

Thaana is the name of the modern script used to write Dhivehi. It looks like a cross between shorthand and Arabic, which is no coincidence, as it came to the Maldives during the Islamic revival of the late sixteenth century, and shares Arabic's right-to-left appearance for words (and left-to-right for numbers). The list below shows the letters of the Thaana alphabet with their nearest English equivalent, and a few words to show the way the letters combine.

(h) ﺯ (sh) ﺵ (n) ﺱﺱ (r) ﺭ (b) ﺡ (lh) ﻝ (k) ﻙ
(a) ﻉ (v) ﻭ (m) ﺝ (f) ﻑ (t) ﻑﺭ (dh) ﻡ (th) ﺕﺡ
(l) ﻝ (g) ﻙ (gn) ﻙﻥ (s) ﺱ (d) ﺩ (z) ﺯ (t) ﻁ
(y) ﻱ (p) ﻱ (j) ﺝ (ch) ﻙﻑ

palm tree	ruh	ﺭﺡ
cat	bulhaa	ﺏﻝ
egg	bis	ﺏﺱ

There is no officially correct, or even consistent, spelling of Dhivehi words in official English language publications.

Maldivians are pleased to help you learn a few phrases of Dhivehi, and, even if you only learn a few words, the locals you meet will be very appreciative of your interest.

The best phrasebook available is *Practical Divehi* by M Zuhair (Novelty Press, Male', 1991). It's available from the Novelty Bookshop in Male' (see p94) and in a number of the resort shops.

GREETINGS & BASICS

Hello.	a-salam alekum
Goodbye.	vale kumu salam
Peace.	salam
Hi.	kihine
See you later.	fahung badaluvang
How are you?	haalu kihine?
Very well. (reply)	vara gada
Fine/Good/Great.	barabah
OK.	enge
Thank you.	shukuria
Yes.	aa
No.	noo
How much is this?	mi kihavaraka?
What is that?	mi korche?

What did you say?	kike tha buni?
I'm leaving.	aharen dani
Where are you going?	kong taka dani?
How much is the fare?	fi kihavare?
I/me	aharen/ma
you	kale
she/he	mina/ena
name	nang, nama
expensive	agu bodu
very expensive	vara agu bodu
cheap	agu heyo
enough	heo
now	mihaaru
little (for people, places)	kuda
mosquito	madiri
mosquito net	madiri ge
bathroom	gifili
toilet	fahana
inside	etere
outside	berufarai
water (rain, well)	vaare feng or valu feng
swim	fatani
eat	kani
walk	hingani
sleep	nidani
sail	duvani
go	dani
stay	hunani
dance	nashani
wash	donani

PEOPLE

friend	ratehi
mother	mama
father	bapa
atoll chief	atolu verin
island chief	kateeb
VIP, upper-class person	befalu
white person (tourist or expat)	don miha
religious leader	gazi
prayer caller	mudeem
fisherman	mas veri
toddy man	ra veri
evil spirit	jinni

PLACES

atoll	atolu
island	fushi/rah
sandbank	finolhu
reef/lagoon	faru
street	magu
lane or small street	golhi/higun

mosque	miskiiy
house	ge

TIME & DAYS

today	miadu
tomorrow	madamma
yesterday	iye
tonight	mire
day	duvas
night	reggadu
Monday	horma
Tuesday	angaara
Wednesday	buda
Thursday	brassfati
Friday	hukuru
Saturday	honihira
Sunday	aadita

NUMBERS

1	eke
2	de
3	tine
4	hatare
5	fahe
6	haie
7	hate
8	ashe
9	nue
10	diha
11	egaara
12	baara
13	tera
14	saada
15	fanara
16	sorla
17	satara
18	ashara
19	onavihi
20	vihi
30	tiris
40	saalis
50	fansaas
60	fasdolaas
70	hai-diha
80	a-diha
90	nua-diha
100	sateka

LANGUAGE

Glossary

animator – scary extroverted person employed in some resorts to promote group activities and 'good times'. Be afraid.

atoll – ring of coral reefs or coral islands, or both, surrounding a lagoon; the English word 'atoll' is derived from the Dhivehi atolu

atolu verin – atoll chief

bai bala – traditional game where one team tries to tag another inside a circle

bashi – traditional girls' team game played with a tennis ball, racket and net

BCD – buoyancy control device; a vest that holds air tanks on the back and can be inflated or deflated to control a diver's buoyancy and act as a life preserver; also called a buoyancy control vest (BCV)

befalu – upper class of privileged families

bodu – big or great

bodu beru – literally 'big drum'; made from a hollow coconut log and covered with stingray skin; *bodu beru* is also Maldivian drum music, often used to accompany dancers

bodu raalhu – literally 'big wave'; when the sea sweeps over the islands, causing damage and sometimes loss of life

bonthi – stick used for martial arts

cadjan – mat made of coconut palm leaves

carrom – popular board game, like a miniature snooker; players use their fingers to flick flat round counters from the edges of a square wooden board, trying to knock other players' counters into the four corner holes

chew – wad of areca nut wrapped in an areca leaf, often with lime, cloves and other spices; commonly chewed after a meal

CMAS – Confédération Mondiale des Activités Subaquatiques; French organisation that sets diving standards, training requirements and accredits instructors

dhiguhedhun – traditional women's dress, full length with long sleeves and a wide collar, usually in unpatterned fabric but sometimes brightly coloured

Dhiraagu – the Maldives telecommunications provider, it is jointly owned by the government and the British company Cable & Wireless

Dhivehi – language and people of the Maldives, also spelt 'Divehi'

Dhivehi Raajje – 'Island Kingdom'; what Maldivians call the Maldives

dhoni – Maldivian boat, probably derived from an Arabian dhow. Formerly sail powered, many dhonis are now equipped with a diesel engine

divemaster – male or female diver qualified to supervise and lead dives, but not necessarily a qualified instructor

fahana – toilet

fandhita – magic, wizardry

faru – also called *faro*; ring-shaped reef within an atoll, often with an island in the middle

feyli – traditional sarong, usually dark with light-coloured horizontal bands near the hem

finolhu – sparsely vegetated sand bank

FIT – fully independent traveller; the name given to anyone not travelling on a pre-paid package

fushi – island

gazi – religious head of atoll

gifili – courtyard with a well; used as an open-air bathroom; a modern version is a popular feature of many resort rooms

giri – coral formation that rises steeply from the atoll floor and almost reaches the surface; see also *thila*

golhi – short, narrow lane

haj – Muslim pilgrimage to Mecca

haveeru – evening

hawitta – ancient mound found in the southern atolls; archaeologists believe these mounds were the foundations of Buddhist temples

higun – wide lane

house reef – coral reef adjacent to a resort island, used by guests for snorkelling and diving

hulhangu – the southwest monsoon period, from May to November, which are the wetter months with more storms and strong winds

inner-reef slope – where a reef slopes down inside an atoll; see also *outer-reef slope*

iruvai – northeast monsoon period, from December to March, which are the drier months

jinni – witch or wizard, sometimes coming from the sea

joli – also called *jorli*; net seat suspended from a rectangular frame; typically there are four or five seats together outside a house

kandiki – sarong worn by women under the libaas

kandu – sea channel; connecting the waters of an atoll to the open sea; feeding grounds for pelagics, such as sharks, stingrays, manta rays and turtles; good dive sites, but subject to strong currents

kateeb – chief of an island
kunaa – traditional woven mat

laajehun – lacquer work traditionally used as containers, bowls and trays to present gifts to the sultan, now popular as small souvenirs
libaas – traditional dress with wide collar and cuffs, and embroidered with gold thread

madrasa – government primary school
magu – wide street
mas – fish
miskiiy – mosque
MTPB – Maldives Tourism Promotion Board; the government tourism promotion organisation
mudhim – muezzin; the person who calls Muslims to prayer
mundu – man's sarong, usually made with a chequered cotton fabric with a darker panel at the back of the garment
munnaaru – minaret, a mosque's tower

nakaiy – period of about two weeks associated with a specific weather pattern; the year is divided into 27 *nakaiy*
namadh – call to prayer for Muslims
NSS – National Security Service; the Maldivian army, navy, coastguard and police force

outer-reef slope – outer edge of an atoll facing open sea, where reefs slope down towards the ocean floor; see also *inner-reef slope*

PADI – Professional Association of Diving Instructors; commercial organisation that sets diving standards and training requirements and accredits instructors
pelagic – open-sea species such as sharks, manta rays, tuna, barracuda and whales

Quran – also spelt Koran; Islam's holy book

raa veri – toddy seller
Ramazan – Maldivian spelling of Ramadan, the Muslim month of fasting

Redin – legendary race of people believed by modern Maldivians to have been the first settlers in the archipelago and the builders of the pre-Islamic *hawittas*
reef – ridge or plateau close to the sea surface; Maldivian atolls and islands are surrounded by coral reefs
reef flat – shallow area of reef top that stretches out from a lagoon to where the reef slopes down into the deeper surrounding water
rhan – bride price

SAARC – South Asia Association for Regional Cooperation; a regional trade and development organisation which comprises Bangladesh, Bhutan, India, Maldives, Nepal, Pakistan and Sri Lanka
SSI – Scuba Schools International; diver accreditation organisation
STO – State Trading Organisation

Thaana – Dhivehi script; the written language unique to the Maldives
thila – coral formation that rises steeply from the atoll floor to within 5m to 15m of the surface; see also *giri*
thin mugoali – 'three circles', a 400-year-old game similar to baseball
thileyrukan – traditional jewellery-making
toddy tapper – person who extracts the sap of a palm tree to make toddy
tundu kunaa – finely woven reed mats, particularly those from Gaaf Dhaal

undholi – wooden seat, typically suspended under a shady tree so the swinging motion provides a cooling breeze

vedhi – large *dhoni* used for trading between Male' and the outer atolls
VSO – Voluntary Service Overseas; British overseas aid organisation

wadhemun – tug-of-war
Wataniya – Kuwaiti mobile phone provider operating one of the Maldives' two networks

Behind the Scenes

THIS BOOK

Robert Wilcox wrote the 1st edition of *Maldives & Islands of the East Indian Ocean* back in 1990. Mark Balla wrote the 2nd edition and James Lyon wrote editions three through five. Tom Masters wrote the 6th edition of the guide, and also updated this edition. The Health chapter is based on text written by Dr Trish Batchelor. The guidebook was commissioned in Lonely Planet's Melbourne office, edited and laid out by The Content Works, High Wycombe, UK (www.thecontentworks.com), and produced by the following:

Commissioning Editor Errol Hunt
Coordinating Editor Lesley McCave
Coordinating Cartographer Alex Leung
Coordinating Layout Designer Alison Rayner
Managing Editors Melanie Dankel, Bruce Evans, Geoff Howard
Managing Cartographer Adrian Persoglia
Managing Layout Designer Sally Darmody
Assisting Layout Designer Nick Colicchia
Cover Image research provided by lonelyplanetimages.com
Indexer Joe Bindloss
Project Manager Ruth Cosgrove
Language Content Coordinator Quentin Frayne

Thanks to Jane Atkin, Lucy Birchley, Yvonne Bischofberger, Jessica Boland, Ellen Burrows, Rebecca Dandens, Diana Duggan, Mark Germanchis, Chris Girdler, Michelle Glynn, Martin Heng, Lauren Hunt, Laura Jane, Evan Jones, Craig Kilburn, Yvonne Kirk, Tracey Kislingbury, Lisa Knights, Chris Lee Ack, Alison Lyall, James Mitchell, Chris Morton, Maryanne Netto, Darren O'Connell, Lisa Plumridge, Jo Stiebel, Aude Vauconsant, Glenn van der Knijff

THANKS
TOM MASTERS

Thanks to Ali Rilwan, Eagan Badeeu, Allo Saeed, Aiman Rasheed, Ahmed Naseer, Ahmed Zahir, Maseem Nazaki, Afshan Latheef, Aminath Huda and Maleeh at MTPB, David Hardingham, Paul Roberts, Maryam Omidi, Sarah Mahir, Vice President Dr Mohammed Waheed Hassan and Minister of Tourism Ahmed Ali Sawad for all their help, advice and time. A huge thanks to all the resorts for their flexibility with my schedule, as well as to all my faithful boat crews in various parts of the country. My work is dedicated to the Maldivian democracy activists who so bravely fought to see an end to decades of dictatorship.

OUR READERS

Many thanks to the travellers who used the last edition and wrote to us with helpful hints, useful advice and interesting anecdotes:
Alexis Broulis, Scott Elliott, Hiroshi Iwasa, Jason Kruger, David Lowe, Evdokimos Tsolakidis, Emily Turner

---

LONELY PLANET AUTHORS

Why is our travel information the best in the world? It's simple: our authors are independent, dedicated travellers. They don't research using just the internet or phone, and they don't accept freebies, so you can rely on their advice being not only well researched, but impartial too.

However, in the Maldives the only way for our author to reach many of the far-flung island destinations was to travel on transport (sea planes, usually) contracted by the resorts themselves for the sole use of their guests. So for this book we sometimes accepted transport assistance from resorts. There simply wasn't any other way for us to ensure we set foot on every atoll, island, islet and sandbar that we needed to visit. We did this on the clear understanding that our editorial independence would remain paramount: that if we didn't think the resort offered good value to travellers, our text would reflect that.

We took this approach because otherwise we were going to have to compromise on our promise to perform on-the-ground research, and because we think this was the best way to serve you, the traveller. We're confident we made the right decision. If you disagree, let us know!

BEHIND THE SCENES

ACKNOWLEDGMENTS

Many thanks to the following for the use of their content:

Globe on title page ©Mountain High Maps 1993 Digital Wisdom, Inc.

Internal photographs p77 (#3) Tom Masters; p74 (#1) Reinhard Dirscherl/Photolibrary; p77 (#5) Mike Christie; p79 (#13) Marco Lijoi/Dreamstime. All other photographs by Lonely Planet Images, and by Michael Aw p73, p76 (#1), p78 (#6, #9), p80 (#3); Casey Mahaney p74 (#2), p75, p78 (#1, #2, #3, #4, #5, #7, #8), p79 (#10, #11, #12, #14), p80 (#1, #2); Chris Mellor p74 (#3); Felix Hug p76 (#2); Dennis Wisken p77 (#4).

All images are the copyright of the photographers unless otherwise indicated. Many of the images in this guide are available for licensing from Lonely Planet Images: www.lonelyplanet images.com.

SEND US YOUR FEEDBACK

We love to hear from travellers – your comments keep us on our toes and help make our books better. Our well-travelled team reads every word on what you loved or loathed about this book. Although we cannot reply individually to postal submissions, we always guarantee that your feedback goes straight to the appropriate authors, in time for the next edition. Each person who sends us information is thanked in the next edition – and the most useful submissions are rewarded with a free book.

To send us your updates – and find out about Lonely Planet events, newsletters and travel news – visit our award-winning website: **lonelyplanet.com/contact**.

Note: we may edit, reproduce and incorporate your comments in Lonely Planet products such as guidebooks, websites and digital products, so let us know if you don't want your comments reproduced or your name acknowledged. For a copy of our privacy policy visit lonelyplanet.com/privacy.

THE LONELY PLANET STORY

Fresh from an epic journey across Europe, Asia and Australia in 1972, Tony and Maureen Wheeler sat at their kitchen table stapling together notes. The first Lonely Planet guidebook, *Across Asia on the Cheap,* was born.

Travellers snapped up the guides. Inspired by their success, the Wheelers began publishing books to Southeast Asia, India and beyond. Demand was prodigious, and the Wheelers expanded the business rapidly to keep up. Over the years, Lonely Planet extended its coverage to every country and into the virtual world via lonelyplanet.com and the Thorn Tree message board.

As Lonely Planet became a globally loved brand, Tony and Maureen received several offers for the company. But it wasn't until 2007 that they found a partner whom they trusted to remain true to the company's principles of travelling widely, treading lightly and giving sustainably. In October of that year, BBC Worldwide acquired a 75% share in the company, pledging to uphold Lonely Planet's commitment to independent travel, trustworthy advice and editorial independence.

Today, Lonely Planet has offices in Melbourne, London and Oakland, with over 500 staff members and 300 authors. Tony and Maureen are still actively involved with Lonely Planet. They're travelling more often than ever, and they're devoting their spare time to charitable projects. And the company is still driven by the philosophy of *Across Asia on the Cheap*: 'All you've got to do is decide to go and the hardest part is over. So go!'

Index

See also separate index for Resorts *(p198)*

INDEX

INDEX

INDEX

MAP LEGEND
ROUTES

...........Primary		.........One-Way Street
.........Secondary		...........Mall/Steps
...........Tertiary		.........Walking Tour
...............Lane		...Walking Tour Detour
.....Unsealed Road		.................Track

TRANSPORT

– – 🚉 – – ....Ferry

HYDROGRAPHY

| ....River, Creek | ....Water |
| ....Reef | |

BOUNDARIES

| ....International | ....Tourism Zone |
| ...Administrative Districts | ....Marine Park |

AREA FEATURES

...............Airport	...............Market
.........Area of Interest	.................Park
.........Beach, Desert	................Rocks
...............Building	...............Sports
..................Land	

POPULATION

⊙ ..CAPITAL (NATIONAL) ● ..CAPITAL (Administrative District)

SYMBOLS

Sights/Activities	Eating	Information
⬛ ....Beach	🍴 ....Eating	⑤ ....Bank, ATM
⬛ ...Diving, Snorkelling	**Entertainment**	⊕ ...Embassy/Consulate
⬛ ....Islamic	⬛ ....Entertainment	⊕ ...Hospital, Medical
⬛ ....Monument	**Shopping**	❶ ....Information
🏛 ....Museum, Gallery	⬛ ....Shopping	@ ...Internet Facilities
● ......Point of Interest	**Sleeping**	⊗ ....Police Station
⬛ ....Ruin	⬛ ....Sleeping	⊗ ....Post Office
⬛ ....Surfing, Surf Beach		⊗ ....Telephone
Sleeping	**Transport**	⊕ ....Toilets
⬛ ....Resort	⬛ ....Airport, Airfield	**Geographic**
		△ ....Telecom Tower

LONELY PLANET OFFICES

Australia
Head Office
Locked Bag 1, Footscray, Victoria 3011
☎ 03 8379 8000, fax 03 8379 8111
talk2us@lonelyplanet.com.au

USA
150 Linden St, Oakland, CA 94607
☎ 510 250 6400, toll free 800 275 8555
fax 510 893 8572
info@lonelyplanet.com

UK
2nd fl, 186 City Rd,
London EC1V 2NT
☎ 020 7106 2100, fax 020 7106 2101
go@lonelyplanet.co.uk

Published by Lonely Planet Publications Pty Ltd
ABN 36 005 607 983

Printed by Toppan Security Printing Pte. Ltd.
Printed in Singapore.